BRAC

W9-CFT-234

JAN - - 2018

THE FIFTH ESTATE

THE FIFTH ESTATE

Think Tanks, Public Policy, and Governance

James G. McGann

BROOKINGS INSTITUTION PRESS
Washington, D.C.

The Brookings Institution is a private nonprofit organization devoted to
research, education, and publication on important issues of domestic and
foreign policy. Its principal purpose is to bring the highest quality independent research and analysis to bear on current and emerging policy problems.
Interpretations or conclusions in Brookings publications should be understood to be solely those of the authors.

Library of Congress Cataloging-in-Publication data

Names: McGann, James G., author.
Title: The fifth estate : think tanks, public policy, and governance /
    James G. McGann.
Description: Washington, D.C. : Brookings Institution Press, 2016. |
    Includes bibliographical references.
Identifiers: LCCN 2016008974 (print) | LCCN 2016020766 (ebook) |
    ISBN 9780815728306 (hardback) | ISBN 9780815728313 (epub) |
    ISBN 9780815728320 (pdf) | ISBN 9780815728313 (ebook)
Subjects: LCSH: Government consultants—United States. | Research
    Institutes—United States. | Policy sciences—United States. | Political
    Planning—United States. | Ex-legislators—Employment—United States. |
    BISAC: POLITICAL SCIENCE / NGOs (Non-Governmental
    Organizations). | POLITICAL SCIENCE / Public Policy / General. |
    POLITICAL SCIENCE / Government / National.
Classification: LCC JK468.C7 M39 2016 (print) | LCC JK468.C7 (ebook) |
    DDC 320.60973—dc23
LC record available at https://lccn.loc.gov/2016008974

9 8 7 6 5 4 3 2 1

Typeset in Garamond

Composition by Westchester Publishing Services

Big, pluralistic America. It's the noisiest political debating society in the world: a babble of voices airing contrary opinions on how this country should be run. For this democracy, where every view is permissible and each faction seeks to persuade—Republicans, Democrats, left, right and centrist. Lobbyists, journalists, scholars, religionists. And think tanks. Dissonant, protean, cacophonous, they are yeast in the ever-fermenting discussion.

—Patricia Linden,
"Powerhouses of Policy: A Guide to America's
Think Tanks," *Town and Country*, January 1987

Contents

Acknowledgments

I WANT TO thank all the individuals and organizations that suggested case examples and the think tank scholars and executives who provided the background information for the domestic and foreign policy cases that are presented in the book.

I would like to thank my very dedicated and able research interns from the University of Pennsylvania, American University, the University of Delaware, the University of Denver, the University of North Carolina, Princeton University, Swarthmore College, Wesleyan University, Haverford College, and Bryn Mawr College for their help in collecting data and background research for this manuscript.

Special thanks goes to Rachel Bailey Scott and her able team, Elizabeth Clinton, Kylee DiGregorio, Jessica Herring, and Tuli Mitra, for their help in preparing the manuscript for publication.

I want to thank my editor, Bill Finan, for encouraging me to publish the book and guiding me through the review process while he was with the University of Pennsylvania Press. When he left Penn Press to join the Brookings Institution Press, it made eminent sense that my manuscript should follow him and be published there.

Finally, I want to thank my wife, Emily, and daughter, Maya, who regularly brought light and laughter into my office after a long day of research and writing.

Introduction

THE IDEA THAT think tanks constitute a Fifth Estate in American society draws on the tradition of European social divisions through the eighteenth century. Given the four existing divisions (the clergy, the nobility, the urban wage laborers and rural peasantry, and the press), it makes sense that a Fifth Estate consists of, as Craufurd Goodwin of Duke University puts it, "organizations that clarify and address the public interest from a wider perspective than any of the first three estates and in greater depth than the fourth."[1] Goodwin includes policy research institutes, scholarly networks, political parties, mass membership organizations, and policy analysts in his definition of the Fifth Estate.

I have both drawn from and narrowed Goodwin's classification to define the role of think tanks in modern American society and how they constitute their own unique Fifth Estate. While Goodwin conceives of the Fifth Estate as a broad collection of nongovernmental, publicly oriented organizations, I contend that think tanks alone ought to constitute the division. They have been instrumental in fulfilling many of the roles that Goodwin assigns to his more broadly defined Fifth Estate, including "provision of discipline and rigor in public debate," "creation of new knowledge," "compensation for inadequacies of government," "strengthening enlightened self-interest," "strengthening the media," and "construction of social and political consensus."[2] This book claims the Fifth Estate for think tanks by explaining their workings and their contributions to U.S. domestic and foreign policy.

1

The U.S. government and its allies face an ever-changing political landscape, wielding policy to combat the problems that plague society and its interests. In the midst of this high-stakes environment, think tanks have carved out a niche in U.S. civil society. They serve as a vital source of new ideas and critical thinking that provide "just in time" information and analysis for the critical decisions that policymakers make on a daily basis. Indeed, these research institutions have become a Fifth Estate in the United States, influencing policy, generating research, informing the public, and creating a revolving door through which scholars and policymakers pass seamlessly between positions in government and leading think tanks.

While think tanks play a vital role in U.S. civil society, it is by no means static. Think tanks constantly evolve, because they are rooted in aspects of U.S. political culture particularly conducive to such dynamism. The election of Barack Obama and the global economic crisis brought a new group of think tanks to the forefront of U.S. politics. These new organizations are challenging the more established think tanks by expanding their power, diversifying their functions, and increasing their efficacy.

Exploring the status and role of American think tanks is also vital to understanding U.S. domestic and foreign policy decisions. Think tanks have a long history of guiding the legislative and executive branches toward informed decisions. Consequently, these institutions have had to adopt the responsibilities of both advocating for the public and providing consultation to the U.S. government across administrations. Think tanks have learned to appeal to multiple audiences, bridging the gap between academics, politicians, and the public. Academics benefit from the immense research capabilities of think tanks and their contributions to knowledge within many different fields. Policymakers appreciate the clear, concise, and direct recommendations of think tanks, which avoid the ambivalence that often characterizes the work of academics and theorists. Furthermore, think tanks act as advocates for particular policies and ideologies, working to convince policymakers to adopt certain courses of action. They also interpret and evaluate policies for the public, endeavoring to publicize information in a manner that avoids both the dense language of academics and the increasingly partisan prose of politicians. Considering these myriad responsibilities, it is no wonder that U.S. think tanks are constantly reinventing themselves and expanding their capabilities to stay in the game.

The think tank landscape is much more complex today and includes traditional academic-oriented research centers and policy activists. Some scholars, however, such as G. William Domhoff, Joseph Peschek, and Thomas Dye, perceive the rising role of think tanks as a negative development for politics. They argue that think tanks have become instruments of what they call ruling-class power. There is also a growing community of scholars, such as Philip Mirowski and Dieter Plehwe, who regard think tanks as closely tied entities that have been given the task of espousing a neoliberal economic and political perspective.

This book concerns itself with these latest trends and changes, chronicling the journey of U.S. think tank scholars into presidential administrations, with a particular focus on President Obama's administration and policymaking. It is a study that is increasingly relevant to the American political arena. The examination of think tanks leads to a greater understanding of the federal policy process, providing insight into some of the tools policymakers use to make better-informed decisions. Moreover, an exploration of think tanks reveals many subtleties of the complex relationships among research, communication, publicity, and policy arenas in the United States. Think tanks join sometimes disparate threads together, weaving a more complete picture of the U.S. political system as a whole. From this perspective, an up-to-date understanding of think tanks is essential for anyone who participates in, studies, or simply wants to stay informed about current U.S. politics.

Chapter 1 begins by defining think tanks and explaining their different categories. This seemingly simple endeavor requires a surprising level of nuance. As think tanks broaden their activities, their sources of funding, and their roles in civil society, defining what a think tank is becomes a challenge unto itself. The chapter also provides a historical account of think tanks in the United States and outlines the many roles think tanks have played since their inception, along with their relationship to civil society and the state of think tanks in the world today. The following section addresses the unique situation of think tanks in the United States. The U.S. political system and culture allow think tanks to flourish, thanks to a reliance on the private sector and highly developed philanthropic culture, among other elements. The think tank atmosphere has also led to diverse think tank activity in both the public and private spheres.

Chapter 2 examines a distinctly American think tank phenomenon: the "revolving door." Through the revolving door, think tank experts rotate into government positions, while politicians often use think tank work as an outlet for their research priorities and ideas, creating an intimate and highly transitional relationship between think tanks and the government.

In chapters 3 and 4, case studies are used to support and complete the portrait of think tanks presented in the previous chapters. Addressing both domestic and foreign policy issues, these case studies illustrate the methods through which think tanks have influenced, contributed to, and developed policy in the past and present.

The book ends with a look at the future of think tanks in the twenty-first century. *The Fifth Estate* draws on a large variety of sources, including academic writings from journals and books, historical content, and case studies. Information and statements from political campaigns, as well as interviews with think tank members, are also used. Data on the names, numbers, and proliferation of think tanks in the United States and throughout the world come from the Think Tanks and Civil Societies Program, which releases an annual database of think tanks worldwide.

The evolution of the American think tank continues daily. While keeping up with these changes and trends is a daunting task, this book represents the latest, most comprehensive attempt to do so. The following work offers a full account of some of America's most unique and important institutions. Most important, it sheds light on some of the lesser-known contributors to the policy world and makes a case for their recognition as an important institution in modern U.S. governance—indeed as a Fifth Estate.

CHAPTER ONE

Think Tanks and Governance in the United States

WHAT EXACTLY IS a think tank, and how is it different from other organizations? Defining the concept is not as easy as it may seem. The broadest definition posits that think tanks are "institutions that provide public policy research, analysis, and advice."[1] That definition casts a wide net and qualifies several different types of both nongovernmental and governmental groups as think tanks. For example, many interest groups, university research centers, and other civil society organizations conduct policy research and provide advice as components of their primary activities. Similarly, many government agencies, such as the Interstate Commerce Commission, the Food and Drug Administration, and the Environmental Protection Agency, are required to conduct policy research and provide advice to the public.

BROAD DEFINITIONS

Scholars who attempt to define the concept of a think tank agree that establishing a clear definition is problematic.[2] According to Thomas Medvetz, the term *think tank* "is a murky, fuzzy concept that cannot be nailed down precisely."[3] Scholars such as Andrew Rich and Hartwig Pautz agree that while achieving a clear definition is problematic, it is also necessary.[4]

Refining the definition is the point at which many scholars diverge. Most describe think tanks as nonprofit, independent public policy research organizations. Some add that they are private organizations. Others also describe them as nonpartisan and tax-exempt. Several scholars, however, point out the complications that arise when using these characteristics to define think tanks.

Defining think tanks as independent excludes many of the world's institutions typically characterized as think tanks.[5] According to Diane Stone, "The notion that a think tank requires independence or autonomy from the state and private interests in order to be 'free-thinking' is a peculiarly Anglo-American predilection that does not travel well into other countries."[6] James Allen Smith's statement that think tanks are "those quintessentially American planning and advisory institutions" would seem to support this argument.[7] In many parts of the world, think tanks are not independent. In Germany and the Netherlands, for example, they often have close political and financial ties to political parties. In some countries, the law requires that think tanks have the sponsorship of a government ministry.

Scholars such as Paul Dickson and I claim that think tanks can be either affiliated or independent, as long as they are permanent and not ad hoc institutions.[8] Stone adds that they can operate within a government, be independent, nonprofit organizations, or be attached to a profit-making corporate entity. Pautz argue that the autonomy of think tanks is relative because they cannot be completely independent and still influence policy. He maintains that three types of relative independence are necessary: legal, financial, and scholarly.[9] I would sharpen this by suggesting that true independence can only be achieved if the following conditions exist: 1) there are laws that recognize and protect the space for civil society organizations; 2) there are regulations that enable civil society organizations to raise funds from a diverse set of domestic and international sources; 3) society recognizes the value and importance of civil society and independent policy analysis; and 4) public policy research organizations value and respect independent analysis and adhere to basic principles of scientific inquiry.

Another reason nailing down a precise definition is so difficult is because think tanks vary drastically in a variety of dimensions. According to Donald Abelson, they are dissimilar in terms of "size, financial resources, staff composition, ideological orientation, areas of specialization, and research programs."[10] They further differ significantly concerning the degree of importance they place on research. Smith argues that they also vary in terms of "the constituencies they choose to serve, the balance they strike between research and advocacy, and the breadth of the policy questions they address."[11] Many scholars, such as Dickson, stress the role that think tanks also play as a bridge between knowledge and power and between science and technology and policymaking. And Howard Wiarda broadly describes all the different functions of think tank fellows, including thinking, writing, publishing, appearing on television, giving congressional testimony, attending White House briefings, and advising the State and Defense Departments and other departments, among others.[12]

The role that think tanks play is essential to clearly defining the concept. Think tanks are formed in response to the need to analyze and organize information in a coherent and relevant way. As I point out, the problem is not that there is a shortage of information but rather that there is too much information, and it is impossible for policymakers to sift through it all and determine what is relevant. I define think tanks as "organizations that generate policy-oriented research, analysis, and advice on domestic and international issues that enable policymakers and the public to make informed decisions about public policy issues."[13]

NARROW DEFINITIONS

Aside from the broad classification, several scholars have attempted to classify the various different think tanks into categories. Kent Weaver breaks them down into three categories: universities without students, the contract researcher, and advocacy think tanks.[14] McGann, Pautz, and Abelson add a fourth category: vanity think tanks. Universities without students rely heavily on academics, as researchers receive the majority of their funding from the private sector and produce primarily book-length studies. As Christopher DeMuth points out, think tanks are different from universities in that they do not produce research for its own sake but rather because they want to affect change in public policy. For this reason, they try to produce and promote interesting and accessible literature. They also try to secure features in newspapers' op-ed pages and to promote their books and magazines "much more aggressively than a university would feel comfortable with."[15]

Contract researchers, like universities without students, rely heavily on academics and emphasize objective analysis. Their research agendas are largely determined by the government agencies that contract their studies. The think tanks' principal products, unlike those of the first category, are usually shorter reports intended for the specific government agencies that initiated the contract. As such, many of the studies produced by these think tanks are not available to the general public except at the discretion of the agencies.

Advocacy think tanks differ from the first two categories in several ways. First, they do not carry out original research. Instead they "synthesize and put a distinctive 'spin' on existing research."[16] Further, they are characterized by a strong policy, partisan, or ideological orientation, which they combine with "aggressive salesmanship and an effort to influence current policy debates."[17] As a result, these think tanks often enjoy a much more influential relationship with policymakers.

Vanity think tanks, which are also called legacy-based think tanks, are created by important individuals, such as former presidents, who seek to leave a lasting legacy on foreign and domestic policy. According to Abelson, "They produce a wide range of publications, hold seminars and workshops, and conduct research in a number of policy areas."[18]

OTHER DEFINITIONS

Other scholars have also attempted to classify think tanks into categories. I have broken them down into four categories or models based on the most influential think tank in each: the Brookings Institution, the RAND Corporation, the Urban Institute, and the Heritage Foundation. The Brookings model "attempts to bring the knowledge and expertise of academics to bear on public policy."[19] These think tanks are staffed by "recognized scholars who engage in empirical, scholarly, and objective analysis of public policy issues in the social sciences."[20] The RAND model is "based on the research and development center model and [is] guided by a systems approach to problem solving."[21] The Urban Institute model focuses mainly on urban and social issues. Finally, the Heritage Foundation model was the last to emerge and is characterized by the politicization of think tanks.

Medvetz offers a different way of defining think tanks altogether. In his view, they are not organizations per se but rather organizational devices used for "gathering and assembling authority conferred by the more established institutions of academics, politics, business, and the media."[22] Medvetz describes them as the "structurally hybrid offspring of the more established institutions of academics, politics, business, and journalism."[23] He calls his definition a relational mode of analysis that overcomes the fallacies that follow from narrowly constructivist and structuralist definitions. Diane Stone, too, promotes a looser definition in *Think Tank Traditions: Policy Research and the Politics of Ideas*, which holds that *think tank* is often used to refer to a function or practice rather than an organizational structure.[24]

The only consensus in the literature on the definition of think tanks is that there is no consensus. The term is difficult to define because the broad definition encompasses other similar non-think-tank organizations, and any attempt to narrow the definition excludes organizations that are commonly accepted as think tanks. Think tanks are most certainly public policy research institutions, but the debate continues as to whether they can be more narrowly defined as private, nonprofit, independent, or nonpartisan. In contrast to lobbyists and columnists, who mainly play an advocacy role, think tanks also play a unique scholarly role in the process of policy formulation, placing them in a category of advocacy separate from others. This perspective sets think tanks in their own place in society, their own separate Fifth Estate.

Challenging the Traditional Definitions

Academic writing has traditionally defined think tanks in the United States as policy research organizations that are independent of government and universities and that operate on a not-for-profit basis. This definition, however, is too narrow on two counts.

First, RAND and many other organizations to which the think tank label is routinely applied are almost totally dependent on government contracts for their revenues and thus are not fully autonomous. They are, however, think tanks, regardless of their financial dependence on the government. Historically they have been considered as such because of their role in conducting original research with the ultimate goal of influencing and affecting public policy. Although active support by the government or a university can be perceived as providing a financial incentive that obliges them to support the donors' own politicized agendas, it does not necessarily distort the research function fundamental to the purpose and the performance of think tanks. The quality of research depends on the culture and working relationships that have developed over time, and on the nature of the subjects being investigated.

Furthermore, in some European countries, notably Germany and the Netherlands, think tanks maintain close financial and personal ties with political parties. Despite this affiliation, their status as research institutions remains both legitimate and untainted by political preferences. In some parts of the world, sponsorship by a government ministry is legally required for a think tank to exist. Moreover, in regions where resources for policy research are extremely scarce, financial support from universities or contracting relationships with the private sector benefit think tanks in that they provide the means to pay core personnel and facilities costs, which is crucial to the functioning of the think tank. Excluding such affiliated organizations from the official definition of think tanks would convey the illusion that certain countries do not have any.

A compromise between a broad definition and a more specific academic definition is therefore the most logical way to define the term. Think tanks are policy research organizations that serve as key civil society actors, also known as the "third sector." The third sector refers to an aspect of the public domain that is significantly autonomous from the government (the first sector), as well as from the corporate world (the second sector). *Autonomy*, however, is a relative, rather than an absolute, term. While some think tanks may make a profit, their main interest in accruing money is based on a desire to generate policy-oriented research, analysis, and advice on domestic and international issues that enable policymakers and the public to make informed decisions about public policy. In the past, think tanks have been referred to as "brain boxes," "idea factories," and "thinking cells"—all of which imply a shared characteristic of contemplation and analysis.

Is there a definition of think tanks that has the flexibility and utility we need for the purposes of this study? Yes, this:

> Think tanks are public policy research, analysis, and engagement institutions that generate policy-oriented research, analysis, and advice on domestic and international issues that enable policymakers and the public to make informed decisions about public policy issues. Think tanks may be affiliated with a political party, a university, or a government; they are independent institutions that are structured as permanent bodies, not ad hoc commissions.

With this definition, we can further sharpen our understanding of the importance of think tanks in governance. These institutions often act as bridges of knowledge between the academic and policymaking communities. They seek to serve the public interest as independent voices that translate applied and basic research into a language and form that is understandable, reliable, and accessible to policymakers and the public. Think tanks perform a variety of critical roles in the policymaking process by offering original research and analysis, as well as generating new information; providing policy advice; evaluating public policies and programs; identifying and training policy analysts; providing a home for public figures who are out of office or planning to assume key positions in future administrations; providing a neutral territory for the conduct of informal diplomacy or to float trial policy balloons;[25] convening experts both inside and outside government to float policy proposals and build consensus; and educating and engaging policymakers, the media, and the public.[26] Think tanks share one common element unconditionally: "the individuals in them attempt to make academic theories and scientific paradigms policy relevant."[27] The ability of think tanks to offer insights into policy formation that are based on research separates them from those organizations whose primary nature is advocacy, who generally lobby governments but who are absent from informing policy research, and it places research institutions in their own unique Fifth Estate position in society.

In the aptly named Information Age, U.S. decisionmakers find themselves besieged by a surplus of data, much of which is irrelevant.[28] The Heritage Foundation's Helle Dale likens policymakers' search for information to drinking water from a fire hose.[29] In response, U.S. politicians and bureaucrats have increasingly turned to think tanks to provide research and systematic analysis that are reliable, policy relevant, and, above all, useful.[30] In fact, Tuğrul Keskingoren and Patrick Halpern argue that think tanks have grown to the point where they are "the intellectual epicenter of the policy planning process" and "provide the research and early policy proposals that eventually find a home on Capitol Hill."[31] The significant role of think tanks in providing relevant information for the public and for public policy represents only the first few ways that think tanks represent a Fifth Estate on their own.

The increase in the numbers and influence of independent public policy research organizations has been noted by a growing number of scholars, donors, and practitioners in the United States and abroad. Regional and global intergovernmental organizations such as the United Nations, World Bank, Asian Development Bank, and NATO have recently recognized the crucial role that think tanks play in the policymaking process. These organizations have organized nascent think tank networks to help develop and assess policies and programs and to serve as a link to civil society groups on the national, regional, and global levels.

TYPES OF THINK TANKS

Think tanks can be classified in two ways: by their strategies and by their sources of funding. The combination of these characteristics results in seven types of think tanks: autonomous and independent, quasi-independent, university affiliated, political party affiliated, government affiliated, quasi-governmental, and for-profit.[32]

An autonomous and independent institution maintains independence from any one donor and from the government of its home country. Therefore, few restrictions are imposed on the research areas it pursues and the positions it takes regarding policy issues. U.S. organizations such as the Peterson Institute for International Economics, the Heritage Foundation, the Council on Foreign Relations, and the Carnegie Endowment for International Peace are all examples of such institutions.[33] It is important to recognize that *autonomous* does not necessarily denote objectivity or nonpartisanship; that is, as a strategic choice, an organization can be autonomous without being objective or nonpartisan.

A quasi-independent institution is autonomous from the government, but an interest group, donor, or contracting agency provides a majority of its funding and exercises significant influence over its operations. The Center for Defense Information and the research arm of the American Association of Retired Persons (AARP) in the United States are quasi-independent in nature.[34]

A university-affiliated think tank is a policy research institute situated under the structure and governance of a postsecondary education institution. As previously stated, more than half of all think tanks are university affiliated, which is especially common outside the United States.[35] These institutions have become prevalent because they are able to take advantage of the academic climate and the vast resources that universities offer. Two leading examples of university-affiliated think tanks within the United States are the Hoover Institution, affiliated with Stanford University in California, and the Baker Institute for Public Policy at Rice University in Texas. A political party–affiliated think tank has an overt, formal association with a political party, such as France's Jean Juares Foundation or the Progressive Policy Institute in the United States, the policy arm of the Democratic Leadership Council. A government-affiliated think tank is part of the formal structure of a government and therefore functions under the government's authority. The leading example is the Congressional Research Service (CRS), which is under the purview of U.S. Congress.[36] CRS staff members work exclusively and directly for members of Congress and their committees and staff to provide confidential public policy research and analysis at all stages of the legislative process. For this reason, it is often referred to as "Congress's think tank."

Quasi-governmental think tanks are funded exclusively by government grants and contracts but are not part of the formal structure of the government. Government agencies commission the research these think tanks carry out and provide the lion's share of their funding, but the institutions are not part of the

TABLE 1-1. Categories of Think Tank Affiliations

Category	Definition
Autonomous and independent	Significant independence from any one interest group or donor and autonomous in its operation and funding from government
Quasi-independent	Autonomous from government but controlled by an interest group, donor, or contracting agency that provides a majority of the funding and has significant influence over operations
Government affiliated	Part of the formal structure of government
Quasi-governmental	Funded exclusively by government grants and contracts but not a part of the formal structure of government
University affiliated	Policy research center at a university
Political party affiliated	Formally affiliated with a political party
Corporate (for profit)	For-profit public policy research organization, affiliated with a corporation or merely operating on a for-profit basis

official structure of government. The Woodrow Wilson International Center for Scholars in the United States and the Korea Development Institute are examples of such think tanks.[37]

For-profit think tanks are organized on a business model and often take the form and characteristics of for-profit consulting firms. They respond to clients' demands, and they tend to drift outside the purely political world occupied by most other types of think tanks (see table 1-1). Good examples include the Kissinger Group, the McKinsey Global Institute, and A. T. Kearney's Global Business Policy Council.

These ideal categories of think tanks have served both as models for newly established organizations and as points of departure for existing institutions that seek to reinvent themselves. But most think tanks do not fit neatly into any one category, and the distinctions among them are becoming increasingly blurred. Hybrids between think tanks and organizational siblings that have some similarities but exist outside the official definition are increasingly common. University research centers mirror academic think tanks; for-profit consulting agencies mirror government research organizations; temporary government commissions mirror some contract researchers; interest groups and public interest lobbies mirror advocacy tanks; and party research departments mirror party think tanks.

STRUCTURES OF THINK TANKS

I have written extensively with Kent Weaver of the Brookings Institution on the strategy and structure of think tanks.[38] Over the last several decades, distinctive organizational forms of think tanks have come into being that differ substantially from their predecessors in operating styles, recruitment patterns, and aspirations to standards of objectivity and completeness in research. Weaver and I agree that all public policy research organizations in the United States can be divided into three broader categories of think tanks: academic, contract research, and advocacy (see table 1-2).

Academic think tanks, or "universities without students," employ staff members with strong academic credentials. They focus on a wide range of issues and seek long-term changes in policy direction.[39] Weaver and I further agree that organizations with comprehensive agendas, such as the American Enterprise Institute (AEI), the Hoover Institution, and the Council on Foreign Relations, fall into this category.

The second category, contract researchers, conducts research and analysis under contract and often develops close relationships with a few government agencies. With a reputation for objective research, these institutions provide a useful external voice to supplement their clients' own work. As contract researchers typically are funded by the government agencies that contract their services, the funding agencies usually play a large role in setting the think tanks' agendas. Output generally takes the form of reports to those agencies rather than publicly circulated books and articles. The best examples of this brand are RAND and the Urban Institute. In my global typology of think tanks, I include political party–affiliated and government-affiliated think tanks, which are more commonly found outside the United States. My recent research suggests that newly established think tanks have blurred the lines between these separate categories, borrowing characteristics from media and marketing organizations to create a new hybrid category.[40]

The first two types, academic and contract research think tanks, have many similarities. Both tend to recruit staff with strong academic credentials (for example, PhDs from prestigious universities), and both tend to emphasize the use

TABLE 1-2. A Typology of Think Tanks

Think tank types	Major characteristics and products						
	Staffing	Financing	Agenda setting	Products and product style	Subtypes	Facilitating conditions	Examples
Academic/ university without students	Focus on staff with strong academic credentials and muted ideology	Primarily foundations, corporations, individuals	Agenda set primarily by researchers and foundations	Academic monographs and journal articles in objective and nonpartisan style	Elite policy club; specialized academic think tank	Culture and philanthropic tradition that support idea of nonpartisan experts	Brookings Institution; Institute for International Economics (U.S.)
Contract researcher	Focus on staff with strong academic credentials, muted ideology, and objective, nonpartisan research	Primarily government agencies	Agenda set primarily by contracting agency	Reports for government agencies and other clients in objective and nonpartisan style	Specialized contract researcher	Government support available for policy research	RAND and Urban Institute (U.S.)
Advocacy tank	Focus on staff with political or philosophical/ ideological credentials	Primarily foundations, corporations, individuals	Agenda set by organization leaders	Brief papers typically focused on currently topical issues	Specialized advocacy tank; vanity and legacy think tanks	Foundation, business and group support available	Centre for Policy Studies (U.K.)
Party think tank	Focus on party members and party loyalty	Primarily party and government subsidies	Agenda closely tied to party platform	Varies	...	Government funding available for political party research	Konrad Adenauer Stiftung (Germany)

of rigorous social science methods so that their research will be perceived as objective and credible by a broad audience. However, they differ largely in their sources of funding, research agendas, and output.

Academic think tanks are typically funded by foundations, corporations, and individuals. Their agendas are usually set internally, in part through a bottom-up process in which the researchers themselves play an important role, although funders are increasingly active in the agenda-setting process. Reflecting the academic training and orientation of their staffs, the research output of academic think tanks most often takes the form of academic monographs and journal articles. These think tanks present a sharp contrast to contract research think tanks, which are funded by the government and whose reports are written for the specific funding agency.

Advocacy think tanks either possess extremely strong ideologies or focus on persuading policymakers and the public on short-term, specific policy debates. Advocacy think tanks, while maintaining formal independence, are linked to particular ideological groupings or interests. They tend to view their role in the policymaking process as winning the war of ideas rather than disinterestedly searching for the best policies. Advocacy think tanks frequently draw their resources disproportionately from sources linked to specific interests (often corporations fund conservative think tanks, and labor unions fund liberal ones, for example). Their staffs, in comparison, are typically drawn more heavily from government, political parties, and interest groups than from university faculties and may be less credentialed in terms of social science expertise, although this is not always the case. The products of their research tend to be policy briefs or white papers that advocate a particular policy rather than the tomes associated with academic think tanks.

The Heritage Foundation and the Heartland Institute on the political right and the Center for American Progress (CAP) on the political left are two examples of advocacy-oriented think tanks. Since policymakers simply do not have the requisite time to sift through lengthy scholarly books and journal articles that are frequently laced with academic theories and jargon, concise policy briefs that clearly illustrate various policy implications and options developed by think tanks such as the Heartland Institute and CAP have proved useful. In this sense, these organizations are better able to influence policy and disseminate information among policymakers than are think tanks that rely solely on academic papers, which are less likely to be read by the time-limited policy world.[41] In addition to the Heartland Institute, Weaver and I place the Economic Policy Institute in this category.[42]

Each of type of think tank—academic, contract, and advocacy—has its relative advantages and disadvantages. Because academic think tanks emphasize
scholarly objectivity and the scientific credentials of their staff, a strong tension
exists between the goals of scholarly objectivity and the completeness and policy relevance of the reports. Academics generally favor the former, while policymakers prefer findings that are brief, clear, and free of the qualifications and
ambivalence with which scholars frequently temper their conclusions.

Contract researchers have an advantage over academic think tanks in terms
of policy relevance since policymakers often outline in fairly specific terms the
questions they want answered. The tension for contract think tanks is primarily
between the goals of scholarly objectivity and the policy preferences of their
clients, especially if contract researchers are heavily dependent on a particular
client. When clients outline their preferences, they are attempting to influence
the final results, or the clients refuse to release research that does not abide by
those preferences. At the very least, this tension may pose a threat to the perceived objectivity of that research. Sometimes the threat is made explicit. In
1995 the U.S. Agency for International Development (USAID) sponsored a
joint research project between a U.S. think tank and a think tank in South
Africa to assess the impact of its programs on civil society in postapartheid South
Africa. One conclusion of the study revealed that USAID programs deferred too
frequently to the ruling African National Congress in South Africa and were thus
stunting the growth of civil society and pluralism in South Africa. In response,
USAID refused to release the study until that conclusion was excised.

Advocacy tanks, which adhere to strong values and often take institution-
wide positions on particular policy issues, face tension between maintaining
consistent value positions and perceptions of objectivity and completeness. As a
consequence, messages perceived to reflect inflexible values rather than "objective" analysis may simply be ignored by a large part of the audience they seek to
reach. Similarly, the party affiliation of think tanks limits their objectivity,
credibility, and independence; when their party is not in power, their access to
and influence on policymakers is limited.

The think tank environment continues to be quite dynamic, requiring further
elaboration and expansion of the think tank typology. The most recent trend in
this ever-changing system is a hybrid that includes features of one or more of the
dominant types of think tanks. Table 1-3 highlights the many types and organizational forms and includes some examples of each.

Diverging from Weaver's and my classifications, Yale political scientist
David Ricci divides the agendas of think tanks into two groups: short-term

TABLE 1-3. Sample Classification of Think Tanks Worldwide

Date established

Political party

Konrad Adenauer Foundation (Germany)	1955
Jaures Foundation (France)	1992
Progressive Policy Institute (United States)	1989

Government

China Development Institute (PRC)	1989
Institute for Political and International Studies (Iran)	1983
Congressional Research Service (United States)	1914

Quasi-governmental

Institute for Strategic and International Studies (Malaysia)	1983
Korea Development Institute (Korea)	1971
Woodrow International Center for Scholars (United States)	1968

Autonomous and independent

Pakistan Institute of International Affairs (Pakistan)	1948
Institute for Security Studies (South Africa)	1991
Peterson Institute for International Economics (United States)	1981

Quasi-independent

European Trade Union Institute (Belgium)	1978
NLI Research Institute (Japan)	1988
Center for Defense Information (United States)	1971

University affiliated

Foreign Policy Institute, Hacettepe University (Turkey)	1974
Institute For International Relations (Brazil)	1979
Hoover Institution on War, Revolution and Peace, Stanford University (United States)	1919

mobilization and long-term mobilization.[43] Short-term mobilization agendas include activities such as participating in television talk shows and news programs; writing editorials or regular columns for newspapers and magazines; and sponsoring a wide variety of meetings, symposia, and conferences. Other short-term activities may include testifying before congressional committees, serving on advisory commissions, and providing informal sources of information for congressional staff members. Anthony Cordesman of the Center for Strategic and International Studies (CSIS), an expert who is often interviewed and cited by broadcast media, is a short-term mobilizer. In contrast, the concept of long-term mobilization consists of writing journal articles, monographs, and books so as to "disseminate scholarly analysis to thoughtful readers on a variety of issues . . . [serving] as important conduits for the more fundamental research that is performed at universities."[44] A specific example of long-term mobilization is reflected in the mission statement of Resources for the Future (RFF), which is to improve environmental and natural resource policymaking worldwide through objective social science research of the highest caliber. This is accomplished by producing academic, peer-reviewed journal articles, monographs, books, *Resources* (a free magazine in publication for more than fifty years), public events, and conferences.

How Think Tanks Are Funded

The variety of sources that fund think tanks is just as diverse a categorization as that of think tanks. Philanthropists such as Robert Brookings and Andrew Carnegie played a crucial role in the birth of think tanks, and individuals, businesses, and foundations continue to provide the bulk of their financial support.[45] Some think tanks, such as the Brookings Institution, are financed through large endowments. Others receive portions of their funding through revenue derived from the sales of publications, such as the *National Interest*, published by the Center for the National Interest (formerly the Nixon Center). Many think tanks, including RAND, bring in revenue through contract work from private or government clients. Institutions that come under the authority of governments or universities, such as the Congressional Research Service and the Center for International and Security Studies at the University of Maryland, derive much of their funding from their parent organizations. Typically, think tanks rely on a combination of these funding sources along with generous contributions from private donors, individuals, corporations, and foundations.

An institution's independence may well be determined by the diversification of its funding base because a think tank with an expanded donor base is not beholden to a single donor and its interests. This principle of diversification of funding is demonstrated well by many of the largest and most prominent think tanks in the United States. The Cato Institute and the Heritage Foundation, for instance, rely mainly on individual contributions, receiving 83 percent and 59 percent, respectively, of their income from such donations. AEI receives 58 percent of its funds from individual and corporate sponsors, and CSIS receives 63 percent from foundations and corporations. Most notably, Brookings has historically drawn about 20 percent of total revenue from its endowment, which is its largest single source of revenue.

Institutes that have traditionally relied on government contracts are now broadening their funding bases as well. For example, James Thomson, RAND president emeritus, explained that the institution uses "a whole set of fund-raising functions, because [it needs] to get more people involved with RAND to have a broader reach."[46] The perception that RAND's funding is largely or exclusively based on defense-related grants and contracts is no longer true, and the organization's fundraising and research programs reflect this new reality.

Nevertheless, diversification of funding has become more difficult because of a new trend in think tank funding. A great deal of funding is now project specific, creating the potential for a wealthy partisan donor to determine a think tank's research agenda.[47] Because of the recent growth in the number and range of think tanks, funding has emerged as a serious issue. In response, many think tanks are now highly specialized, focusing on specific issues or ideologies.[48]

According to some scholars, right-wing think tanks have benefited strongly from a proactive approach to collectivizing and organizing their search for funding.[49] Conversely, left-wing think tanks have suffered because, historically, progressive individuals and foundations have been more reluctant to provide financial support for policy research. Further, conservative donations have been more integrated than progressive donations, simultaneously supporting conservative think tanks, academic programs that sponsor conservative thinkers, conservative-friendly media, powerful lobbies, and a strong Republican Party. These various elements work together successfully to implement conservative policy. In the wake of this widespread success, conservative funding strategists now face their biggest challenge in combating a sense of complacency among conservative donors.

Given the 2008 financial crisis, some scholars, such as Peter Singer, a former Brookings fellow, wonder if conservative think tanks have begun to feel financial strain.[50] AEI has been a frequent target of speculation about its fragile financial condition, since it relies heavily on donations instead of an endowment and is one of the few major think tanks in Washington, D.C., that has not owned its own building for most of its history. (In 2007, however, it launched a capital campaign and will move into a newly renovated building in 2016 on "think tank row" on Massachusetts Ave in Washington, D.C.) The General

Motors Foundation was recently required to cut its regular contributions to AEI because of the ongoing financial crisis and the competitive issues facing the automobile industry in the United States. This exemplifies the volatility facing conservative think tanks that depend on large donations from corporate foundations and philanthropists. Nevertheless, the sheer number of donors and the integrated nature of the conservative funding network will likely soften any blow to the budget of think tanks. Furthermore, the Heritage Foundation has proved that an aggressive marketing campaign, featuring tactics such as direct mail, can financially sustain conservative think tanks. Such a strategy secures small donations from hundreds of thousands of American citizens instead of relying exclusively on larger donations from fewer sources.[51]

The progressive funding strategy, in contrast, was weak until the first decade of the twenty-first century. In 2005 Rob Stein founded the Democracy Alliance to serve as a financial clearinghouse for liberal donors. The alliance of eighty critical donors, which includes George Soros and Tim Gill, seeks to establish a long-term and cohesive financial strategy to fund progressive policy advocacy. Soon after its establishment, the Democracy Alliance received pledges for more than $80 million in contributions over a five-year period.[52] The donations have been used to fund organizations that are endorsed by the alliance and "that are building a more robust, coherent progressive movement at the local, state, and national level."[53] It remains to be seen how this strategy will affect the future financial stability of liberal think tanks and advocacy groups.

Establishing a long-term commitment from a set of core donors is crucial to funding. As previously noted, this strategy can, however, reduce a think tank's independence if relied on too heavily. RAND's Silvia Montoya and Rachel Swanger caution that think tanks must "strive to find the right balance" between their joint objectives of developing close relationships with policymakers and "maintaining adequate independence to preserve integrity (real and perceived) of the research" they generate.[54] This is a particularly troublesome situation for conservative think tanks such as the Cato Institute, which at one time received more than 50 percent of its budget from various Koch family foundations. Although this has changed over the years, Koch is still a major contributor to Cato as evidenced by the much publicized battle between Cato founder Ed Crane and the Koch brothers for control of the organization. Ultimately, diversification through small and midsize donors is a more sustainable and healthy way of receiving funding. Nevertheless, as the Cato Institute demonstrates, the desire for diversification is still overshadowed by the strong focus on large foundations.

THE HISTORY OF THINK TANKS

To govern well, governments need information, knowledge, and the means of implementation to connect informed policy to the relevant theater of social operations. Information should be distinguished from knowledge. While information is data collected from the world, knowledge comes from the integration of information into an inherited cognitive framework meaningful to human beings. Means of implementation are often unaddressed by the academics and policy intellectuals generating research and are instead the domain of government officials. Without the necessary administrative, budgetary, and legal means to implement a policy, nothing is accomplished. The "theater" in which information and knowledge need to be translated into real-world policy implementation may concern the economy, defense and foreign policy, environmental issues, public health, and any number of other public policy domains. Think tanks partially evolved over time to fill the gaps between information and knowledge and policy generation and implementation.

For all practical purposes, the first think tanks were largely a product of the Progressive Era in the United States (1890–1920), during which these institutions gained prominence as important players in U.S. policymaking. While several think tanks existed before the onset of World War II, the United States and Western Europe saw an explosion both in the number and activities of their think tanks during the 1960s and 1970s. These think tanks recommended policy pertaining to the Cold War, foreign aid, and domestic issues such as the health of the economy. They became increasingly specialized and influential in the policymaking process. This specialization increased after the end of the Cold War in 1990, and think tanks began to research and recommend policy on a variety of highly technical and specialized issues. Their growing prominence in different fields of research has contributed greatly to the decision-making process by allowing policymakers and the public to offer expert advice on key policy issues. While the activity and presence of think tanks have grown immensely, the study of think tanks as important actors in the policymaking process is rather new, having started in the 1980s.[55]

Before the twentieth century, institutions that are similar to today's think tanks existed in the United States. One of the earliest meetings that shared characteristics similar to modern think tanks occurred in 1865, when a group of roughly one hundred people from a variety of professions—including various government officials—converged in the Massachusetts State House in Boston to discuss a plan of national recovery following the Civil War.[56] During that meeting, a number of Progressives interested in issues such as unemployment and public health discussed and analyzed the problems facing the war-ravaged nation. Several professional organizations, such as the American Political Science Association and the National Conference on Charities and Correction, trace their origins to that meeting. Although not a think tank meeting per se, the event in Boston signified one of the first recorded instances of policy experts' assembling in one place to discuss contemporary issues.[57]

Some scholars believe that the government's reliance on expert assistance began even earlier in the nineteenth century. Paul Dickson asserts that the adviser-advisee relationship began in 1832, when the secretary of the treasury contracted the Franklin Institute of Philadelphia to solve technical issues American steamboats. Although these scholars were not yet conscious of the significance of their work, Dickson argues that the Franklin Institute was the first functional think tank. But because of Dickson's lack of documentation, academics like Donald Abelson doubt that the institute was the first to interact with government actors to solve governmental or societal issues.[58] Rather than focusing on the ambiguity regarding the creation of think tanks, it is arguably more relevant to track their continued progress and their relationship with the executive and legislative branches.

The influence of think tanks on government administrations and policy-making was substantial by the early twentieth century. According to James Smith, the weight of experts had grown so great by the turn of the century that President Woodrow Wilson began to harbor "distrust" of experts by 1912. Wilson, a graduate of the University of Virginia and Johns Hopkins University and onetime president of Princeton University, saw the role of experts as a potential threat to democratic institutions and the people's responsibility to govern themselves. White House officials, former presidents, and government administrators had begun to rely informally on the expertise of scholars in specialized fields such as economics and statistics. The way experts were consulted during this period is markedly different from the way they are consulted now. Presidents and policymakers customarily called on these experts only for private meetings, instead of requesting publicized testimonies, which is the norm today. Even President Wilson eventually put his mistrust aside, using think tanks' professional expertise during World War I.[59] The historical distrust of big government placed severe constraints on the size of the federal bureaucracy and the civil service. As the demands on the government increased and the number and complexity of policy problems grew, policymakers increasingly turned to scientists and outside experts to help them manage the domestic and foreign policy challenges they faced.

Think tanks attempted to meld the realms of social science and politics. The Progressive belief that the social sciences could solve the public policy problems of the time helped shape the notion that think tanks were created to help "government think." Neither ideological nor promotional, "the new think tanks had missions consistent with the scientific, knowledge-based movement toward efficient government."[60]

In a period highlighted by scandals involving corporations and politicians, think tanks were hypersensitive about accepting any funding that could potentially lead to a loss of independence and credibility. It is, however, ironic that the major philanthropists of the time were captains of industry who created the leading foundations and think tanks in the United States. Think tanks derived most of their funding from the Second Industrial Revolution, but, more specifically, they received financial support from industrial-era businessmen such as John D. Rockefeller, Andrew Carnegie, and J. P. Morgan. These businessmen were driven by enlightened self-interest and were primarily concerned with promoting a more professional, business-oriented facet of government—one capable of both addressing the social problems that accompanied industrialization and easing the growing discontent of their workers. Big business, in other words, had its own agenda. Nonetheless, the fact that the businessmen trusted the private sector more than the public sector helped engender a healthy, balanced relationship between the newly founded think tanks and their funders.

The generosity of private philanthropists helped create many of the leading think tanks that exist in the United States today. The donors and reformers shared a common goal of bringing knowledge to bear on public policy. Their goal was to fight corruption and promote efficiency within government, or, as some have suggested, to "help government think." Throughout the early twentieth century, social science experts were relied on for their unbiased counsel. These experts demonstrated the value of distinguished, independent voices, which contributed to the rise of think tanks such as the Carnegie Endowment for International Peace, established in 1910, and the Brookings Institution, whose origins date back to 1916.[61] These institutions filtered information to key stakeholders in the United States to keep them informed on the government's wide-reaching actions. The outbreak of World War I energized these institutions, allowing them to become leading voices in the passionate debates concerning the proper role of the United States in a rapidly changing world. The mission and purpose of the Carnegie Endowment for International Peace, for example, were clearly positive and intended to benefit the United States as well as those states that had suffered the violence and ravages of World War I. Andrew Carnegie's $10 million founding donation demonstrated his (and the think tank's) commitment to "hasten the abolition of international war, the foulest blot upon our civilization."[62] The Great Depression and the government's response to this domestic crisis catalyzed the establishment of a group of now well-established think tanks.

While several think tanks were born out of the Great Depression, the survival of those that predated the financial crisis (despite the loss of their absolute neutrality and independence) attested to the stability of think tanks more broadly. Andrew Bird argues that "with the onset of the Great Depression, faith in purely scientific analysis and detached administrative solutions to social problems diminished." In the severely depressed U.S. economic and political environments, the impact of think tanks withered. The development of knowledge became superfluous when the basic necessities of survival—food, water, and shelter—were threatened. Bird explains that "direct expert intervention in political decisionmaking became more common," however, because the extreme circumstances of the Great Depression enabled the experts, who had established themselves up to that point, to play a vital role in the process of policy formulation. Because of the extent of the crisis and the need for immediate action, they abandoned their traditional role as advisers and were directly engaged in shaping and helping implement key policies and programs. Bird concludes that "think tanks had become effectively established in American politics, but intellectual and ideological currents were changing."[63] Think tanks were evolving in response to major historical events.

As the United States took on a greater role in global leadership, early think tanks sought "to advance the public interest by providing government officials with impartial, policy-relevant advice."[64] During the later postwar isolationist period of the 1920s and 1930s, think tanks kept the discussion of world affairs alive within U.S. intellectual and policy circles.[65] In many ways, Andrew Carnegie's philanthropic legacy made this financially possible. A Carnegie Corporation grant of $1.65 million in 1922 laid the groundwork for a 1927 merger of the Institute for Government Research, founded by Robert Brookings, and its two sister organizations, the Institute of Economics and a graduate school, to form the modern-day Brookings Institution.[66] Rather than taking on the task of lobbying, however, this period's new institutions concerned themselves with enhancing and sharing their nonpartisan policy expertise. Their research found a wide-ranging audience and helped solidify think tanks' relationships with government decisionmakers.[67]

By the mid-twentieth century, Congress began to reorganize the structure of various governmental departments, placing greater emphasis on specialized research. The 1947 reformation, by revamping the legislative committees, extended the staff capacity and research resources of the General Accounting Office as well as the CRS within the Library of Congress. During the 1970s Congress created the Congressional Budget Office and the Office of Technology Assessment and equipped each with modest staffs. The executive and legislative branches were simultaneously maintaining "contractual relationships" with universities and independent research institutions, including RAND and the Urban Institute.[68]

Three Waves of Think Tanks

As previously mentioned, the term *think tank* was introduced in the United States during World War II to describe the protected state in which military and civilian experts were situated so that they could develop invasion plans and other military strategies. The end of World War II ushered in a new understanding of international relations, and thus a new wave of think tanks emerged outside the realm of military policy and strategy. Institutionalized policy advising became a permanent feature of U.S. politics.[69] Scholars of social, environmental, domestic, and foreign policy became more readily available to presidents, cabinet members, the legislature, and one another. Government departments such as the Department of Defense hired organizations to conduct research that addressed specific concerns of policymakers and others in the government.[70] The organizations became "government contractors" and, by serving as consultants to policymakers, influenced government policies and programs from the inside. Perhaps the best example of one of these government-contractor think tanks is RAND. Established first as "Project RAND" by the United States Army Air Forces under a contract to the Douglas Aircraft Company, RAND separated from Douglas in 1948 to become the independent, nonprofit organization it is today.

A second wave of think tanks emerged following World War II and the beginning of the Cold War. After World War II, a variety of new, specialized, nongovernment contractor think tanks began to appear in response to the growing public sector and the establishment of the United States as a global superpower. In 1952 RFF received initial funding from the Ford Foundation for the study of conservation, development, and the use of natural resources. The Mid-Century Conference on RFF in 1953, sponsored by a wide variety of private organizations, provided an open forum for President Dwight Eisenhower, RFF, conservationists, businesspeople, and policymakers to discuss new approaches to environmental policy in the next generation. The conference spearheaded RFF's name as the first premier think tank with an environmental focus.[71]

After the war, the term still mainly applied to contract researchers such as RAND that performed a mixture of deep thinking and program evaluation for the military. The use of the term was expanded in the 1960s to describe other groups of experts who formulated policy recommendations, including some research institutes concerned with the study of international relations and strategic questions. Other examples of "government contractors" include the Hudson Institute and the Urban Institute, founded in 1961 and 1968, respectively. Think tanks established during this era were often characterized by a "typically long bureaucratic birth," as was the case for the Urban Institute, whose foundations stretch back to the Kennedy administration, but who was not brought into being until the domestic troubles of the 1960s.[72] President Lyndon Johnson was an outspoken advocate for think tanks, noting their growing value and saluting Brookings for influencing his own Great Society reforms. Johnson named Brookings as a "national institution, so important to . . . the Congress and the country . . . that if [it] did not exist, we would have to ask someone to create [it]."[73] By the 1970s, the term *think tank* was applied to those institutions focusing not only on foreign policy and defense strategy but also on current political, economic, and social issues.

According to Donald Abelson, a combination of several factors explains the proliferation of think tanks after World War II, as well as the increasing diversity of their interests. The United States becoming a superpower and accepting its new status, with all the new global responsibilities that it entails, brought foreign policy—and thus the need for foreign policy advice—to the forefront. The expansion of the federal bureaucracy provided experts with more avenues to share their input. The antiwar and civil rights movements broadened the public's consciousness of social issues and generated several liberal think tanks. Simultaneously, conservative backlash against the perceived liberal bias within U.S. universities in the late 1960s and early 1970s created a demand for a friendlier environment in which conservative scholars could pursue their research.[74] The moderate conservative movement gained popularity following Richard Nixon's election to the presidency in 1968. William Simon, secretary of the treasury for Presidents Nixon and Ford, was an advocate of the movement calling for "a radical rethinking of conservative principles."[75]

The conservative movement further matured during President Ronald Reagan's years in office.[76] Reagan, a Hollywood actor turned politician, relied extensively on the research and advice of conservative think tanks during both his governorship in California and his presidency in the 1980s. The Hoover Institution even named Reagan a distinguished fellow of the organization.[77] Reagan also looked to these conservative think tanks for affiliated individuals to fill seats in his campaign organization and in his administration. James Smith points out that experts like Richard V. Allen, who served as a foreign policy adviser during the campaign and the national security adviser, and Martin Anderson, a conservative economist educated at MIT and Columbia University and a senior fellow employed at the Hoover Institution, were indispensable to both Reagan's campaign and his grasp of domestic and foreign policy. In addition to his work on Reagan's presidential election in 1976, Anderson was engaged in Barry Goldwater's presidential campaign in 1964 and Nixon's election in 1968. Anderson personally presided over twenty-five domestic and economic policy task forces and twenty-three foreign policy and national security projects. Moreover, more than 450 policy experts in total were involved in Reagan's election campaign as surrogates, advisers, briefers, and speechwriters.[78] Evidently, the guidance of thinks tanks was crucial to Reagan's formation of his own version of U.S. conservatism during the so-called Reagan Revolution.

In this new political environment, a third wave of think tanks—advocacy think tanks—began to dot the policy research landscape.[79] Unlike their contract-driven predecessors, advocacy think tanks actively sought to involve themselves in policy debates and influence "the direction and content of foreign and domestic policy."[80] This influence is achieved in part through "aggressive marketing techniques" that promote the think tank's specific interests among policymakers and the general public.[81] Richard Haas describes the Heritage Foundation, founded in 1973, as the prototypical advocacy think tank. Other examples include the liberal Institute for Policy Studies (IPS), founded in 1963, and the libertarian Cato Institute (or Cato), founded in 1977. IPS played an active role in the civil rights movement, the women's movement, and, most notably, the anti–Vietnam War movement. IPS's *Vietnam Reader* became "a kind of text-book for anti-war teach-ins," according to Lee Michael Katz.[82] While Haass may describe Heritage as the prototypical advocacy think tank, IPS is the original one. According to a 1986 *Washington Post* piece by Sidney Blumenthal, "The Heritage Foundation . . . was modeled directly on IPS."[83]

A more recent arrival on the advocacy think tank scene is CAP.[84] Just as Heritage followed the precedent set by IPS, CAP followed the precedent set by

Heritage, searching for a more "muscular political influence" that was missing on the political left. CAP's strategy and structure was modeled after Heritage's and was consciously designed to be policy and advocacy oriented, as well as to serve as a progressive counterweight to Heritage. Its establishment by "Clinton administration refugees" in 2003 demonstrates CAP's prolific relationship with the Obama administration. Katz describes CAP as "the zenith" of the pinnacle of the recent rise of think tanks. While CAP's stock has skyrocketed with the number of its officials appointed to the Obama administration, this surge in appointments could also be "a death knell" if too many of the organization's scholars leave for government posts.[85]

"Legacy-based think tanks" are considered by some scholars to be the fourth wave of policy research institutions. These are usually established by former officeholders who actively seek to impart their legacy on domestic and foreign policy. Perhaps the best example is the Carter Center, which was started by President Jimmy Carter in 1982 to continue his work on the advancement of human rights. Another such think tank is the Center for the National Interest, formerly the Nixon Center for Peace and Freedom, founded by President Nixon in 1994, which is committed to "developing new guiding principles for United States global engagement in a dramatically new international environment."[86] In a previous publication, I labeled legacy-based institutions as "vanity think tanks" and defined them as institutions that bear the name of the individual who serves as the driving and defining force behind the institution and its research agenda. While some institutions that were created and led by former presidents manage to be sustained after their deaths, many of these "vanity tanks" prove short-lived.[87] Senator Bob Dole's Better America Foundation is a prime example.[88] Although the Better America Foundation was initially established as a charitable organization in 1993, it acted increasingly as a think tank to advocate for Republican positions, including those of Senator Dole. After the foundation spent one million dollars on a Dole television campaign in 1994, numerous Democrats complained that the foundation was serving the purpose of supporting Dole's bid for the presidential election, prompting Dole to close it down in 1995.[89]

A Change in the Kinds of Issues Faced by Think Tanks

While think tanks have taken on a variety of roles over the course of their evolution during the nineteenth and early twentieth centuries, they certainly have not been immune to problems upon inheriting their new broadened range of responsibilities. Think tanks were forced to compensate for having been historically more subdued and often unaccredited for their work. It was not until the 1960s that think tanks took on their higher profile as actors in the policymaking process. Previously, their research was "not intended to grab headlines but rather to become infused into the political lexicon over time. This low profile [had] contributed to their attracting little scholarly attention." During the following two decades, literature appeared that denounced interest groups and their biases; however, it did not consider the ideas and the expertise supplied by think tanks or the inevitable ideological cleavages that existed in the policymaking process that had to be taken into account. As time progressed, think tanks were forced to adapt to the competitive environment in which policy is formulated and implemented. Unlike interest groups, they did not have a constituency to represent them before policymakers; instead they were forced to compensate by means of research, self-promotion, and conformity with the existing system of policymaking. According to Andrew Rich, "As think tanks have themselves become more often ideological . . . and aggressively promotional, think tanks and their products have come to warrant greater attention."[90]

The nature of think tanks, however, became less grounded in rationality toward the end of the twentieth century. As the spectrum of think tanks and their varying characteristics grew, so did the discrepancies among the institutions, which in turn fueled a more competitive atmosphere. Rich states that today "many experts now behave like advocates. They are not just visible but highly contentious as well. They more actively market their work than conventional views of experts would suggest; their work, in turn, often represents preformed points of view rather than . . . rational analysis."[91] By the beginning of the twenty-first century, policy experts within the think tank infrastructure had become staunch advocates for their fields of research, further emphasizing the chasm between the acts of providing neutral political advice and imposing a specific ideology. Rich elaborates, explaining that "many contemporary policy experts do seek an active and direct role in ongoing political debates. Far from maintaining a detached neutrality, policy experts are frequently aggressive advocates for ideas and ideologies; they even become brokers of political compromise."[92] The think tank industry has become more multifaceted in its attempts to adapt to the changing times, in terms of both its function and its sources of funding.

On the one hand, some think tanks became more concerned with visibility—raising funds and media attention—in the late twentieth century, thus accentuating their loss of impartiality as they compete for limited resources and the attention of the public and policymakers. Placing more emphasis on the numbers of mass media appearances, legislative testimonies, and news coverage citations, these institutions have devoted more resources to ensuring name recognition than in previous decades. In exchange, fewer resources were allocated for generating new policy solutions. On the other hand, increased communication between think tanks has contributed to the effective utilization of professional resources. Staff members from different institutes often cooperate, pooling their resources and participating in joint research projects. Such collaborative work further promotes name recognition and overall credibility within think tank circles.

THINK TANKS FROM THE LATE TWENTIETH CENTURY TO TODAY

As think tanks have become more visible, they have also become more global. Although think tanks abroad are not an entirely new phenomenon and have arguably been around longer than their U.S. counterparts, they only began to take on a true global presence in the 1990s as they were established around the world at an exponentially increasing rate. Globalization, the growing needs of the Information Age, and the extraordinary complexity of global public policy problems have made it possible for think tanks and scholars to scan the world for bigger and better ideas. In particular, the increase in globalization has corresponded to an increase in the worldwide spread of think tanks. From 1991 to 2000, the think tank proliferation phenomenon peaked with an astounding number of new institutions arising each year. Beginning around the year 2000, the forum of public policy research expanded globally and gave rise to global think tanks, which have formed networks or physically expanded across the world. In addition to its primary staff, a global think tank has a large number of collaborators who come from a myriad of sectors such as international organizations, nongovernmental organizations (NGOs), corporations, and academia and who assist the institution in its various functions. Furthermore, growth in structurally independent public policy networks has shown similar characteristics, arguably surpassing even the global think tank phenomenon and providing an influential alternative and complement to the traditional one-headquarter think tank.

The sharp spikes in the establishment of think tanks between 1991 and 2000 can be largely attributed to the democratization of formerly closed societies after the conclusion of the Cold War, increased trade liberalization, and the expansion of both market-based economies and globalization.[93] As noted, before

1991, most think tanks were located in the United States and Canada. The democratization and liberalization that occurred during the 1990s in effect created a more hospitable atmosphere for the rise of independent think tanks in other regions of the world.

In contrast, North America experienced a gradual decrease in the number of new think tanks established in the decade following the peak in the 1980s, and then a sharp decline in the first decade of the twenty-first century. Think tank proliferation in Western Europe followed another path entirely: whereas most regions witnessed a marked increase in the number of think tanks at least until the 1990s, Western Europe experienced two peaks of expansion followed by sharp declines in the 1960s and 1990s. The recent declines in the number of think tanks forming in these two regions have called into question the direction think tanks will take in the future.

As the number of international think tanks saw an upsurge in the 1990s, domestic institutions faced their own challenges within the United States. Domestic think tanks tackled various controversial problems throughout the decade, including welfare reform and the health care debate. Legislators and Clinton administration officials frequently relied on the work and guidance of experts from the leading think tanks in and around Washington, D.C., for fresh approaches to these problems. In addition to bringing an academic dimension to the welfare debate, the analysis provided by these esteemed researchers contributed constructive, practical critiques of the cash-assistance system during the process of welfare reform. However, in the case of President Bill Clinton's health care reform proposal, the variation in the research results, the lack of agreement among experts on the recommended course of action, and the complications caused by special interests and party politics led to the eventual defeat of the proposal in 1994.

Following Clinton's tenure in office, the George W. Bush administration provided numerous opportunities for think tanks to influence policy, particularly those institutions with a more conservative tendency. In contrast to the problems faced by the Clinton administration, Bush encountered success in invoking the advice of policy experts and ultimately enacting it into law.

Controversial topics such as health care and tax reform were at the heart of many scholars' research agendas as Bush came to office. The fight over tax cuts and tax reform began before Bush's election and continued after it. Experts from various institutions made their years of research expertise available to advise both sides of the debate. Although their combined knowledge failed to establish concurrence among policymakers, think tanks, and specifically the

Hoover Institution, played a vital role in advising the executive branch during this dispute. Bush's primary adviser (and thus an essential member of his administration), Lawrence Lindsey, was a Federal Reserve Board governor and a fellow at AEI. Lindsey solicited advice from various universities and think tanks on the economic implications of the proposed tax cut (President Bush pushed for a $1.35 billion tax cut following his inauguration). On the basis of the Congressional Budget Office's estimated $5.6 trillion budget surplus over a ten-year span, the House of Representatives passed the tax cut on March 8, 2001, and the Senate followed suit on May 18, 2001. The tax cut was officially signed into law on June 7, 2001.[94]

In sum, experts are involved in more than just the agenda-setting process. According to Rich, they are also indispensable during policy deliberation, enactment, and implementation. Experts may play radically different roles at different stages of the policymaking process. Consequently, they often become the virtual backbone during policy debates. The significance of policy research and the functional dimension of scholarly expertise have become widely respected domestically and internationally.

Today, the United States, Canada, and Western Europe host nearly 60 percent of the world's think tanks. Historically, the political and institutional environment in these regions has differed from that of Latin America, central and eastern Europe, and the former Soviet Union. Nations that experience authoritarian regimes and military dictatorships—as have been nearly ubiquitous in the latter group of regions—have a tendency to stifle "the voicing of independent opinions and any form of political or policy dissent."[95] As such, the evolution of knowledge and its dissemination throughout the public sphere has suffered under such political systems. As Weaver and I have said, "It is certainly no accident that the rapid growth of think tank activity in Latin America, Central and Eastern Europe, and the former Soviet Union coincided with the decline of military government in Latin America and the fall of communism."[96] Although the 1940s saw a gradual increase in the number of think tanks worldwide, the period of largest growth occurred from 1991 to 2000. This explosion was particularly observable in Africa, the Middle East, and eastern Europe, where governments were in transition and civil society was asserting its potential as a legitimate actor in both national and world politics. Starting around 2005, a dramatic change occurred, and countries such as Russia, China, and Zimbabwe began to engage in what I describe as NGO "pushback," which was a systematic effort to limit the number, role, and influence of think tankd in countries around the world.[97]

As this brief history shows, think tanks rose from humble beginnings about one hundred years ago to gain important international visibility as players in civil society and the policymaking community today. While the direction and role that think tanks will take in the years ahead remains uncertain, it is certain that think tanks have proven themselves to be irreplaceable and active participants in civil society and governance in the United States and worldwide.

THINK TANKS IN THE WORLD TODAY: THE UNITED STATES AND THE EUROPEAN UNION

Although the United States and Europe have close economic, historic, and cultural ties, the role of think tanks as policymaking organizations differs greatly between the two regions. On the one hand, think tank activity in the United States is more centralized. Although think tanks can be found in almost every state, all the major think tanks in the United States are located in either Washington, D.C., or New York City, with RAND, the National Bureau of Economic Research, and the Hoover Institution notable exceptions. Activity of think tanks in the European Union, on the other hand, exists across several capital and noncapital cities, and they are often located near major universities. Brussels is specifically trying to become a hub for those think tanks that concentrate mainly or solely on the European Union. These think tanks will be given specific consideration later in the book.

European and U.S. think tanks also differ in organizational structure, sources of funding, and degree of policy orientation. In part this reflects the differences that distinguish the political environments within each region, such as number of political parties and types of parliamentary system. The individual scholars who work at U.S. and European think tanks therefore have different degrees of job security and move between academia and government to varying degrees. This can be partially explained by the much stronger presence of the revolving door phenomenon in the United States, in which scholars and policymakers move freely between government jobs and positions in the think tank sector. Additionally, think tanks in the United States are much more visible in the media than those in Europe and consciously use the media to advance their ideas and policy proposals.

Given that the European Union and the United States share common political systems, cultural backgrounds, and levels of economic development—as well as a common history of think tanks and other civil society organizations— they lend themselves naturally to a comparative study. However, a comparison of single member states within the European Union with the United States would prove more problematic. This study seeks to compare think tanks in the United States and the European Union on several aspects. This is a macrolevel look at think tanks and is not focused on any specific institutions. Thus, both the opinions of experts in the field as well as empirical research data from the Think Tanks and Civil Societies Program's report *2007 Survey of Think Tanks* and Notre Europe's survey of EU member states will be used to gain a comprehensive understanding of the two regions.[98] As part of the research for this book, a study of a small but representative group of European think tanks was also conducted to capture some of the more recent trends. European research organizations were asked a set of fourteen questions, and the responses were compiled and analyzed (see appendixes for survey). It should be noted that trends can be deduced from the data and research, but not every think tank will follow the pattern. Indeed, as dynamic institutions, think tanks change and act on their own accord.

CURRENT LITERATURE ON THE GLOBAL STATE OF THINK TANKS

Think tanks now operate in a variety of political systems, engage in a range of policy-related activities, and include a diverse set of institutions that have varied organizational forms. While their organizational structure, modes of operation, audience or market, and means of support may vary from institution to institution and from country to country, most think tanks share the common goal of producing high-quality research and analysis that are combined with a form of public engagement.

All think tanks face the same challenge: how to achieve and sustain their independence so that they can speak "truth to power" or simply bring knowledge, evidence, and expertise to bear on the policymaking process. Unfortunately, not all think tanks have the financial, intellectual, and legal independence to enable them to be truly independent and operate as strong, effective, and constructive institutions that can assess policies and inform public policymaking. This problem is most acute in developing and transitional countries where the means of financial support for think tanks is limited, the legal space in which these organizations operate is poorly defined, and the channels for influencing public policy are narrow. It is these characteristics that distinguish think tanks in the Northern and Western Hemispheres from their counterparts in developing and transitional countries.

FIGURE 1-1. Worldwide Growth of Think Tanks, 1919–2009

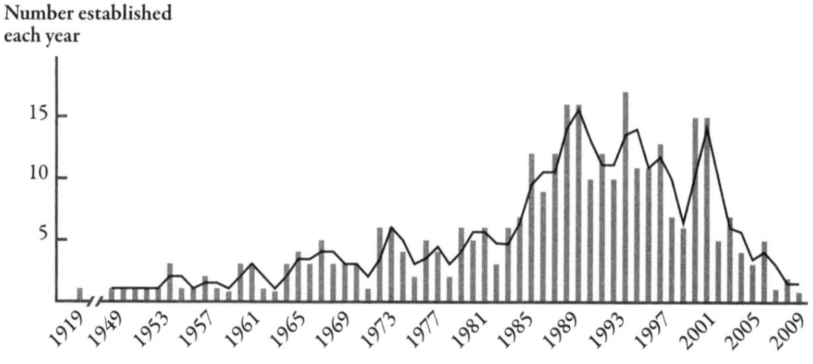

Number established
each year

Source: Think Tanks and Civil Societies Program database, 2010.

Although the number and overall impact of policy research organizations have been growing and spreading (see figure 1-1), data from the 2006–07 *Global Think Tank Trends Survey* indicate that the rate of establishment of new think tanks may be declining for the first time in twenty years. The reasons for this trend will require greater research and analysis, but the decline may be the result of a combination of complex factors: shifts in funding, lack of start-up grants and capital, and unfavorable government regulations that attempt to limit the number and influence of think tanks. While think tanks are one of the many civil society actors in a country, they often serve as catalysts for political and economic reform. The indigenous think tank sector can also function as a key indicator for the state of the civil society in that country. If analysts and critics associated with think tanks are allowed to operate freely, so too can the rest of civil society.

There has been an increasing amount of research highlighting the rise of broad European think tanks, as well as a sizable amount of criticism on the current state of EU think tanks.[99] The notion that there is disunity within the European Union and that the European community needs to find one voice or a set of coherent voices that effectively advance the interests of Europe has been a continuing topic of discussion. This is particularly important for the European Union, which wants to strengthen its role on the world stage. In the absence of a single voice, the European Union would be overshadowed or overlooked as an important player in the international arena.

There have been few significant scholarly projects on the specific topic of EU think tanks, but some efforts do stand out in recent years. A Notre Europe report, *Europe and Its Think Tanks: A Promise to Be Fulfilled,* is one of the more extensive discussions to date. In the report, Stephen Boucher outlines the current state of EU think tanks and their involvement in EU policymaking. Boucher states that there is general agreement on three categories for European think tanks: national, European specific (concerned with only European issues), and European oriented (addressing European issues among others). A growing number of think tanks follow the Anglo-American think tank model, which is more advocacy focused; the remaining number of European think tanks are predominantly academic-type research institutions. According to the Notre Europe report, EU think tanks want to be a part of the policy-initiation stage, when they are most likely to have the greatest impact. There is a focus on public debates, discussions, conferences, academic research, and publications, which are all employed to amass support and enhance visibility. With competition growing as more think tanks enter the arena, there is a need to be seen as relevant, which for some requires developing a niche market. Think tanks achieve this objective by specializing in a particular issue area or developing a political or philosophical brand. Notre Europe recommends five strategies for think tanks to maintain their relevance and effectiveness in the future:

- Strategically and actively cultivate private sources of funding.
- Develop performance measurement tools.
- Welcome new entrants and develop synergies through networks and cooperation.
- Consider greater focus and, perhaps, further specialization.
- Develop a better awareness of potential audiences.

Much of the other noteworthy research on the subject is found in discussions of the think tank world in general. *Think Tanks and Civil Societies: Catalysts for Ideas and Action* contains a number of relevant chapters on think tanks in Spain, Portugal, and France, as well as those in central and eastern Europe.[100] Alan Day gives an overview of think tanks in which he notes a trend toward advocacy think tanks and an increasing focus on issues that affect the European Union. Jonathon Kimball offers a comparison of think tank activity in Albania, Hungary, Poland, Slovakia, and Bulgaria. He notes that think tanks in central and eastern Europe face similar challenges to those in the rest of Europe: the search for influence, independence, and sustainability. In *Comparative Think Tanks, Politics and Public Policy,* the authors note that despite increasing European integration, there still exist profound ethnic, economic, and political divisions.[101] Despite these issues, the authors note that Europe is able to provide "a relatively

healthy and stable environment for independent analysis and advice."[102] They
focus their analysis on Russia, Germany, and Hungary, identifying a number of
indicators that have affected the think tank communities in these countries: the
existence of strong higher education systems, economic strength, and political
and press freedom. Last, *Think Tank Traditions: Policy Research and the Politics
of Ideas* devotes chapters to holistic European Union think tanks, as well as to
think tanks in Germany, Italy, France, and eastern Europe.[103] In the book Heidi
Ullrich gives a broad typology of EU think tanks and discusses the positive effect of think tank networks, while also mentioning that little collaboration and
competition exists among Brussels-based think tanks. A distinction is also made
between German think tanks, which are mostly academic and have been established by the government, and French think tanks, which do not have as much of
a foothold in French civil society.

Much of the current literature on EU think tanks finds that their financial
transparency and sources of funding are seriously inadequate. For example,
Open Europe suggests that the European Union funds think tanks to justify its
own existence and cement the European Commission's view that continued
European integration is the best, or even the only, future path for progress.[104]
At the other extreme, Stephen Boucher and Martine Royo mention the risk of
some think tanks becoming "submarines of private interests."[105] Both can be
viewed as an overreaction because most think tanks are organized to serve the
public interest and are designed to support the public policy process. In general,
too close of a relationship to any sector, whether it is government, business, or
unions, can affect the independence and effectiveness of a think tank. This was
perhaps a concern when, at a conference, members of the European Policy Institutes Network and several other think tank representatives concluded that there
is a need for think tanks to develop a code of conduct, to clarify where their
researchers come from, and to reveal the sources of funding.[106] According to the
members, there is a distinction between European think tanks, which have a
limited set of rules that regulate their operations, and U.S. think tanks, which
often must comply with a complex set of regulations to maintain their nonprofit
status and must provide annual tax returns to the U.S. Internal Revenue Service. While these regulations are cumbersome and time-consuming, they provide a great deal of transparency and tax advantages for nonprofits in the United
States as individuals are encouraged to support think tanks by receiving a tax
credit for making contributions to a nonprofit organization.

The intended focus of literature on EU think tanks, however, is on the ability
of think tanks to help deal with current and future challenges for government

and civil society. Despite the challenges of European integration, or perhaps in response to it, there exists a clear need for European think tanks with a truly regional perspective, whose programs are exclusively focused on issues surrounding European-level policymaking and the issues confronting Europe.

THINK TANKS NORTH, SOUTH, EAST, AND WEST TODAY

The Think Tanks and Civil Societies Program at the University of Pennsylvania catalogues and maintains the most comprehensive database of think tanks worldwide, which consists of 6,846 think tanks from 206 countries. It features specialized global databases of think tanks in areas such as development, environment, security, and international affairs. Information in the database can be sorted by geographic region, subregion, country, and subnational entity (for the United States and Canada). As of August 31, 2015, of the 6,846 global think tanks: 615 were located in Africa; 1,262 in Asia; 1,770 in Europe; 774 in Central and South America; 398 in the Middle East and North Africa; 1,931 in North America (with 1,839 located in the United States); and 96 in Oceania (see figures 1-2 and 1-3).

Policy research organizations have been growing in numbers and impact in recent years. A survey of think tanks conducted in 1999 found that two-thirds of all public policy research and analysis organizations in the world were established after 1970, and half have been established since 1980. Data from the 2006–07 *Global Think Tank Trends Survey* indicate that the number of think tanks in the United States may be declining for the first time in twenty years, as previously mentioned. Discovering the specific drivers of this trend will require further research and analysis. It is likely, however, that the result of a combination of complex factors—shifts in funding, underdeveloped institutional capacity, and unfavorable government regulations—will act to further limit the number and influence of think tanks. While think tanks are only one of the many civil society actors in any given country, they often serve as catalysts for political and economic reform.

Policy research centers have been growing rapidly in developing and transitional countries in sub-Saharan Africa; eastern and central Europe; and East, South, and Southeast Asia, which are regions where the majority of these institutions were established in the last ten to fifteen years. Similar centers have also appeared throughout Latin America and the Caribbean, where their operations began as early as the 1960s and 1970s.

Think tanks in developing countries, however, are currently faced with a unique challenge. As systems of communication have become more comprehensive

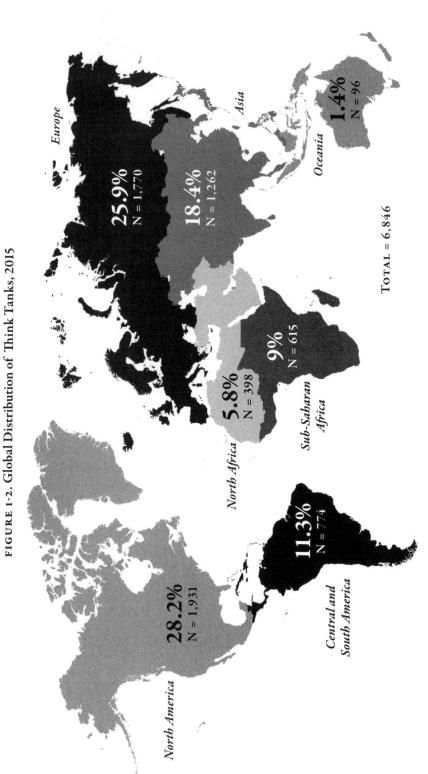

FIGURE 1-2. Global Distribution of Think Tanks, 2015

Europe

25.9%
N = 1,770

18.4%
N = 1,262

Asia

1.4%
N = 96

Oceania

9%
N = 615

5.8%
N = 398

North Africa

Sub-Saharan Africa

TOTAL = 6,846

28.2%
N = 1,931

North America

11.3%
N = 774

Central and South America

Source: Think Tanks and Civil Societies Program database, 2015.

FIGURE 1-3. North America Think Tank Distribution, 2014

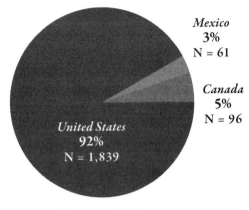

Mexico
3%
N = 61

Canada
5%
N = 96

United States
92%
N = 1,839

TOTAL = 1,996

Source: Think Tanks and Civil Societies Program database, 2015.

owing to technological advancements, salient issues that nations seek to resolve are more accessible to the stronger, older external think tanks that have established themselves as respectable and efficient international actors when compared with the fledgling, indigenous think tanks. In short, the latter are potentially overlooked when it comes to resolving conflicts and solving problems in their home countries. A certain degree of competitiveness between sprouting indigenous think tanks and more advanced, industrial ones is therefore instilled and reinforced by globalization.[107]

Table 1-4 lists the countries with the largest number of think tanks—those with ten or more; not included are the countries that do not have any think tanks currently in operation. Countries without think tanks include Antigua and Barbuda, Brunei, Comoros, Djibouti, Equatorial Guinea, Guinea-Bissau, Kiribati, Macao, Marshall Islands, Micronesia, Monaco, Myanmar, Nauru, Oman, Palau, San Marino, São Tomé and Príncipe, Solomon Islands, Tonga, Turkmenistan, Tuvalu, and Vanuatu. For a more complete picture of the global distribution of think tanks by country, consult appendix C.

THE THINK TANK ENVIRONMENT

Think tanks are not islands in a sea; rather, they are born within a larger socioeconomic framework and must remain responsive to any changes within the greater society to stay relevant. An analysis of the environments in which think

TABLE 1-4. Global Distribution of Think Tanks by Country

Sub-Saharan Africa

Angola	4	Gabon	2	Nigeria	48
Benin	15	Gambia	6	Rwanda	7
Botswana	13	Ghana	37	Senegal	16
Burkina Faso	16	Guinea	2	Seychelles	3
Burundi	5	Guinea-Bissau	1	Sierra Leone	1
Cameroon	21	Kenya	53	Somalia	6
Cape Verde	2	Lesotho	4	South Africa	86
Central African		Liberia	3	South Sudan	5
Republic	2	Madagascar	5	Swaziland	4
Chad	3	Malawi	15	Tanzania	15
Congo	3	Mali	12	Togo	4
Congo, Democratic		Mauritania	2	Uganda	28
Republic of	7	Mauritius	8	Zambia	13
Côte d'Ivoire	12	Mozambique	4	Zimbabwe	26
Eritrea	5	Namibia	15		
Ethiopia	25	Niger	4		

Asia

Afghanistan	6	Indonesia	27	Pakistan	20
Armenia	14	Japan	109	Philippines	21
Azerbaijan	13	Kazakhstan	8	Singapore	12
Bangladesh	35	Kyrgyzstan	10	South Korea	35
Bhutan	9	Laos	3	Sri Lanka	14
Brunei	1	Macao	1	Taiwan	52
Cambodia	10	Malaysia	18	Tajikistan	7
China	435	Maldives	6	Thailand	8
Georgia	14	Mongolia	7	Turkmenistan	1
Hong Kong	30	Nepal	12	Uzbekistan	8
India	280	North Korea	2	Vietnam	10

Central and Eastern Europe

Albania	14	Bosnia and		Bulgaria	35
Belarus	21	Herzegovina	14	Croatia	11

Czech Republic	27	Lithuania	19	Russia	122
Estonia	17	Macedonia	18	Serbia	24
Finland	28	Moldova	9	Slovakia	18
Hungary	42	Montenegro	4	Slovenia	19
Kosovo	3	Poland	42	Ukraine	47
Latvia	11	Romania	54		

Western Europe

Andorra	2	Ireland	14	Portugal	21
Austria	40	Italy	97	San Marino	1
Belgium	53	Liechtenstein	2	Spain	55
Denmark	41	Luxembourg	6	Sweden	77
France	180	Malta	4	Switzerland	73
Germany	195	Monaco	2	United Kingdom	288
Greece	35	Netherlands	58	Vatican City	1
Iceland	7	Norway	15		

Central and South America

Anguilla	1	Cuba	19	Panama	12
Antigua and		Dominica	3	Paraguay	27
Barbuda	2	Dominican		Peru	33
Argentina	138	Republic	31	Puerto Rico	6
Aruba	1	Ecuador	18	St. Kitts and Nevis	1
Bahamas	2	El Salvador	13	St. Lucia	3
Barbados	9	French Guiana	1	St. Vincent and the	
Belize	4	Grenada	1	Grenadines	1
Bermuda	3	Guadeloupe	5	Suriname	3
Bolivia	59	Guatemala	12	Trinidad and	
Brazil	89	Guyana	4	Tobago	12
British Virgin		Haiti	2	Turks and Caicos	
Islands	1	Honduras	9	Islands	1
Cayman Islands	1	Jamaica	6	U.S. Virgin	
Chile	44	Martinique	2	Islands	1
Colombia	40	Montserrat	1	Uruguay	21
Costa Rica	37	Nicaragua	10	Venezuela	20

(*continued*)

TABLE 1-4. (*continued*)

Middle East and North Africa

Algeria	9	Kuwait	14	Sudan	5
Bahrain	4	Lebanon	19	Syria	6
Cyprus	6	Libya	2	Tunisia	18
Egypt	35	Morocco	15	Turkey	32
Iran	59	Oman	3	United Arab	
Iraq	31	Palestine	28	Emirates	7
Israel	58	Qatar	7	Yemen	22
Jordan	21	Saudi Arabia	4		

North America

Canada	99	Mexico	61	United States	1,835

Oceania

Australia	63	New Zealand	5	Samoa	1
Fiji	1	Papua-New Guinea	1	Vanuatu	1

tanks operate is crucial toward understanding their influence on policy. This includes studying the movement of scholars within think tanks and the government, as well as recent trends within the think tank community. This comparison is an expansion on a section in one of my earlier works, "National Interest vs. Regional Governance: Think Tanks, Policy Advice and the Future of the EU."

Think tanks in the United States have held an extremely influential position in the policymaking process for at least fifty years. Most notably, the 1960s and 1970s saw an influx of think tanks fulfilling crucial roles in government processes as social, environmental, and economic departments of government expanded or were created. As time went on, these institutions became larger, more complex, and more dynamic than ever before. They exist in ever greater numbers, and even institutions founded more recently have garnered successes. Today, think tanks interact with both the public and the government to ensure that their policy recommendations are adopted. Think tanks in the United States are an important part of civil society and are independent from the government, work in the public interest, and offer policymakers practical and effective policy recommendations.

While the vast majority of think tanks in the United States are focused on foreign relations and economic affairs, there is truly a think tank for every issue area. As more than mere advocacy groups, they unite scholars and policymakers so that they can discuss and debate pressing issues to create relevant and applicable policies for the government to adopt.

Some top U.S. think tanks are very well funded relative to those in other regions of the world. This is in part due to the many philanthropic organizations in the nation that seek to influence policy and participate in the political system. Institutions such as the Carnegie Corporation of New York, Hewlett Foundation, Ford Foundation, and the Pew Charitable Trusts made and continue to make important and lasting funding contributions. However, while many philanthropists hope to simply create a better world by giving to organizations that strive for the public good, others give money so think tanks can produce research and analysis that advances a particular agenda. As a result, partisan politics have at times narrowed the space in which think tanks operate in the United States by limiting the range of policy choices that they might consider. While some think tanks do not like to be branded, most of them can be characterized as favoring a singular political ideology.[108] The large number of think tanks and the diversity that exists among them helps guard against any one institution from undue influence on the president or on Congress.

A defining characteristic of American think tanks is that they often serve as a source of qualified staff for key positions when there is a change in administrations in Washington. This was the case most recently with both George W. Bush and Barack Obama, both of whom relied on the help and expertise of think tanks such as the conservative AEI and the progressive CAP, respectively. These think tanks helped shape the ideas and policy of the administration in power.[109] Indeed, many government officials participate in the "revolving door" and move between positions within the government and in the think tank community, usually depending on which party is in power in the White House and in both houses of Congress. This movement is not new, either; the "revolving door" phenomenon has helped form "governments-in-waiting" since 1961.[110]

The ease of entry between the government sector and think tanks allows scholars and public officials to maintain a healthy balance between hectic, purely policy-focused work and more abstract, scholarly pursuits. Lee Hamilton, a former member of Congress who now directs the Woodrow Wilson International Center for Scholars, contends, "Many of the think tanks are developing talent for a new administration. You will see a large number of people leaving the think tanks to go into the Obama administration."[111] Indeed, Phillip J. Crowley, formerly of CAP and former assistant secretary of state for public affairs, explains, "There's a lot more sanity in the think tank world than there is in government. You're not on the treadmill as much. . . . It is a chance to step back, to actually think. If you're in government, you're dealing with those boundaries that have already been set. In a think tank, you start with a blank piece of paper."[112] This ends up benefiting the policymaking process as a whole. In their own words, academics who straddle the academic and policy worlds can attest to the importance of the "revolving door": "One of the most effective transmission belts for ideas to travel from the academy to government might be called 'embedded capital' in the minds of 'in and outers'. . . . As Henry Kissinger once pointed out, the pressure on time that bears upon policymakers means that they rely on ideas and intellectual capital created before they entered the maelstrom."[113]

Despite increasing competition for outreach, several think tanks hold high profiles in the media, and some can even become household names. To assert better control over their public images, many think tanks deal directly with the public and media. While many prominent journalists serve as fellows for various think tanks, institutions such as the Heritage Foundation, the Carnegie Endowment for International Peace, and CSIS even maintain their own television studios. The Peterson Institute inaugurated its media center in 2008.

Financial transparency is a major feature of U.S. think tanks, as briefly mentioned before. Partly because the U.S. Internal Revenue Service requires that all nonprofits, including think tanks, to submit financial reports each year to maintain their nonprofit status, U.S. think tanks are often very forthcoming about their main sources of funding, and the records of many institutions are available to the public through the Internet. Overall, the U.S. public and media generally demand a greater degree of transparency and accountability than do their European counterparts.[114] Many think tanks even have their own public relations representatives, and websites often provide public access to the leaders of these organizations and enable them to engage with the scholars on staff. With the ability to scrutinize these political intermediaries, the public has grown to believe that think tanks are working in the public interest.

Partisan U.S. Think Tanks

As was discussed earlier in the history of think tanks, not all think tanks are nonpartisan. Some represent nearly every possible position on the political spectrum, with four main categories encompassing most U.S. think tanks:

FIGURE 1-4. Ideological Breakdown in U.S. Think Tanks

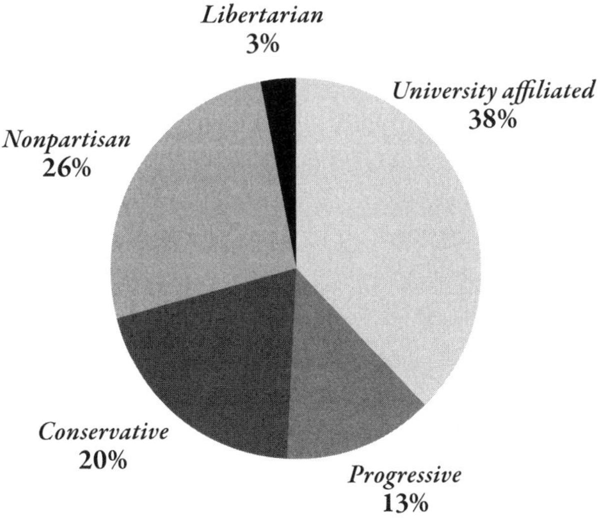

Libertarian
3%

University affiliated
38%

Nonpartisan
26%

Conservative
20%

Progressive
13%

Source: Think Tanks and Civil Societies Program database, 2015.

conservative, libertarian, centrist, and progressive. In addition, a large number of think tanks classify themselves as "university affiliated" and self-identify as nonpartisan (see figure 1-4).

Over the last decade, right-of-center think tanks have had a commanding presence and influence in Washington. This influence was in part due to their superior funding advantage and to the effectiveness of conservative organizations such as the Heritage Foundation and Cato.[115] Recently, however, liberal-leaning donors, most notably George Soros, have helped even out the partisan imbalance with the creation of organizations such as CAP, which has a close relationship with the Obama administration. John Podesta, the chair and counselor of CAP, made clear "his plan for what he likes to call a 'think tank on steroids.'" The objective was to create more advocacy oriented think that that focused on policy products with a quicker response time, shorter in length and clear and direct position on key policy issues. "Emulating those conservative institutions," he said "a message-oriented war room will send out a daily briefing to refute the positions and arguments of the right. An aggressive media department will book liberal thinkers on cable TV. There will be an 'edgy Web site' [thinkprogress.org] and a policy shop to formulate strong positions on foreign and domestic issues."[116] The reemergence of liberal think tanks has brought about a balance of power in Washington's partisan playing field.

Another characteristic of U.S. think tanks is the well-developed national networks of progressive and conservative think tanks, such as the U.S. Public Interest Research Group (U.S. PIRG) and HI. For example, established in the 1970s as an outgrowth of the consumer movement spearheaded by Ralph Nader, U.S. PIRG is now a nationwide movement of state-based think tanks, primarily concerned with environmental issues, consumer protection, and political and social justice. Nonetheless, U.S. PIRG differs from other think tanks in that it was founded as a student group and still remains one today. Indeed, most of its members and financial resources come from student-driven organizations. It often employs grassroots methods to get its voice heard, which other think tanks might not find effective.[117]

The conservative HI was established in Chicago in 1984. According to its website, it received 71 percent of its income from foundations, 16 percent from corporations, and 11 percent from individuals in 2007. No corporate donor gave more than 5 percent of its annual budget. HI maintains a network of 125 academics and professional economists serving as policy advisers to it, including members of the faculties of Harvard University, University of Chicago, and Northwestern University.

Finally, another characteristic of U.S. think tanks is their geographical distribution and the variety of topics they cover. While there are 398 think tanks in Washington, D.C., alone, every single state in the United States, with the exception of Wyoming, which is the least populous state, has at least one think tank (see table 1-5). Although commonly thought of as national institutions, think tanks also research topics pertaining to state and local issues. Indeed, power has increased in the hands of the states in recent decades, and it is often up to the states to balance large and complex budgets and administer complex programs. As with national policy, think tanks research and debate issues to make recommendations to policymakers at the state and local levels. Although think tanks operating at the local level do not operate in as competitive an environment as those working on national issues do, these think tanks work just as hard to convey their messages.[118] Generally, think tanks have played an important role in the policymaking process in the United States, influencing the activities and policies of the government, yet remaining responsive to issues of the public.

TABLE 1-5. U.S. Think Tanks by State and the District of Columbia, 2014

State/D.C.	Number	State/D.C.	Number
District of Columbia	398	Kansas	17
Massachusetts	177	Alabama	16
California	169	Oregon	16
New York	144	New Hampshire	13
Virginia	105	Hawaii	12
Illinois	62	Kentucky	11
Maryland	50	Oklahoma	11
Texas	47	Iowa	10
Connecticut	44	Louisiana	10
Pennsylvania	42	Mississippi	10
New Jersey	36	Arkansas	8
Colorado	31	Montana	8
Florida	31	Nebraska	7
Michigan	31	New Mexico	7
Georgia	29	Utah	7
Washington	27	South Carolina	6
Ohio	25	West Virginia	6
Minnesota	23	South Dakota	5
North Carolina	23	Vermont	5
Wisconsin	22	Idaho	4
Arizona	21	Nevada	4
Indiana	21	North Dakota	4
Maine	21	Alaska	3
Rhode Island	20	Delaware	3
Tennessee	19		
Missouri	18	**Total**	**1,839**

COMPARATIVE THINK TANKS, POLITICS, AND PUBLIC POLICY IN THE UNITED STATES AND EUROPE

A comparison of think tanks in the United States with those in Europe brings into focus the unique elements of U.S. politics, political culture, and institutions. It is precisely these characteristics that help explain why there are more think tanks in the United States than in any other country in the world. It also explains why

Americans have a proclivity for advice that is independent of government and why think tanks play such an important role in policy debates and policymaking.

U.S. think tanks hold a unique role in U.S. society as independent institutions that is unmatched by comparative think tanks in Western Europe. Why do they have greater independence, influence, and resources than European think tanks do? The political culture in the United States differs from what is found in Europe in the following ways:

Porous and highly decentralized system of government
- Separation of powers (legislative, executive, and judiciary).
- Federal, state, and local governments.
- Fear of an imperial Congress or president.

Weak civil service and strong reliance on independent advice
- "The government that governs best, governs least."
- Desire to avoid centralized power and giving too much power to unelected bureaucrats.

Strong two-party system but weak party discipline
- Members of Congress elected by popular vote.
- No viable third party—Democrats and Republicans dominate.
- Personal attributes, power base, and financial support matter more than party affiliation.
- Candidates use party label but are not defined by or bound to the party.

President's candidacy not tied to a party
- President elected by popular election, not by the majority party.
- Primary elections are open for all candidates for president and members of Congress, attracting a wide range of candidates.

Hyperpluralistic and individualistic society
- Most religiously and ethnically diverse country in the world.
- Every interest has a group to represent it.

Highly developed philanthropic culture
- Individuals, private corporations, private foundations, unions, and other interest groups fund and support nongovernmental organizations.
- More wealthy donors in the United States, examples include Bill Gates ($48 billion) and George Soros ($7.6 billion).
- Well-established legal and tax rules and public support for independent, nongovernmental organizations.

Think tanks in the United States have been carving out their own Fifth Estate for at least seventy-five years, playing increasingly crucial roles in the policymaking process. Notably, the 1970s saw an influx of think tanks fulfilling crucial roles in government processes. As time progressed, think tanks became larger, more complex, and more dynamic. Today, think tanks exist in ever-greater numbers and have garnered successes in influencing public policy; they interact with both the public and the government, ensuring the adoption of their policy recommendations. Largely independent from the government, working primarily in the public interest, and offering policymakers practical and effective policy recommendations, think tanks in the United States are an essential component of U.S. civil society.

How did think tanks rise from the maelstrom of World War I to achieve their prominent perch in American foreign policy formulation? Since 1945 the promise of think tanks as a means of ameliorating the shortcomings of the government's ability to adapt and to plan in policy domains has been largely borne out. It is not that think tanks are immune to error, theoretical cul-de-sacs, bias, and fads, but rather that they have successfully integrated themselves into the preexisting political arena and became integral to the way that the U.S. government functions. The reasons, however, are not all obvious, and the implications are not fully understood even by the participants in the arena of think tanks. Nevertheless, it is known that the U.S. political environment has enabled the influx of think tanks in the United States.

There are institutional reasons for the strength of U.S. civil society and the national environment's conduciveness to think tanks. In contrast to authoritarian regimes, where power is consolidated in the hands of a single individual or an exclusive group of individuals, the United States was founded on a system of separated and fragmented powers, including the fragmentation of power within the legislative branch. As a result, policymakers frequently consult organizations charged with creating knowledge relevant to policy formulation—that is, think tanks. I explain that "each member of Congress is concerned with building a record of legislative accomplishment and position taking," which spurs legislators to consult heavily with think tanks before making policy decisions. This relationship between think tanks and the legislative branch is distinct from that found in most parliamentary systems. Typically in a parliamentary system, governmental departments are relied on more systematically than other sources of policy advice (including think tanks).[119] Coupled with the nature of political parties, the U.S. government structure provides a prime environment for civil society organizations.

CIVIL SOCIETY AND GOVERNANCE

Civil society is made up of a range of associations that occupy the space between a government and its citizens. As objective, independent producers of policy and analysis, representing neither the public nor the private sector, think tanks are an important feature of a strong civil society. This is significant when one considers the generally accepted notion that a strong and vibrant civil society is an essential component of any healthy democracy. The organizations that constitute civil society can span sports teams, labor unions, and policy research organizations. While civil society ideally touts itself as a force separate from the state, it rarely enjoys complete independence from the state.[a]

Naturally, the extent to which states interfere with the operation of civil society depends on the legal, political, social, and economic contexts, as well as the type of civil institution concerned. It is no surprise that given their proximity to government and the nature of policy advice, think tanks are often targets for government intervention in countries where there are authoritarian, corrupt, or nontransparent governments. Moreover, it is vital to recognize that the conditions that enable think tanks to operate as an effective counterweight to the state and the market are not necessarily present in every civil society.

Within civil society, significant trust is invested in the research produced by universities and think tanks, as these institutions influence policymaking and directly affect the population. According to Andrew Rich, "The role of experts tends to be greater in debates that take on a high public profile, that move at a relatively slow pace, and that do not elicit the mobilization of organized interests with much to lose in the decisions under consideration."[b] The success, visibility, and funding of these institutions directly correlates with the concerns of their constituents. The think tanks' research and counsel to the legislative and executive branches are intended to reflect the prerogatives of the public and provide a voice to civil society. However, this constitutes only one element of the relationship between think tanks and civil society.

---

a. As Kent Weaver and I have noted, "Although it may be an area of organized activity, civil society is bound to be liable to state intervention even in democracies." See James McGann, *Democratization and Market Reform in Developing and Transitional Countries: Think Tanks as Catalysts* (London: Routledge, 2010).

b. Andrew Rich, *Think Tanks, Public Policy, and the Politics of Expertise* (Cambridge University Press, 2004), p. 107.

The extent of political parties' control over policy decisions varies according to the political system in place. The power of political parties in the United States, for example, is not comparable with that of parties common in countries such as Germany and the Netherlands, where party-funded think tanks play a prominent role in civil society. Because think tanks in these countries rely heavily on political parties, the results of elections are sufficient to affect their influence and funding. In contrast, political parties in the United States are relatively weak. They "function primarily as campaign vehicles and party platforms [that] often vary considerably over time depending on the positions taken by the party's presidential candidates." Because they do little to fund think tanks and other such organization, parties do not significantly influence the policymaking process postelection; their priorities are constantly shifting with various party nominees, rendering their research transient in comparison with that of U.S. think tanks.[120]

Think tanks occupy an important position in the policymaking process because they offer comprehensive advisory services to the legislative and executive branches of the U.S. government. America's long-standing tradition of trusting the private sector to assist the government, coupled with its equally long-standing tradition of distrusting the government, have contributed to the prominent role that think tanks hold in policymaking. Most recently, reliance on think tanks for policy research and analysis has gained prominence because of their demonstrated efficiency, independence, relevance, and access to key government officials.

Another factor that has increased U.S. reliance on think tanks is their proven efficacy in the policy research they conduct. Think tanks can produce sound analyses of policy problems faster than their counterparts in the public sector, who must contend with the distraction of political maneuvering and a bureaucratic culture that strives to maintain the status quo. Think tanks are often more efficient than government bureaucracies at collecting, synthesizing, and analyzing information. Think tanks are free to be forward-looking, because they do not reward the creative disruptions otherwise known as bureaucratic politics. As they are mostly unencumbered by political constraints, they tend to produce bolder reconfigurations of policy agendas than their public sector counterparts are able to achieve.

Another structural benefit is the wide reach of think tanks, which enables them to engage relevant policymakers better than government agencies can. These agencies are often laden with specific concerns, and the inherent hierarchy that exists within an agency can sometimes swallow information rather than disseminate it efficiently. In contrast, think tanks are independent of the executive and legislative bureaucracies. This allows them more freedom to design their own agendas, adapt to the needs of their clients, and increase collaboration both within and among institutions inside and outside government. Their broad scope empowers think tanks to conceive of policy implementation better than the government bureaucracies that are limited by specialization and segmentation can.[121] The breadth of their influence coupled with their independence from executive and legislative bureaucracies assures skeptical policymakers and citizens alike that think tanks' findings are legitimate.

Additionally, the independence of think tanks from the U.S. government renders them capable of expanding their data sources. Think tanks use data provided by government agencies, but they also draw on resources such as journalistic outlets and NGOs and intergovernmental organizations such as NATO and the World Bank. According to the Heritage Foundation's Helle Dale, a think tank's independence from governmental interference enables it to incorporate as many credible and well-established sources as possible.[122] Moreover, the independent nature of think tanks allows them, as Richard Haass explains, to "give candid assessments of pressing global challenges and the quality of government responses [to them]."[123] Unlike government agencies, think tanks are not formally hindered by official positions or conflicts of interest. Therefore, they are consulted frequently by the public and private sectors for objective judgments and alternative policy options. Yet, despite attempts to court members of Congress with particular policy ideas, think tanks remain independent from the U.S. government.

As suggested, Congress frequently uses think tanks to inform policymaking. Under the legislative system, each member of Congress is responsible for casting one vote on each piece of proposed legislation. Therefore, policy advisers, often from think tanks, are provided an opportunity to personally influence legislators. As Donald Abelson explains, "Think tanks have employed several strategies to attract attention, ranging from testifying before congressional committees and delivering by hand concise summaries of key policy issues to members of Congress to inviting representatives and senators, as well as their staff, to participate in seminars and workshops."[124] Because members of Congress are not held accountable to a specific party, their financial and ideological support of particular think tanks does not "undermine party cohesion," making them open to policy advice.[125]

Think tank culture offers the opportunity to circumvent governmental inertia for six reasons:

1. They are often are more future oriented than government research functionaries, who work in an environment in which efforts at creative disruption are rarely rewarded, if tolerated at all.

2. They are more likely to generate new policy agendas, while bureaucracies thrive on the security of standard operating procedures.

3. They are better able to facilitate collaboration among separate groups of researchers for a common purpose because they have no permanent vested interest in any one domain.

4. They promote the intellectual synthesis that comes from breaking down bureaucratic barriers.

5. They can better disseminate relevant policy research within government than can government agencies themselves, which are subject to bureaucratic politics and turf wars.

6. They can often telescope the policy function from data collection to formation of knowledge to conceiving a means of implementation better than government bureaucracies, which may be segmented along functional lines, can.

Think tanks hold a unique position in political and civic life in America as evidenced by their prominent role and profile in the print and electronic media, in the halls of Congress, and in the briefing rooms of the executive branch. Deeply ingrained in the political and civic culture is a desire for weak bureaucracy and government where powers are divided and decentralized ("a government that governs best, governs least"). All of these characteristics stand in stark contrast to our European counterparts and help explain why think tanks are the Fifth Estate.

Additionally, state and federal tax credits and tax deductions encourage private and corporate support and a policy environment that accommodates their flourishing.[126] In contrast, funding differences and alternate affiliation patterns in Europe have resulted in a strong focus on academic research rather than on policy creation in European think tanks. As opposed to U.S. think tanks, there is no real "revolving door" or personnel exchange back and forth from think tanks to government.[127] Moreover, think tanks in Europe are not as visible in the media, thus highlighting the unique position U.S. think tanks play in bridging the divide between civil society and government.

Scholars have pointed out that think tanks in the United States have more of an impact on public policy compared with their counterparts in other countries. The nature and structure of the American political system creates an open system where there are many points of access to policymakers and the policymaking process. This porous system creates a fertile environment where think tanks, special interest advocacy groups, lobbyists, and other policy actions can operate. What distinguishes think tanks from for-profit corporations are their missions, which are designed to serve the public interest; they are governed by independent boards that are charged with serving the public interests; and their activities and financing are required by federal law to be in the public interest.

While commonly thought of as national institutions, think tanks also research topics pertaining to state and local issues. Just as with national policy, these think tanks research and debate issues in order to make recommendations to policymakers on the local level. While the environment they operate in is not as competitive as that of national think tanks, state-focused think tanks work just as hard to convey their recommendations.[128]

The varied abilities of U.S. think tanks to focus on global, national, and local issues make them a powerful tool in the nation's policymaking process and places them in a position to influence policy while bridging the divide between government and civil society. Because of U.S. think tanks' unique focus on policy research, their overlap with governmental organizations, and their high profile in media, they separate themselves from their European counterparts and have created a position in society as a linkage between government and civil society. Unlike the European think tank model that renders research institutions as an appendage of a political party, this position carves out an independent niche or a separate estate in society that differs from other civil society actors such as the media or lobbyists.

Duties in the Public and Private Spheres

As the use of think tanks has grown, so too has the range of their duties. As think tanks have begun to serve increasingly diversified roles, Donald Abelson has divided the work of think tanks into two spheres of influence: public and private. Think tanks are influential in the public sphere through such venues as public conferences, seminars, and published media, all of which are strategically carried out to draw the attention of policymakers, academics, and the public to the institutions and their experts.

Diane Stone asserts that today's think tanks play active roles in training government officials, sponsoring conferences and seminars, and providing expert testimony. Additionally, many institutions regularly produce books, journals, newsletters, newspaper articles, and online blogs in an effort to disseminate their ideas and improve public education and advocacy. Many think tank scholars have even become regular media pundits who share their experiences with television and radio audiences. *Foreign Affairs* is the journal produced and published by the Council on Foreign Relations, which is itself, among other things, a powerful think tank with offices in New York and Washington, D.C. The *National Interest* does not belong to a large institution or perform research functions, but its editor and executive editor have worked at think tanks and served in government positions. *The Journal* gets many of its articles from former, present, and future think tank scholars as well. *Orbis* is published by the Foreign Policy Research Institute, a Philadelphia-based think tank that increasingly disseminates its research in abridged form over the Internet. As a result of these new developments, the people affected by think tanks "are just as varied as their services and products."[129]

Despite increasing competition in their outreach efforts, several think tanks have high profiles in the media to retain control over their public images. Some think tank scholars have even become household names: Michael O'Hanlon (Brookings Institution), Richard Haass (Council on Foreign Relations), Steven Clemmons (New America Foundation), Norman Ornstein (AEI), and C. Fred Bergsten (Peterson Institute for International Economics) are quoted frequently in the press and are regulars on the nightly news and 24-7 cable news networks. Many prominent journalists serve as fellows for various think tanks, and, as previously mentioned, many institutions maintain their own television studios. Still, as think tanks have become increasingly focused in their efforts to ensure visibility, questions have surfaced pertaining to the reliability and credibility of published and publicized work.

The demand for accessible information online has pressured think tanks to develop technologically. According to Kathleen McNutt and Gregory Marchildon, "Web-based impact refers to the visibility (popularity) and relevance of an organizational or individual website or web page, and it is usually measured by analyzing hyperlinks."[130] This becomes problematic when organizations compromise the quality of materials published online to increase the quantity. Popularity, in turn, is often misconstrued as validity. To measure efficiently the impact of think tanks, "the correlations between an institute's research or recommendations and particular policy outcomes" should be considered first and foremost; they constitute the most valid evidence of a think tank's legitimacy.[131]

As think tanks have become increasingly concerned with their visibility, they have coincidentally served as a vehicle for public relations for government actors as well, having modified their traditional role of providing government officials with policy ideas. Kent Weaver has noted that think tanks have recently been employed by government officials and political figures to promote revolutionary ideas that, for political reasons, they do not want to publicly advocate themselves. Examples include the Heritage Foundation's early calls for widespread privatization of various government agencies and services as well as propositions to deregulate the U.S. transport industry in the late twentieth century, an issue championed by AEI, Hoover, and Brookings.[132]

U.S. RELIANCE ON THINK TANKS

As previously mentioned, a unique characteristic of U.S. civil society is its strong skepticism of government entities. Citizens and public officials are inclined to trust the private sector to assist the government. This willingness to go outside official channels for solutions makes it easy for private policy analysts, ideologues, entrepreneurs, or those with a strong interest in policy formation to influence government decisionmaking.[133] An early notable example occurred during the post–World War I peace conference in Paris. Colonel Edward House, a top adviser to President Woodrow Wilson, assembled a group of ex officio advisers from academia to explore the implications of any potential peace treaty. By 1921, this ad hoc corps of consultants became the Council on Foreign Relations—an organization that continues to influence U.S. foreign policy today.[134]

Another example of America's willingness to rely on think tanks is the Department of Defense's ongoing relationship with RAND. The organization's founding enabled the U.S. Air Force to replicate the cadre of civilian researchers who were recruited during World War II so that they could continue to provide objective views and expertise during the growing chill of relations with the Soviet Union. Since its foundation, RAND has expanded its agenda to include non-defense-related issues such as health care and education.[135] In the mid-1990s, RAND further strengthened its domestic activities, which had existed since 1965 or earlier, as defense funding continued to shrink.[136] Today, half of RAND's work is focused on domestic, nonmilitary issues.

U.S. think tanks nurture the government's willingness to rely on the private sector by playing an active role in advising government officials in both the executive and legislative branches. Think tanks rapidly provide foreign policy information to members of Congress and their staffers, helping those who may lack prior experience in domestic and international issues.[137] For example, the Natural Resources Defense Council (NRDC) has played a crucial role in educating legislators. Hugh Gusterson of George Mason University explains:

> Many Congressional leaders complained that they could not participate in any meaningful way in debates about nuclear arms reductions

without knowing the details of the [Single Integrated Operational Plan] SIOP, since they knew neither how many weapons were required for the various attack options war planners have built into the SIOP nor the strategic logic of the various menus within the SIOP. One of the primary purposes of the NRDC study was to produce a briefing on an NRDC simulation of the SIOP that could be offered to members of Congress as a way of inciting more informed debate about nuclear arms reductions and about Congressional appropriations for nuclear weapons.[138]

The relationship between the policy scholars of think tanks and the legislative actors responsible for enacting those policies serves the agendas of both entities simultaneously. Anthony Bertelli and Jeffery Wenger speculate on the chain of command between think tanks and Congress today, advancing the claim that "the nature of debate in legislative committees drives a demand for strategic information, and the benefactors of think tanks, seeing a market opportunity, create and maintain the organizations which supply that information."[139] As policymakers in the legislative branch contemplate new policy trends and the political climate of today, they are bound to seek consultation from experts and ensure that they have perpetual access to such information. Bertelli and Wenger continue, "Think tanks are specialist, expert suppliers of information that target legislators who are unlikely to substitute support for the think tank's policy position with an opposing stance. Such legislators are the think tank's ideological 'allies.'" Richard Hall and Alan Deardorff predict that "legislators who share the same policy objective' will receive free information-based resources from groups because 'allies will use resources to work toward progress on [an issue], not against it.'"[140] By creating alliances, both think tanks and legislative policymakers maintain a certain degree of solidarity in the face of opposing political ideologies. In a sense, the particular relationship mimics that of a market—a market of knowledge. The demand for think tanks' policy research is driven by the legislative demand for relevant information regarding the debate at the time; to satisfy this demand, political entrepreneurs have increasingly pegged the market by founding think tanks.[141]

Many think tanks have become highly skilled at providing information and analysis in the right form—concise reports or policy briefs—when the legislative agenda is being developed or a critical piece of legislation is being considered. It is at these times that think tanks are most effective.[142] In addition, they maintain a corps of experts who remain ready and willing to testify in congressional hearings and to share their expertise with legislators and the general public on a wide range of topics in foreign policy.[143] Foreign policy think tanks often testify in congressional hearings, as do experts from RFF, whose fellows are often called on to give expert testimony for Senate committees and to brief House representatives and Capitol Hill staffers on a wide range of energy, health, and environmental policies.

Think tanks often work outside government to educate and persuade policymakers through their publications, testimony, and appearances in the print and electronic media to adopt or shift the course of a policy—to "help government think." Meanwhile, they work behind the scenes to draft reports and recommendations that often translate directly to public policy.[144] The case study titled "The Buy America Provision in the 2009 Stimulus Package," discussed later in this book, showcases the response of the Peterson Institute for International Economics to what C. Fred Bergsten described as blatantly protectionist legislation. This case study highlights the think tanks' ability to respond quickly and succinctly to a vote.

The importance of think tanks lies in their ability to provide expertise on a particular item in a policy agenda. Through their work, "issue networks" are established between government officials in the public sector and policy actors from the think tank community.[145] Think tanks become, in the words of French researcher Robert Ranquet, "the places where [government officials] find the opportunity to formulate, elaborate, confront, enrich, validate, and finally diffuse their ideas through their collaboration with the regular scholars that constitute the permanent core of the organizations."[146] Thus, by providing expertise and in-depth scholarly research to governments from an independent position, think tanks position themselves separately from advocacy-based organizations that lobby for their beliefs but are not party to direct policy creation.

The most fundamental element in explaining the continued influence of think tanks in U.S. political culture is the relationship maintained between civil society actors and government actors; the process of recruiting retired political officials as consultants in think tanks and recruiting think tank scholars for positions in the government has become a norm in U.S. political culture. The United States has a less exclusive governing class than do many other political systems and places a premium on independent advice. As a result, former politicians are more likely to indulge in the realm of public policy research and the culture of think tanks than they are in institutions in other regions of the world. Numerous scholars have noted the new role of think tanks as a source of government personnel for incoming administrations. Experts from think tanks increasingly fill empty positions available in government. Their specialized knowledge and reputation regarding specific issues greatly assist their incoming policy-maker colleagues. Richard Haass refers to this as the "revolving door" effect found in the U.S. policymaking environment.[147] Haass links the success of think tanks to the fact that many policymakers serve multiple tours of duty in think tanks and government throughout their careers. Their circular career track means that those in the private sector have access to government officials, and those officials know who to turn to for critical information. Haass has high-lighted the high turnover rate of staff members at all levels between congressional and presidential terms.[148] Similarly, Weaver notes that think tanks can serve as holding tanks for outgoing officials seeking to maintain policy influence until they are able to reenter government service.[149] The personal and professional con-nections and insider's perspective of certain agencies and policies that former gov-ernment officials can bring to these institutions raise the profile and influence of the institutions themselves. The effects of the "revolving door" are further dis-cussed in chapter 2.

In short, greater efficiency, independence, and connections all contribute to the continued success of think tanks as a Fifth Estate that addresses issues in U.S. politics and civil society from a far-reaching, in-depth perspective.

CHAPTER TWO

The Revolving Door

WHILE THE OBAMA administration professed to usher change into Washington—new people with new ideas—many of the administration's greatest minds have also been recycled minds or, as they might prefer to say, experienced minds. In this respect the Obama administration is not different from previous administrations. This mix of new ideas and experienced policy hands, however, proved critical for Obama given the economic crisis the country faced in the fall of 2008 during the transition from one administration to another. This chapter seeks to better explain the "revolving door" phenomenon by profiling prominent officials who walked through that door from their positions in government to roles at think tanks and then back to government once more. The chapter looks in particular at policy advisers who aided the 2008 presidential candidates and further examines why presidential candidates seek policy advice from think tanks. It also explores the pluses and minuses of the circulation of policy elites in Washington.

THE REVOLVING DOOR BETWEEN THINK TANKS AND PRESIDENTIAL ADMINISTRATIONS

Despite the assertion by many scholars that think tanks are objective, that they are "third-party scholars" without political affiliation, there is an undeniably close relationship among think tanks, politics, and public policy in Washington, and this adds to the hypothesis of the Fifth Estate model. Richard N. Haass's revolving door concept, introduced in chapter 1, asserts that think tanks function as a consistent source for talented administrators and congressional staff members and as a haven for personnel departing government office either for an "intellectual breather" or because the administration under which they served failed to be reelected.[1] Regarding the former, think tanks function as "political training grounds," helping presidents and cabinet secretaries respond to the re-generation of the staffing landscape that occurs after each governmental transition.[2] As for the latter, these institutions also offer a "short- or long-term landing place" in which personnel who have left office can remain involved in the policy debates in a way that has a tangible practical impact.[3] Further, it allows those whose political party is out of power to think and exercise "long-range vision" in a manner unaccommodated by the pressures of government leadership.[4] The continuous circulation of government officials and think tank staff members and scholars who move seamlessly between the White House, Capitol Hill, the federal bureaucracy, and think tanks is deeply imbedded in American political culture and institutions. The revolving door is unique to the United States and can be attributed, in part, to the American public's distrust of government, the public's proclivity to seek advice from outside experts, and a desire to bring new faces and new ideas to every new administration. The United States is home to more than 1,800 think tanks, which means that politicians and policymakers have a wide range of ideas and institutions to choose from when they are look-ing to fill key posts.

Haass offers substantial insight into the twenty-first-century meaning of think tank by way of his approach to the term, one that could be taken only by a policymaker, not a detached scholar. To this end, he conducts an empirical assessment of the observable influence of think tanks as opposed to a normative one that would focus primarily on their agendas. For Haass, think tanks affect foreign policymakers in five different ways: "by generating original ideas and options for policy, by supplying a ready pool of experts for employment in gov-ernment, by offering venues for high-level discussion, by educating U.S. citizens about the world, and by supplementing official efforts to mediate and resolve conflict."[5] Diane Stone echoes Haass's observation that think tanks function as a source of policy discussion when she asserts that think tanks have one thing in common: individuals in them seek to make "academic theories and scientific paradigms policy relevant."[6] Stone does not see the interplay between govern-ment and politics as a concern; rather, in *Think Tank Transnationalization and Non-Profit Analysis, Advice, and Advocacy*, she supports a blurred sense of independence, arguing that relative, as opposed to absolute, independence and autonomy are necessary prerequisites for think tanks to fulfill their function. Haass and Stone both embrace the notion that think tanks serve as a bridge between the world of ideas (academia) and the world of power (politics).

For Haass, aside from acting as a source of scholars to enter government as policymakers, think tanks intermittently function as venues or passive entities that facilitate informed discourse among policymakers. He notes that the Council on Foreign Relations is an example of a think tank playing a convening role, hosting hundreds of meetings annually in major cities across America.[7] This concept of think tanks as conveners is a novel one and has been adopted by a number of scholars.[8] In my meetings with think tanks and policymakers around the world I often ask them what the value added of think tanks is. The most common response is think tanks play a track two (unofficial) role by convening key stakeholders to explore policy options and float trial balloons. Their role as independent actors makes it possible for them to convene and engage policy actors in a way that often cannot take place in official meetings and negotiations. Think tanks' role as convener and knowledge/policy broker is greatly enhanced by the revolving door when a former government official, now a scholar at a think tank, provides a briefing or convenes a meeting.

Hartwig Pautz agrees that they are instruments for consensus building amid the corporate, military, and administrative policy communities, noting that they "contribute to the creation of discourse coalitions."[9] Howard Wiarda expands on this notion by labeling think tanks sites of "cross-fertilization" among think tank scholars, journalists, and government officials who attend the conferences, lectures, and forums hosted by think tanks.[10] Think tanks are constantly meeting, formally or informally, with policymakers themselves. Haass asserts that this function extends to the public domain, too, contending that think tanks enhance U.S. civic culture by informing both policymakers and the public about the dynamics of the world that surrounds them.[11] Thus, as a site for collaboration and consensus, think tank scholars can facilitate discussions between the government and civil society, thereby encouraging greater exchange between the two. Think tanks not only serve as a bridge between academic and policy communities but as a bridge between government and the public.

Some scholars regard this close relationship between government and think tanks as a hindrance to objectivity, even though the nonprofit and nongovernmental character of think tanks constitutes an ideal situation in which these institutions are free to conduct independent analysis. The growing influence of funding institutions such as governments, foundations, international lending organizations, and others has led, however, to questions as to whether think tanks can produce independent policy analysis that does not, in some way, reflect the perspectives and interests of their donors. Stone argues that, ultimately, "complete autonomy and independence for think tanks is illusory" but necessary to fulfill its policy-creation goals.[12] The United States is distinctly different from most of the countries in the world because the lion's share of the funding for think tanks is provided by private sources. Over the past thirty years the funding has shifted from general, core support to support for specific projects. This shift has compelled many think tanks to become more specialized and change their fundraising strategies to secure a more diversified base of support from the private sector and, to a lesser degree, from the government. A large proportion of the funding provided has been donor-defined, project-specific grants, and as a result think tanks have been obliged to narrow their research agendas and programs so they are consistent with a donor's interests and guidelines.

Although the rise of short-term, project-specific funding by donors has had a deleterious effect on think tanks, it has not necessarily affected their independence. What it has done is made raising funds more difficult. Finding the funds to cover the core operations is a major challenge. The new reality is that think tanks have to raise funds from a large number of donors so they can cover the core operations. Previously donors either endowed think thinks like the Carnegie Endowment for International Peace or they would provide grants in support of the general operations of a think tank, which gave them greater degrees of freedom in defining their research priorities. The net result of these shifts in the funding patterns has forced these institutions to become more specialized and has narrowed the range of issues that might be analyzed. It is wrong and overly simplistic to suggest, as some authors have, that these funding shifts have resulted in a loss of independence. These claims ignore the diversity of institutions and opinions present in the think tank landscape in the United States and overstate the influence donors exert on them. It is also possible that the need to raise funds from a larger pool of donors has democratized funding: consider that most think tanks now have many hundreds of donors as opposed to one golden donor.

Lost in these discussions is the fact that the nearly 2,000 think tanks in the United States employ more than 20,000 scholars and executives who are dedicated to independent analysis on major policy challenges. They do this, day in and day out, to help policymakers and the public make informed decisions on a wide range of policy problems. The advocacy-oriented think tanks that engage in opinion mongering and advocacy notwithstanding, the vast majority of think tanks are committed to producing evidence-based, policy-relevant research that is not influenced by donor interests or priorities.

One by-product of the donor demands is the increasing specialization of a growing number of think tanks. This often involves branding by research specialization, ideology, policy products, and high-profile policymakers and scholars who are recruited to work at a think tank. One of the unfortunate side effects is specialization by ideology (progressive, Libertarian, conservative) because it often mirrors and at times intensifies the partisan politics in the nation's capital.

Partisan politics is on the rise in the United States because policymakers are faced with a set of tough policy issues: a domestic economy that continues to exhibit slow growth, intense competition from the emerging economies, shrinking tax revenues, and a federal budget largely consumed by the mushrooming cost of entitlements. This limits the policy options for the legislative and executives branches of government, which has contributed to the political polarization and paralysis in Washington. The partisan warfare is so intense because the policy choices are tough. Rather than seek a common ground and innovative solutions, some think tanks have chosen to align with partisan donors often more interested in rancor than reason and constructive rhetoric. If some think tanks continue to mirror the dysfunctional aspects of politics in Washington, they may become casualties in the war of ideas that is being waged by the political parties and advocacy groups in the United States.

It is important to point out that while this trend toward specialization is undeniable, it can be attributed to a number of environmental forces, not just money and politics. The increased competition, project-specific funding, growth of social media, 24-7 news networks, and mobile technologies have forced think tanks to adapt to the changes in the political economy. Yes, donor support has become more specialized, and openly partisan think tanks like the Center for American Progress and the Heritage Foundation are now permanent fixtures; however, this does not mean all think tanks have abandoned their commitment to objective, evidence-based research and given control of their missions and research agendas to donors and partisans. The simple reality is that the leading think tanks in Washington have anywhere from 500 to thousands of separate donors (individuals, corporations, private foundations, and so on), and most constitute a small percentage of the total support provided on an annual basis. In addition, the number of private donors in the United States is large and diverse, and they often have competing and offsetting interests. This, by the way, is also true for political parties and interest groups that reflect the hyperpluralistic dimensions of American politics. The issue of donor influence on public policy research needs to be carefully monitored, and the forces affecting the independence and integrity of think tanks should be studied more thoroughly so it can be properly understood. Failure to do so leaves unchallenged the assertion, unsupported by data or evidence, that think tanks in general have given up their independence to donors and partisan politics. This does a great disservice to the thousands of institutions and scholars dedicated to evidence-based research and serving the public interest. To remain effective, think tanks must actively seek to uphold their intellectual independence and objectivity and avoid being sucked into ideological warfare.

Think tanks may not be totally free of political bias because their work involves politics, public policy, and public discourse. Political bias is an obvious occupational hazard that must be kept in check. However, the defining characteristic of public policy think tanks is their relative intellectual independence, and this should not be forgotten—even during this era of increased politicization. I have been encouraging think tanks to develop ways to bridge the partisan divide so political paralysis and policy gridlock can end in Washington. It is critical that think tanks be perceived as part of the solution and not as part of the problem. Their independent expertise needs to be viewed as a source of insight and sound policy advice in Washington and across the country.

Presidential Advisers, Surrogates, and Appointees

The United States has seen considerable recycling of talent through administrations and think tanks, perpetuating the revolving door phenomenon. The Brookings Institution's and Harvard's impact during the Kennedy and Johnson administrations and the influence of the Heritage Foundation, the Hoover Institution, and the American Enterprise Institute (AEI) during the Reagan administration have been widely documented.[13] The revolving door is now a well-established feature in the institutions of government and presidential campaigns as demonstrated by the Clinton, Bush, and Obama administrations. Today, many policy experts from one party spend time researching and publishing while the other party is in power; they return to executive office when their party returns to the White House.

An interim position at a think tank is not solely a means of biding time, however. Brookings alumnus and University of Virginia scholar William Antholis believes think tanks are a place for exiting government officials to recharge "their intellectual batteries." As "idea havens" they allow for the reflective thinking a hectic government post does not. According to former Secretary of State George Shultz, "You're drinking from a fire hose of information and events . . . but you don't have time to reflect on it. You do here" at the Hoover Institution.[14] Still, Brookings President Strobe Talbott views the revolving door as "two-way." When Obama became president, Brookings scholars left for posts in the new administration; at the same time Talbott recruited exiting officials from the Bush administration.[15]

Think tanks can become strategic partners in staffing key posts and helping generate policy proposals for any new administration. By recruiting policy experts outside government, the Obama administration solidified the relationship between prominent think tanks and policymakers. For example, the Center for American Progress (CAP) was founded to push a Democratic Party agenda and its work toward Obama's eventual election allowed it to form a close relationship with the new administration and to become a key player in influencing policies. By forming a close relationship with the administration, CAP and other D.C.-based think tanks were able to ensure their eventual role in helping shape policy decisions. As Lee Katz has noted, the "early period [of a presidential administration] is a time when new policy is made."[16] Therefore, CAP, Brookings, the Peterson Institute for International Economics, and others making it a priority to assist in Obama's election were a more likely candidate to be consulted by the administration immediately upon its formation. And in the case of CAP, the revolving door was a key factor given that John Podesta was its president and had served as chief of staff in the Clinton administration. For this reason, CAP was able to become a key player in influencing policies enacted by the Obama administration.

While the importance of think tanks may have reached a pinnacle under Obama, the revolving door has a long and nonpartisan history (Presidents Carter, Reagan, Clinton, and Bush I and II all pulled experts from think tanks to give advice and serve in their administrations).[17] The result has been a U.S. phenomenon of stable think tanks that are able to produce research independent of political parties, governments, or even universities. The infrastructure of these think tanks is enormous compared with that of those outside the United States. For example, Brookings has at its disposal a budget of more than $90 million, while the average budgets of most think tanks outside the United States are in the $5 to $10 million range.

More important to the discussion of the revolving door is the fact that policy experts who are ideologically opposed to the administration can continue to voice their opinions. In addition, think tanks provide the perfect atmosphere for these experts because they provide the funding and staff necessary for research.

Certain fields lend themselves particularly well to the revolving door effect. For example, economists have an enormous rate of exchange between think tanks and government: about half of the Brookings Institution's economic policy researchers were recruited to work for President Obama. Many of these economists maintain their ties with universities, think thanks, and the government all at once, providing an enormous wealth of information. However, the relationship between political scientists and the government is rapidly changing. Social scientists from universities are increasingly being left out of the policymaking arena. As Harvard professor Joseph Nye points out, "Scholars are paying less attention to questions about how their work relates to the policy world, and in many departments a focus on policy can hurt one's career."[18] Instead, there is a much greater emphasis on theory. Although this can benefit the academic world, much of this theory is not readily accessible to politicians or others outside the academy. Nye's point is that scholars from departments of political science, security studies, and international affairs are no longer attractive to policymakers because they have become too arcane. Thus, the scholars at think tanks who are more policy relevant are gaining importance because they can fill the void left by universities and bridge the gap between the world ideas and power.

The revolving door trend is likely to continue. This phenomenon ensures that think tanks will remain key players in all facets of the policymaking process as exhibited by the case studies discussed in the following chapters. As think tanks continue to gain prominence in the United States, the links between government and these independent research groups will only strengthen.

U.S. PRESIDENTIAL CAMPAIGNS

To fully appreciate the revolving door phenomenon, we must give attention to the increasing role of think tanks in presidential campaigns. The contributions think tank scholars make to presidential candidacies can act as stepping-stones for scholars to enter the administration of the winning candidate. Despite the risk of losing objectivity by siding with a candidate, advising a winning candidate can pay tremendous political dividends.

In some instances, however, a think tank's survival is tied to its independence from the U.S. government and political entanglements. Associating an institution too closely with a political party or politician can be dangerous.

Robert Boorstin warns that when a think tank wades into the morass of party politics, it often attaches its fortunes to a presidential candidate. If the candidate fails, Boorstin continues, the institution will fail with him or her and can potentially lose funding and influence. In short, involvement in party politics can destroy a think tank.[19] This does not mean that think tank scholars cannot work for presidential candidates. Many scholars do get involved with campaigns. It is seen as an opportunity for the think tank to actively participate in the development of policies without overstepping boundaries. As Donald Abelson points out, during elections "think tanks appear to make the greatest contribution to the development and refinement of ideas" since during this period candidates solicit the most advice.[20]

However, U.S. tax laws prohibit think tanks from supporting a candidate or overtly advocating on behalf of a specific piece of legislation. To keep their nonprofit status and remain tax exempt, these institutions must steer clear of party politics.[21] The limits of tax regulations have been tested in recent years as many of these institutions have taken on a more activist role in the pursuit of greater influence and impact.

While it is true that think tanks cannot support political candidates, they are not barred from developing policies and educational programs that are consistent with the general platform of a party or candidate. In addition, when candidates are elected president, they frequently turn to the think tanks whose scholars and ideas have the greatest currency with the American electorate to take the appointed posts that each incoming administration can fill at their discretion. Furthermore, scholars are free as individuals to support and advise campaigns and candidates.

Abelson attempts to predict those presidential candidates who will seek the advice of one or more think tanks and those who are likely to appoint the junior and senior staff members of the think tanks to key positions in their administrations. Abelson argues there are two main characteristics that can predict the recruitment patterns of think tanks: their status as a Washington insider or outsider and the strength of their ideological views, as viewed by the public.

Abelson tempers this profile as not being "exhaustive of all potential factors," but through case studies of elections from 1976 to 1992 he shows the conjunctions of criteria that may be predictors of why a candidate seeks advisers from think tanks.[22] The "Washington outsider" who is a "strong ideologue" is cited as the most likely type of candidate to solicit policy advice from think tanks, and the "Washington insider" who is a "weak ideologue" is least likely to rely on outside contributions from think tanks. Abelson reasons that Washington outsiders need to solicit expertise because they lack a full understanding of the inner process of federal politics and are most likely to need supplementary information to complete their policy on domestic and foreign issues. Depending on the strength of their ideological leanings, they may desire the outside validation that a think tank can provide, which usually leads a candidate to advocacy think tanks. When the qualities are separate, the "Washington outsider" or "strong ideologue" will not form significant ties to a think tank (and often relies on a university research institute if a relationship is created). The combination of both qualities indicates a readiness to rely on a think tank.

The opposite of the "Washington outsider" and "strong ideologue" is the "Washington insider" and "weak ideologue" who is logically seen as least likely to rely on think tanks. These individuals are viewed as requiring little policy expertise, and because they are not marketing themselves as ideologues, they do not need the outside validation.

Abelson's book does not make predictive claims about the behavior of a candidate once elected, and the evidence presented is inconclusive. In addition, the data collected from the 2008 presidential election tend to challenge Abelson's findings and conclusions. There is a complex set of factors that goes into a candidate's choice of advisers and surrogates. What is undeniable is the increase in the number of candidates for each party and their inclination to seek the advice of scholars who are affiliated with the leading think tanks in the United States.

In the final analysis, an incoming administration recruits the best and brightest from the institutions it knows and trusts, and this often involves those inside the beltway as well as the more than 1,400 think tanks that are outside the nation's capital. The simple reality is the think tank landscape in the United States is expansive and covers a range of policy expertise and political perspectives; every newly elected president has an endless supply of talent to draw on when selecting key staff members.

The U.S. presidential campaign of 2008 began with a call for a candidate with foreign policy experience, and its end was overshadowed by a dramatic response to the economic crisis. However, the foreign policy expertise that candidates gather around them reveals the importance of foreign policy credibility on the campaign trail and the willingness of some think tank scholars to attach their names to a particular candidate. The following sections focus on foreign policy advisers affiliated with the think tank community and whether or not they served as formal or informal advisers. It will not list every foreign policy adviser each candidate used. Individuals from the think tank community who *endorsed* but did not *advise* candidates will not be discussed.

If we carefully analyze the presidential candidates in the 2008 presidential election, we can get a clearer sense of the role think tank scholars play in helping shape the positions, policies, and platforms for the leading candidates in the race for the White House. The erosions of party discipline, seniority rules, and the rise of Political Action Committees (PACs) have led many candidates to operate independently and to have their own bases of support and teams of advisers. Thinks tanks have become the "go-to" place for advice and advisers for presidential candidates in both parties. In the following sections I attempt to demonstrate how the Republican and Democratic candidates in the 2008 campaign relied on think tank scholars for inspiration and ideas on key policy questions in the campaigns of both parties. The examples provided in the next sections are also intended to illustrate the revolving door phenomena.

The Republican Ticket in the 2008 Presidential Election

The analysis of the leading Republican presidential candidates reveals their personalities, policy preferences, and where they fall on the political spectrum within the Republican Party.

John McCain

During his presidential campaign, Senator McCain claimed that the most important foreign policy priorities for the next president were to revitalize the purpose and standing of the United States in the world, to defeat terrorists who threaten liberty on U.S. soil and overseas, and to build an enduring peace. An interesting characteristic of McCain's advisory team is just how many notable names from the foreign policymaking stage served as "informal" advisers. They included high-profile figures such as Richard Armitage, former deputy secretary of state in President George W. Bush's administration; Bernard Aronson, former assistant secretary of state for inter-American affairs; Max Boot, a Council on Foreign Relations senior fellow and former editorial page editor at the *Wall Street Journal*; Niall Ferguson, Harvard historian and Hoover Institution senior fellow; Robert Kagan, senior fellow with the Brookings Institution and *Washington Post* columnist; Henry A. Kissinger, President Nixon's and President Ford's secretary of state; and before his highly publicized endorsement of Barack Obama, General Colin L. Powell, President George W. Bush's former secretary of state.

McCain's formal advisers included Michael J. Green, former Asia adviser to President George W. Bush and now Japan chair at the Center for Strategic and

International Studies (CSIS); Gary Schmitt, former staff director of the Senate Intelligence Committee and now an AEI scholar; and Lieutenant General Brent Scowcroft, national security adviser to Presidents Ford and George H. W. Bush and now a counselor and trustee at CSIS. McCain's advisers reveal a reliance on a group of scholars from a group of centrist, establishment think tanks. They also tended to be what might be described as traditional or establishment Republican advisers and institutions on foreign policy. McCain is a Washington insider who drew heavily from the leading scholars and institutions in the Beltway.

Mike Huckabee

Governor Huckabee vowed to change "the tone and attitude" of U.S. foreign policy while reaching out to the rest of the world. As a presidential candidate, Huckabee had one notable foreign policy adviser, Richard N. Haass, who currently serves as president of the Council on Foreign Relations and was the State Department's director of policy planning from 2001 to 2003 during President George W. Bush's administration.[23] The selection of Haass as a key adviser appears to have been intended to add intellectual and foreign policy weight to a candidate known more for his evangelical roots and views on social policy.

Mitt Romney

Mitt Romney's priorities concerning U.S. foreign policy included strengthening the U.S. military and economy, achieving energy independence, reenergizing civilian and interagency capabilities, and revitalizing alliances. A prominent scholar advising Romney on Latin American policy was Mark Falcoff, who was AEI's Latin America scholar emeritus and onetime consultant to President Reagan's Commission on Central America. The Romney campaign sought to include the conservative establishment in Washington to bolster his conservative credentials and to increase his policy expertise by tapping the scholars at one of the most venerable conservative think tanks in Washington, AEI. Romney was an outsider and weak ideologue who consciously surrounded himself to bolster his conservative credentials.

Rudy Giuliani

Rudy Giuliani believed that the three major challenges confronting the next president in the realm of foreign policy were winning the fight in the terrorists' war on global order, strengthening the international institutions that "the terrorists seek to destroy," and extending the benefits generated by the international system—the World Bank, the International Monetary Fund, the World Trade Organization, and the United Nations—to people worldwide. As a presidential candidate, Giuliani was advised by an impressive roster of think tank–associated personnel.

Charles Hill of the Hoover Institution was the campaign's chief foreign policy adviser. Other notables who advised Giuliani included Gerard Alexander, an AEI visiting scholar; Peter Berkowitz, Hoover Institution senior fellow; Robert Conquest, a Soviet-era historian and former adviser to British Prime Minister Margaret Thatcher and a Hoover Institution researcher; Lisa Curtis, a Heritage Foundation senior research fellow; and David Frum, a former resident fellow at AEI and former speechwriter for President George W. Bush.[24] Kim R. Holmes, the Heritage Foundation's vice president of foreign and defense policy studies, served as a senior foreign policy adviser to the campaign.[25] Furthermore, Stephen Yates, former deputy assistant to Vice President Dick Cheney for national security affairs and now a lobbyist and American Foreign Policy Council senior fellow, served as a senior Asia adviser to the campaign.[26]

The Hudson Institute boasted a large presence in the Giuliani campaign. Hudson senior fellow Charles Horner advised the campaign on Asian affairs.[27] Norman Podhoretz, a fellow and the former editor of *Commentary* magazine, served on the campaign's Senior Foreign Policy Advisory Board. Kenneth Weinstein, Hudson's chief executive officer, served as a foreign policy adviser. Finally, S. Enders Wimbush, Hudson Institute's director of future security strategies, served as a senior public diplomacy adviser for the campaign. Unlike Huckabee and Romney, Giuliani was able to enlist a broad range of scholars from virtually all the leading conservative think tanks in the United States to advise his campaign. In Giuliani we have an outsider who was also a weak ideologue who put together a strong team of conservative establishment advisers.

The Democratic Ticket in the 2008 Presidential Election

The Democratic candidates for president exhibited the same proclivities for think tank experts who reflected the Democratic establishment when selecting the advisers for their campaigns as illustrated by the examples of foreign policy advisers provided below.

Barack Obama

Barack Obama campaigned on a foreign policy platform that stated that "the security and well-being of each and every American is tied to the security and well-being of those who live beyond our borders. The United States should provide global leadership grounded in the understanding that the world shares a common security and a common humanity."[28] Indeed, the new president's first television interview with the pan-Arab network Al-Arabiya seemed, at the time, to be the delivery of a campaign promise. Two key characteristics of Barack Obama's campaign advisory team were the team's association with President Bill Clinton and its ties to key think tanks. Obama's advisers included numerous officials appointed under the Clinton administration, as well as scholars affiliated with think tanks such as CSIS, Brookings, and CAP.

Advisers included Jeffrey Bader, a former U.S. ambassador and President Clinton's National Security Council Asia specialist and then head of Brookings's China Center; Ivo H. Daalder, National Security Council director for European affairs in the Clinton administration, a former Brookings senior fellow, and former U.S. ambassador to NATO; Richard Danzig, President Clinton's secretary of the navy and now vice chair of the board of trustees of the RAND Corporation; Lawrence J. Korb, assistant secretary of defense from 1981 to 1985 under Ronald Reagan and now a senior fellow at CAP; Denis McDonough, a former CAP senior fellow and former policy adviser to Tom Daschle and Susan E. Rice, President Clinton's Africa specialist at the State Department and National Security Council; and Mona Sutphen, former aide to President Clinton's national security adviser, Samuel R. Berger, and to former UN ambassador Bill Richardson.[29] The choice of seasoned foreign policy advisers from the some of the leading centrist and progressive think tanks reflected Obama's need to bolster his defense and foreign policy credentials and help garner the support of the foreign policy and political establishment in Washington.

Hillary Clinton
During her campaign, Hillary Clinton stressed "multilateralism, with unilateralism as an option when absolutely necessary to protect our security or avert avoidable tragedy."[30] Clinton pledged to work with international institutions like the United Nations. In the event that international bodies failed to act, she believed that the United States "should bring [international institutions] in line with the power realities of the twenty-first century and the basic values embodied in such documents as the Universal Declaration of Human Rights."[31] As this country's chief diplomat, Clinton had the opportunity to turn her presidential campaign promises into action. In addition, she had the unique advantage of drawing from her husband's legion of experienced advisers. They included chairwoman of the National Democratic Institute and President Clinton's former

secretary of state, Madeleine Albright, his former national security, adviser Sandy Berger, and former UN ambassador Richard Holbrooke.

Hillary Clinton also benefited from her informal advisers, including Leslie Gelb, president emeritus of the Council on Foreign Relations, and Strobe Talbott, president of the Brookings Institution. Another Brookings presence was Martin S. Indyk, formerly President Clinton's ambassador to Israel and former director of the Brookings Institution's Saban Center for Middle East Policy. Clinton's advisers demonstrate her deep connections within the think tank community and the foreign policy establishment in Washington.

John Edwards

John Edwards sought a U.S. foreign policy of reengagement and a new diplomatic initiative to repair relations with U.S. allies and other nations in the world, specifically the United Kingdom and the nations of the European Union and Latin America. Edwards received foreign policy advice from two think tank–affiliated advisers, Barry M. Blechman and Irving N. Blickstein. Blechman, formerly President Carter's assistant director of the U.S. Arms Control and Disarmament Agency, is cofounder of the Henry L. Stimson Center and chairman emeritus of its board of directors. Blickstein is a former assistant deputy chief of naval operations and a RAND researcher.

Edwards's advisers reflect his specialized foreign policy experience and interest. For the most part his advisers were focused on a narrow set of issues and did not reflect the depth and breadth of the advisers to the two front-runners, Clinton and Obama. Edwards was an outsider who was a weak ideologue who did not seek the type and range of advisers expected from a candidate who is not a Washington insider.

CLINTON, BUSH, AND OBAMA

Appendix D charts the career movements more than 100 well-known political actors who have circulated through the think tank and government revolving door. This chart offers clear examples of journeys made from the Clinton administration to the think tank universe and back up Pennsylvania Avenue to the Obama administration. In reverse, other high-profile officials pass them on their way from the think tank universe to the Bush administration and back again to a think tank.

The revolving door effect is a major part of the advisory function that think tanks provide to policymakers. With each successive administration, the new president replaces many of the midlevel and senior executive branch personnel. A great number of the incoming bureaucrats are drawn from the think tank community, and many of the departing officials land at the desks of similar institutions. This revolving door phenomenon has helped form "governments-in-waiting" since 1961.[32] President Barack Obama's administration is no exception to this rule. His National Security Council has two former senior fellows at CAP, Mara Rudman and Denis McDonough. Susan Rice, current national security adviser and former U.S. ambassador to the United Nations, also reflects the revolving door phenomenon. Rice was previously a senior fellow in the Foreign Policy and Global Economy and Development programs at the Brookings Institution and was an assistant secretary of state in the Clinton administration before joining the Obama administration.

Richard Haass, the Council on Foreign Relations president and former State Department director of policy and planning in the George W. Bush administration, writes that the revolving door is a source of strength in U.S. foreign policy formulation. He believes that think tanks are a forum in which government officials can remain involved in ongoing foreign policy debates and are a means to staff an informal establishment that provides advice and commentary on world affairs.[33] In addition, the revolving door offers think tank scholars the ability to reach policymakers and provides a reliable source of independent information free from political taint to those in power (further examples of this phenomenon are found in appendix B). Lee M. Katz supports Haass's assertion that the revolving door provides independent and reliable scholarship, arguing that CAP played a crucial role in President Obama's transition and is now a source of personnel for his administration. Abelson is another proponent of this notion, noting that think tanks "often serve as 'holding tanks' where policy experts congregate in hopes of being recruited into senior government positions."[34] This revolving door trend, Haass acknowledges, is unique to the U.S. political system; in other developed democracies such as Britain, France, and Japan, a new government finds continuity of available personnel in the professional civil service.[35] Indeed, in the words of P. J. Crowley, a CAP fellow, think tanks are the closest thing that the United States has to a shadow government. In the English political system, for example, there exists a formalized government-in-waiting for the political party that is out of power.[36]

The revolving door between government and think tanks underscores the significance of these institutions in supplying Washington with critical thinkers and policy creators. Unlike other civil society entities such as corporations or nonprofits, think tank scholars flow in and out of government easily. As administrations transition, think tanks act as an incubator for scholars previously in government, offering an opportunity to investigate, inform, and produce insights. Conversely, with new administrations, leaders select the brightest minds from policy institutions, seeking their expert opinions and discerning ideas. This inextricable link between research institutions and the government through personnel overlap reaffirms the position of think tanks as a Fifth Estate.

CHAPTER THREE

Think Tanks in Action

DOMESTIC POLICY CASE STUDIES

THE FOLLOWING CASE studies were chosen to demonstrate the different ways think tanks affect the formulation and direction of U.S. domestic policy. Each case study provides a short summary of the situation and the involvement of different think tanks. Each conclusion identifies how the think tank influenced the final decisions made by the administration at that time.

DOMESTIC POLICY IS discussed through studies of Social Security reform and welfare reform during the Clinton and George W. Bush presidencies, health care reform during the first Clinton term and the Obama administration, and recent economic policy under Obama.

CASE STUDY 1: SOCIAL SECURITY REFORM

A number of congressmen and congresswomen have acknowledged that the Social Security Trust Funds in its current state is unsustainable, but reform of the existing system has never been treated as an urgent need. Nevertheless, several think tanks have repeatedly offered advice, so reform has stayed on the agenda for much of the past twenty years. Social Security is an excellent example of both the influence on policymakers of traditional think tank activities, such as policy research and advocacy, and how these encourage further debate on key political issues.

Since 1935 the Old-Age, Survivors, and Disability Insurance program, commonly referred to as Social Security, has provided a guaranteed income to Americans who have ceased working because of age or disability and to the dependents of deceased workers. The program is largely funded through a payroll tax paid by employers and employees. The U.S. Treasury spends the money and issues bonds to the Social Security Trust Fund. Benefits are paid out to individuals from this trust fund.[1]

In 1983 the Social Security system faced a crisis of insolvency; benefits being paid out were beginning to outgrow payments into the fund. President Ronald Reagan and congressional Democrats reached a political compromise and made a variety of reforms, including raising the retirement age and increasing the flow of taxes into the system.

Today the Social Security system faces a similar crisis. Approximately three workers pay into the system for every one person receiving benefits. By 2034 the worker-to-beneficiary ratio will fall to nearly two to one as the baby boomer generation ages and life expectancies rise. This will nearly double the number of older Americans, from 38.6 million to 74 million.[2] The growing number of individuals entitled to benefits, in addition to inflationary effects and rising income equality, will soon cause the deficit produced by the current system to skyrocket.

Recognizing the dire long-term situation, both the Clinton and George W. Bush administrations worked to develop solutions to ease the strain on the system's funds. Clinton commissioned the 1994–96 Advisory Council on Social Security, which offered various suggestions such as increasing the payroll tax, raising the age of eligibility to receive benefits, extending the benefit computation period, and establishing individual accounts to combat benefit growth. Although these measures were proposed to Congress, none was enacted.[3] Bush's efforts to establish individual accounts and progressive price indexing proved similarly fruitless.

In 2010 President Obama created the National Commission on Fiscal Responsibility and Reform (often referred to as Bowles-Simpson, or Simpson-Bowles, after the names of the cochairs Alan Simpson and Erskine Bowles). The five major steps outlined in the draft proposal in November 2010 are the following:

1. "Sharp reduction" in discretionary spending
2. Tax reform
3. Reduction of health care cost
4. Cuts in farm subsidies

5. "Overhaul" of Social Security, where savings would be used for the program's solvency and not for deficit reduction in the government's general fund[4]

As of now, however, the proposal has not been consolidated into a recommendation because of a failed vote in Congress in December 2010.[5]

The Input of Think Tanks

Since its role on Clinton's advisory council, the American Enterprise Institute (AEI) has been a strong voice for privatizing Social Security. A member of Clinton's council, AEI resident scholar Carolyn L. Weaver has led this effort. She notes that under the current system, workers are given the promise that upon reaching retirement age they will receive regular payments, financed by future generations of workers. Under privatization, in contrast, Social Security would be provided through individuals paying into guaranteed retirement accounts that they own and control themselves.

Private retirement accounts, whether as a supplement to or a full replacement of the Trust Fund, have been promoted by other scholars of conservative, market-minded think tanks. Maya MacGuineas of the New America Foundation testified before the President's Commission to Strengthen Social Security in 2001 that national saving could be facilitated and incentivized through a "progressive" form of privatization in which the investments of low-income workers are matched by the government. Senior fellow at the Cato Institute Michael D. Tanner has played an instrumental role in keeping privatization on the table in recent years. Tanner maintains that, in addition to combating insolvency, private accounts would allow workers to decide how their savings are invested, give low-income workers the opportunity to accumulate a "nest egg" of inheritable wealth, and improve young workers' rates of return.[6]

During his 2000 presidential campaign, then-governor George W. Bush made Social Security reform a central campaign issue. Taking cues from AEI, the New America Foundation, and the Cato Institute, he advocated creating private accounts as a necessity for Social Security's long-term survival and as a way to provide workers with better retirement options. Once in office, President Bush continued to work on implementing private retirement savings accounts, creating the President's Commission to Strengthen Social Security. He charged the commission with developing reform proposals that incorporated private retirement accounts that would not raise the payroll tax or any other taxes, that avoided investing the Trust Fund in the stock market, and that maintained benefits for workers nearing retirement.[7]

The commission included scholars from several well-known conservative think tanks who had professed their support for privatization, including AEI's Weaver. Also appointed were Tim Penny and Sam Beard, board members of the Cato Institute's Project on Social Security Privatization and advocates for combining privatization with a higher retirement age and a reduction in benefits. John Cogan of the conservative Hoover Institution, who previously had advocated publicly for privatization, also served on the commission.[8] Although the commission was bipartisan in its makeup, former congressman Bill Frenzel, a former guest scholar with the Brookings Institution and chairman emeritus of the Ripon Society, was the only member who was not pro-privatization. While none of the three individual account proposals presented in the commission's report were ultimately implemented, Bush kept Social Security on his domestic agenda. By April 2004 Social Security poll ratings had worsened, and arguments abounded over whether diverting 4 percent of payroll taxes to private accounts might actually hasten the Trust Fund's insolvency.[9] In response, Bush called a press conference to announce an addition to his original reform proposal: progressive price indexing. Benefits for low-income recipients would remain linked to wages, while those of the high-income recipients would become linked to prices. Middle-income recipients would face an indexing mixture. Because prices usually grow more slowly over time than wages do, wealthier citizens would face hidden cuts in their benefits upon reaching retirement age. Ultimately, Democratic opposition, Republican division, and public disinterest impeded the president's efforts. Nevertheless, Bush's proposal remains alive today. In a recent memo to President Obama, the Heritage Foundation pushed for reconsidering progressive price indexing and raising the retirement age.[10]

Senator John McCain has also been a proponent of privatization. In his 2000 presidential bid, he strongly supported private accounts, remaining very much in line with the advice of conservative think tanks. In his 2008 presidential bid, McCain was a less enthusiastic proponent of Social Security reform. Still, he maintained that privatization must be a part of any solution. At the same time, he expressed a willingness to work together with Democrats, who generally oppose privatization, stating that he would consider increasing the payroll tax wage cap as part of a reform compromise.[11]

Other think tanks have disagreed with the proposals of Bush and the conservative think tanks that champion privatization, benefit reduction, and a raised retirement age. For instance, the Center on Budget and Policy Priorities (CBPP) criticizes progressive price indexing for its negative impact on middle-income workers. Former CBPP senior fellow Jason Furman, current chairman of Council of Economic Advisers under Obama, suggests that policymakers couple smaller overall benefit reductions with a progressive increase in payroll tax payments. Such a plan would place a larger share of the burden on wealthier citizens.[12]

Another liberal think tank, the Center for American Progress, has claimed that privatization would prove costly to average workers because of the inherent administrative fees, insurance premiums, transition costs, and labor market risks.[13] Moreover, CAP has highlighted that Social Security is more than old-age income insurance. Disabled workers and their families, widows, widowers, and dependent children of deceased workers may all receive Social Security. Privatization plans could leave these groups without protection, an outcome CAP calls an "abandonment of family values."[14] As an alternative to private investment accounts, CAP suggests that the Social Security shortfall and growing deficit be reduced by raising or eliminating the income cap on the system-funding payroll tax. Under current law, the 12.4 percent payroll tax is charged only on the first $106,800 of a worker's salary, effectively resulting in a tax break for those who earn above this mark. Christian Weller of CAP asserts that this system violates the principal of tax fairness because the wealthiest workers pay only a small percentage of their total earnings, while lower-income individuals shoulder a much heavier burden. Weller claims that raising the wage cap to cover 90 percent of wages would significantly reduce the Social Security shortfall. Eliminating the cap entirely and taxing 100 percent of all wages would completely get rid of the shortfall and generate enough revenue to keep Social Security solvent for the next seventy-five years.[15]

Scholars at the Economic Policy Institute (EPI) have also advocated eliminating the payroll tax cap. EPI president Lawrence Mishel notes that because of disproportionate wage growth for top earners, 15 percent of all wages are exempt from the payroll tax under the current capped system as opposed to 10 percent just two decades ago. Additionally, EPI's John Irons highlighted before the Senate Special Committee on Aging that erasing the wage cap would negatively affect only 6 percent of workers.[16] Other reforms, such as raising the tax rate or cutting benefits, would have more widespread effects on U.S. workers.

Also against privatization were Brookings Institution senior fellows Peter A. Diamond and Peter R. Orszag (Orszag later the former director of the Office of Management and Budget under Obama). In a 2003 book published by Brookings,

Diamond and Orszag proposed gradual and progressive cutbacks in benefits amounting to a 1 percent decrease for today's forty-five-year-olds and more substantial cuts for younger workers. However, when wage increases and inflation are factored in under the plan, the authors stated that real benefits would still be larger than those of today's retirees. In addition, Diamond and Orszag proposed gradually raising the payroll tax rate and taxable earnings cap as well as increasing the number of taxed workers by expanding the program to include all state and local government workers.[17]

In line with the liberal think tanks, President Obama supports adjusting the payroll tax cap and opposes privatization and a higher retirement age. His viewpoint differs in that he is considering creating a "donut hole" in which income between $106,800 and $250,000 would not be taxed at all and income above $250,000 would be taxed at a reduced rate. Overall, Obama's position more closely resembles those of CAP and EPI than that of Brookings since he rejects calls to cut benefits.[18]

Conclusion

AEI, the Cato Institute, the New America Foundation, the Hoover Institution, the Heritage Foundation, CBPP, CAP, EPI, and the Brookings Institution have been providing ammunition for the debate on Social Security and have offered advice to presidential candidates through articles, proposals, conferences, and congressional testimonies over the past several decades. The impact this advice has had on the proposed policy of George W. Bush and Barack Obama indicates the many ways in which think tanks use traditional methods to have an effect on policy. Bush depended on the work of AEI and the New America Foundation to promote privatization during his presidency. Even after the battle was lost, the Cato Institute and the Heritage Foundation kept privatization and progressive price indexing on the table. The strong public policy orientation of these organizations highlights the importance of think tanks in legislative outcomes, not just lobbyist persuasions. They are unique from the other bodies in civil society that remain largely outside policymaking decisions. President Obama is currently supporting measures that reflect those proposed by CAP, EPI, and, to a lesser extent, Brookings. Whatever measures are eventually brought before Congress under President Obama's term, any solution will have the fingerprints of public policy research organizations on it.

CASE STUDY 2: WELFARE REFORM

In the 1990s, there was agreement across the political spectrum that the U.S. welfare system had become ineffective. While most politicians agreed that change was necessary, the proposals for reform varied tremendously. Prominent think tanks assessed the situation and crafted proposals of their own. By helping further the debate on welfare reform, think tanks filled a hole in the dialogue and ultimately allowed for a successful compromise to be reached. When it came to welfare reform, think tanks were especially effective at working within the private-public sphere, demonstrating how policy research from many different groups, delivered at the perfect moment, could help policymakers make an informed decision.

The United States administers welfare through tax cuts, such as the earned income tax credit (EITC), as well as through assistance programs, such as Medicaid, Food Stamps, and Aid to Families with Dependent Children (AFDC). AFDC, the most contentious welfare program, was administered as cash payments to families with children in need of support because of the death, continued absence, or incapacity of the primary wage earner and was funded through the federal government's tax revenues. During the 1990s, payments to beneficiaries of AFDC totaled nearly $2 billion.[19] Since its creation, the program has been a lightning rod for criticism. At the time, Charles Murray's 1984 *Losing Ground* was one of the most famous works calling for reform of the program.[20] His claim, echoed by others, was that the system created a welfare culture populated by a dependent underclass that relied on cash payments and had no incentive to work and end its dependence on the system. As a presidential candidate in 1992, Bill Clinton promised that, if elected, he would institute drastic reforms of the welfare system. His initial proposal, issued in 1994, which emphasized the investment in training and educational programs, was reminiscent of the 1988 welfare reforms in the Family Support Act. However, with the 1994 Republican takeover of Congress came the proposition of competing legislation that would have given states greater ability to administer and more stringently restrict citizens' eligibility to receive grants. These new restrictions included denying welfare checks to unwed mothers and children born to mothers already receiving welfare, as well as a five-year time limit on receiving benefits.[21]

The Personal Responsibility and Work Opportunity Reconciliation Act, signed into law in 1996, was not only a significant act of bipartisan compromise between the plans proposed by the Republican-controlled Congress and President Clinton; it was also the most thorough reform of the welfare system since its inception. The Temporary Assistance for Needy Families (TANF) program gave state governments more responsibility and freedom in administering welfare to their citizens and placed five-year limits on receiving federal funds—reforms aimed at encouraging people to move from welfare to gainful employment. At its height in 1994, 5 million families were enrolled in AFDC. As of 2000, the enrollment in TANF dropped to 2.2 million families. Nearly 60 percent of those who left welfare found jobs. By these measures, many claimed that the 1996 welfare reform was a success. However, critics contend that the low wages of those who left welfare and entered the workforce—earning just $7.00 per hour in 2000—are far below the living wage.[22] Despite these reservations, Congress and President Bush reauthorized TANF in 2003.[23] Although Congress failed to reauthorize TANF in 2010, it has extended the program several times since then.

In July 2012 the Obama administration introduced a major change to the current welfare system under which the states now had the option of applying for a waiver to the existing work requirements embedded in TANF. The rationale provided was that in so doing the Department of Health and Human Services allowed the states to "test alternative and innovative strategies, policies and procedures" to "improve employment outcomes."[24] This spurred significant debate of the proposal to cut the work component of the current welfare mechanism because critics claimed that the waiver option would further reduce people's incentive to work while giving the government even greater discretionary power in welfare distribution.

The Input of Think Tanks

As the reform debate became more heated in the early and mid-1990s, think tanks took a proactive role in pushing it forward. Because welfare reform is such an open topic, major think tanks took radically different approaches in their attempts at reform. Robert Rector of the Heritage Foundation published research suggesting that AFDC was ineffective.[25] Through statistical analysis, he showed that federal social spending had increased as child poverty also continued to increase. Rector largely attributed this situation to an increasing number of households, headed by unemployed mothers, who were dependent on the system. Current Brookings Institution senior fellow Isabel Sawhill issued studies that concurred with Rector's assessments and that were echoed by other researchers and politicians on welfare dependence and ineffectiveness. Cato Institute scholar Michael Tanner also testified before the Senate Finance Committee, unequivocally labeling the welfare system a complete failure.[26]

Although criticism of the welfare system before 1996 spanned the entire ideological spectrum, suggested resolutions did not; rather, they were highly contended across think tanks. While serving as a research fellow at the Urban Institute in 1995, Sawhill expanded her work from critiquing the system to prescribing remedies. She expressed reservations about the Republican plan, which aimed at reducing federal costs, contending that it could result in the dismantling of the welfare system at the expense of the most poor. Instead of supporting a policy that simply issued checks, Sawhill advocated policies that promoted job training and used federal funding to provide child care credits, health insurance, and other benefits.[27] Studies by the Urban Institute, which were rereported by the CBPP with its endorsement, further called into question the potential outcomes of the reformatted version of the Republican plan that passed through Congress in mid-1996.[28] The two institutions believed that the plan would greatly increase the number of individuals living in poverty. CBPP called on President Clinton to veto the Republican plan, as he had for an earlier version that was deemed equally destructive.[29]

On the other side of the issue, the Cato Institute's Tanner urged Congress to avoid "reforming" welfare and to be skeptical of the so-called workfare initiatives. He claimed that there was little evidence of the effectiveness of these programs. Rather, Tanner posited that private charities and religious organizations are more effective at reducing poverty and providing assistance. Therefore, he proposed that the federal government offer dollar-to-dollar tax credits to encourage more private donations to charity, which would fill the void left by the elimination of federal welfare programs.[30] The Heritage Foundation did not go as far as the Cato Institute in calling for the complete elimination of the welfare system, but it did call for reforms resembling those proposed in the Republican plan. The think tank was a vocal advocate for the reforms that were debated in Congress.[31]

Although neither Clinton's initial proposal nor the Republican plan was ever implemented, the compromised welfare reform bill constituted a major system change in the United States. As TANF approached its expiration in 2003, scholars from a number of major think tanks approached Congress and the public to present their assessments of the program. The Urban Institute found that TANF spurred work among adult recipients but that the jobs they took were low wage with few associated benefits. CBPP stated that the reforms had positive effects on poverty reduction. Brookings Institution scholar Ron Haskins also presented testimony before the House Committee on Finance on the successes of welfare reform and supported its reauthorization, while offering recommendations for its potential improvement. Scholars at the Heritage Foundation also claimed success for welfare reform and called for its swift reauthorization.[32]

Conclusion

Although the eventual Personal Responsibility and Work Opportunity Reconciliation Act of 1996 was the result of a compromise between congressional Republicans and President Clinton more than the work of think tanks, the civil society institutions still had played a significant role. The Urban Institute, the Brookings Institution, the Cato Institute, the Heritage Foundation, and others had long called for welfare reform, thereby highlighting the important role think tanks serve as evaluators of governmental policy. They took issue with its failures and made it a fixture on the domestic political agenda. When President Clinton and congressional Republicans proposed their competing reform bills, it was think tanks on both sides of the political divide that exposed the potential costs, drawbacks, and failures of the plans. They encouraged Congress and President Clinton to block the other's proposals, thus paving the way for the eventual legislation. As its reauthorization approached, think tanks evaluated TANF again, declared it to be a success, and urged Congress and President Bush to reauthorize it. Again, while think tanks did not directly codify the reforms to the modern welfare system, their ability to keep the issue prominent, along with the provision of evaluative feedback on the program's success and congressional testimony in debates on welfare reform, indicates their influence and value in policy formation. The case of welfare reform demonstrates the critical ability of think tanks working in the private sphere to provide the right information at the right time and to significantly influence policy outcomes from a position outside government.

CASE STUDY 3: CLINTON'S HEALTH CARE REFORM

Health care reform had strong support both within the Clinton administration and among the U.S. populace in the 1990s. However, many government leaders were opposed to the implementation of a system of universal health care. With the support of several prominent conservative think tanks, Republicans were able to mount an assault against the legislation proposed in that decade. Thanks to the work of a number of major think tanks, opponents of the legislation were able to craft a potent argument that eventually condemned universal health care. This assault displays the influence of think tanks on policy using more than just well-timed briefs. Conservative think tanks flexed their muscles in the public sphere, disseminating their research to the public and leading the specific interpretation of a proposed policy.

Health care reform in the United States has been one of the most politically controversial subjects in the past few decades. The United States as a whole spent approximately $2.5 trillion on health care in 2009 (about 17.6 percent of the GDP)—which amounts to almost $8,000 per capita—more than any other country worldwide. Still, the United States is the only developed Western country that does not provide universal health care coverage for its citizens.[33] The political debate centers on the push for the United States to develop a single-payer universal health care system or a similar program that would provide coverage to currently uninsured Americans.

The Clinton health care plan proposal, then known as "Hillarycare," stands as one of the most stunning political defeats in modern U.S. politics. The issue was so decisively defeated in the public mind that the notion of universal health care or any major health care reform was effectively silenced until the 2008 presidential race. The defeat was a major factor in the Republican Revolution in the 1994 midterm elections when Republicans won overwhelming majorities in both houses of Congress for the first time since the Eisenhower administration.

On January 25, 1993, President Clinton announced the formation of the President's Task Force on National Health Care Reform to "prepare health care reform legislation to be submitted to Congress within one hundred days of our taking office."[34] Clinton also announced that his wife, Hillary Clinton, would be heading the task force. The task force formed immediately and quickly grew in complexity and to 500 advisers. It was disbanded on May 31, 1993, after completing an intricate universal health care plan that was to be written into legislative language over the summer.

The Health Insurance Association of America (HIAA) began a $4 million advertising campaign to attack the plan, which as yet did not exist on paper.[35] The well-known "Harry and Louise" commercial of a middle-class family struggling to choose a government-mandated health care plan ran across the country. A campaign powered by the HIAA and small-business interest groups launched dubious claims about the plan throughout the summer to sow the seeds of defeat.[36] On September 22, 1993, President Clinton addressed a joint session of Congress to launch the Clinton health care plan. The speech was a major hit with the public and national press.[37] The First Lady testified in front of several congressional committees the following week, skillfully presenting the Clinton plan and swiping at Republican opponents. The final legislation, which would be almost 1,300 pages long (a number that opponents would continuously repeat to emphasize the plan's complexity), was introduced the following month.

President Clinton's chosen political strategy was to introduce a plan on the far left and later deal away unwanted provisions in committees to reach the moderate policy that the administration wanted and felt they could pass.[38] Every time the president moved toward the political center on a specific policy, the press and opponents declared the plan was collapsing and that the president was becoming increasingly desperate for a victory. Republican leadership continued to draw the policy to the center so that they could effectively kill it. The bill officially died in Congress in October 1994, just weeks before a stunning midterm victory for Republicans.

The debate altered the American public's perception of health care, which many had viewed as a serious crisis during the 1992 election. Afterward the debate was seen as a manufactured crisis. In a final blow to the credibility of the plan, a *Wall Street Journal* poll in late 1994 found that 76 percent of Americans were favorable toward a health care reform plan identical to the Clinton plan, with one exception—it did not include a disclosure that it was Clinton's plan. When the plan was identified as the Clinton plan in the poll, favorable responses fell to 37 percent.[39] Clearly President Clinton's name was toxic to the plan's success. The endless process stories, special interest advertising, and political bickering had taken their toll on the debate.

The Input of Think Tanks

The Heritage Foundation, AEI, the Cato Institute, and several other think tanks played a major role in generating opposition to the Clinton health care plan and, in some cases, helped to craft the Republican strategy to defeat it. From 1992 to 1994, these think tanks produced an array of scholarly research, editorials, studies, and books that criticized the plan and provided valuable ammunition to its opponents. The work produced by these think tanks attacked the Clinton proposal from a variety of policy positions, criticizing the plan for failings that spanned from not addressing the root problems in the health care industry to creating too much federal control of the industry and making comparisons to European "socialist" systems to denying the existence of a health care crisis by claiming that the proposal was nothing more than a federal government power grab.

The Cato Institute produced six scholarly works during the health care debate that directly addressed the Clinton plan or universal health care coverage more broadly. The think tank's work attributed the rising costs of health care to the lack of patient power in decisionmaking and an absence of market incentives for patients to control their own spending. The Cato Institute even produced its own plan for health care reform elaborated on in the book *Patient Power: Solving America's Health Care Crisis* by John C. Goodman and Gerald Musgrave, which specifically addressed the Clinton plan:

The health care reform proposals favored by the Clinton administration do nothing to address the third-party payment problem that is the root of the health care crisis. In fact, the administration's plan for "managed competition" would worsen the problem by creating a new third-party payment system that would be universal in coverage. To try to keep costs down, managed competition would impose onerous new bureaucratic controls and limitations on patients' choices.[40]

The arguments presented in the book lay at the heart of the opposition to the Clinton plan. Many of the plan's opponents used this or similar arguments to support their claim that the Clinton plan either did not address the actual problems with the U.S. health care system or took away patients' freedom to choose their health care providers. The condensed version of the book sold 300,000 copies during the health care debate and is credited by the National Center for Policy Analysis with playing a "pivotal role in the defeat of the Clinton administration's plan to overhaul the U.S. health care system."[41]

The Heritage Foundation produced dozens of policy papers from 1993 to 1994 that addressed the Clinton plan and other Democratic health care reform bills. Heritage's official response to the Clinton plan was led by Robert Moffit, then director of Heritage's Center for Health Policy Studies. His team created a massive work entitled *The Guide to the Clinton Health Plan*, which scrutinized every aspect of the president's proposal. Opponents of the plan, who were in turn covered by the *Washington Post* and other newspapers nationwide, frequently quoted many of the *Guide*'s talking points.[42]

AEI and the Project for the Republican Future (PRF) had perhaps the most profound impact on the defeat of the Clinton plan. PRF, was a Washington, D.C.–based independent conservative strategy and advocacy think tank, had strong ties to AEI.[43] PRF was led by William Kristol, a former staff member to President George H. W. Bush and Vice President Dan Quayle and a rising star in conservative academia. In a memo, he urged the Republicans to "capitalize on [the Clinton plan's] obvious flaws and kill it outright."[44] Kristol's memo was

widely circulated among Republican members of Congress, and he was in communication with Senate Majority Leader Bob Dole and House Minority Whip
Newt Gingrich, continually writing strategy memos for Republicans.[45] Senator
Dole used Kristol's arguments verbatim when he pronounced that "there [was]
no healthcare crisis" in response to President Clinton's 1994 State of the Union
Address. Kristol also advocated that the Republicans refuse to compromise with
the Democrats on a health care deal and instead wait to reform it on their own
terms, a strategy that was carried out.[46] Although relatively small and new compared with other prominent think tanks, PRF played a critical role in organizing
the Republican opposition and stirring such a response by senior Republicans.
PRF eventually evolved into the *Weekly Standard*, a weekly neoconservative
magazine funded by Rupert Murdoch, which serves as a singular case of a think
tank becoming a media outlet.

In the midst of this debate, the National Legal and Policy Center (NLPC)
sued Hillary Clinton and the task force, in addition to several other plaintiffs,
for the release of their complete records and to open their meetings to the public. NLPC argued that the secrecy of the task force was in violation of the 1972
Federal Advisory Committee Act, which stated that if nongovernment employees
advise the president, then their records must be made public.[47] NLPC won the
lawsuit in late March 1993, and subsequently the Clinton administration pub-
lically released the records. By then, however, they had already been leaked and
widely distributed. NLPC's strong criticism of the Clinton health care plan and
its successful lawsuit seriously damaged the task force's image in the national
media, adding to the growing number of opposing arguments that claimed that
the Clinton administration was trying to reform the health care industry without any public debate. The NLPC believed that it played a pivotal role in the defeat of health care reform, asserting that "in their 2002 books, both Hillary
Rodham Clinton and former White House aide Sidney Blumenthal acknowledged NLPC's role in sinking the plan."[48]

Experts from the Urban Institute were deeply involved as on-the-scene analysts in health care reform and at least four Urban Institute scholars participated in the president's Task Force on National Health Reform.[49] Because of its
direct involvement with government employees drafting legislation and policy,
the Urban Institute was not simply another think tank sitting on the sidelines of
policy creation; rather, it was intimately involved in the policymaking process.

The 2008 presidential election brought the issue of health care reform back
into the national limelight. The Democratic candidates generally proposed
health care reform that would lead to universal coverage or a program to cover

the 44 million uninsured Americans and lower costs for the others. Most of the Republican candidates proposed plans that included lowering health care taxes, providing tax credits for health care costs, or allowing states to create market-based insurance. Virtually every major campaign of the 2008 presidential election had veterans of the 1993–94 health care debate. This is predictable in a modern presidential race, where think tank scholars act as advisers, media surrogates, and political directors. However, the sheer number of participants who fought in the trenches in the 1990s health care debate and subsequently participated in the 2008 presidential election is startling. Examples include some prominent names:

- William Kristol (formerly of PRF) served as an informal foreign policy adviser to Senator John McCain's presidential campaign.[50]
- Daniel McKivergan (formerly of PRF) was the deputy director of the Project for the New American Century until leaving in 2007 to serve as the policy director on Senator John McCain's presidential campaign.
- Helen Halpin (Center for Health and Public Policy Studies, University of California at Berkeley) served as a health care policy adviser to Senator Barack Obama's presidential campaign and previously had served on the President Clinton's Task Force for Health Care Reform.
- Richard Brown (formerly of the Center for Health Policy Research, UCLA) served as a health care policy adviser to Senator Barack Obama's presidential campaign, after "he served as a full-time senior consultant to Clinton's Task Force on National Health Care Reform, for which he cochaired the work group on coverage for low-income families and individuals."[51]
- Robert Moffit (Heritage Foundation) worked on the Massachusetts health care plan with then governor Mitt Romney. Although not an official adviser to the Romney campaign, he strongly supported and influenced Romney's health care proposal with research and media statements.

Conclusion

The impact of think tanks on the health care policies of the United States government has been enormous. Although the roles of think tanks as researchers and policy advocates are made clear by the impact that many institutions have had on formulating proposed health care policy and continuing the debate, the defeat of "Hillarycare" reveals some of the less obvious aspects of how U.S.

think tanks can work. The Cato Institute, the Heritage Foundation, AEI, NLPC, and PRF virtually led the opposition against Clinton's task force, demonstrating the ability of think tanks to create "issue networks" and collaborate research among several different groups with similar positions. These institutions also worked effectively in the public sphere, showcasing the ways in which think tanks interpret policy for members of the public. The health care debate during this time established think tanks, and specific members, as high-profile players in the media and as more than just policy advisers operating behind the closed doors of government. Perhaps most important, think tanks during this period played off the public's trust of the private sector and associated distrust of a big government—two aspects of U.S. culture that have proved especially beneficial to the growth of think tanks. From spearheading lawsuits, providing counter-research, and advising congressional Republicans on how to defeat health care legislation, think tanks played a vital role in the defeat of health care reform and perhaps permanently altered the American political landscape after the 1994 widespread midterm defeat of the Democrats in Congress.

Case Study 4: Health Care Reform: The Patient Protection and Affordable Care Act

The health care debate that initially surfaced during the Clinton administration roared back to life during the 2008 presidential campaign, continuing into the current Obama administration. As it did before, debate around health care reform spurred a flurry of think tank research, contention, and advocacy. Although an act has been signed into law, think tanks continue to act out their roles as policy researchers, evaluators, and interpreters. Most important, these institutions constantly provide new research and opinions on health care, keeping the issue on the table and the debate alive.

During the 2008 presidential campaign, then candidate Barack Obama stated that if elected, fixing America's health care system would be one of his top priorities. On March 5, 2009, Obama formally started the health care reform process, vowing that a plan would be passed by the end of 2009.[52] After passing through the Senate in December 2009 and the House of Representatives in March 2010, Obama signed the act into law on March 23, 2010. Notably, the law prohibits insurance companies from denying coverage on the basis of preexisting conditions, provides incentives for businesses to provide their employees with health care benefits, subsidizes insurance premiums, and establishes health insurance exchanges.

Finally, on June 28, 2012, most components in the Patient Protection and Affordable Care Act (PPACA) or the Affordable Care Act, informally referred to as "Obamacare," were ruled constitutional by the Supreme Court, thus ushering in a new era of the U.S. health care system.[53] Aiming mainly to extend insurance coverage among Americans and to cut health care costs for the less wealthy, Obamacare consists of major provisions such as an expansion of Medicaid eligibility and increased federal subsidies to extremely poor families, as well as a penalty for those who fail to pay their due care.[54] A major shock even to certain Democratic constituencies, the Affordable Care Act remains a highly volatile point of contention between the two camps in the current presidential campaign (see case study 5 below).

The Input of Think Tanks

As in the health care debate during the Clinton administration, numerous think tanks were involved in providing research and outputs both in support of and against the proposed health care reforms. Those supporting the health care reforms proposed by President Obama include the Brookings Institution, CAP, and the Progressive Policy Institute, among others. Think tanks opposed to the proposed health care reforms, as they were in the previous political debates on the topic, include AEI, the Heritage Foundation, the Claremont Institute, the Hudson Institute, and the National Center for Policy Analysis.

In a July 2009 report, *Show Me the Money: Options for Financing Health Reform*, Mark McClellan of Brookings advocated the promotion of high-quality, high-value health care. He called for a politically viable and budget neutral policy, as well as a sustainable financial approach. Likewise, in September 2009, the Engelberg Center for Health Care Reform called for the need to focus on lowering costs while improving quality. It argued that government subsidies are necessary to foster competition in the market and that incentives or rewards are also important to encourage people to achieve measurable health goals.[55]

CAP argued that the new bill would result in better health care. Ellen-Marie Whelan and Lesley Russell based their argument on the proposition that less is more when it comes to health care. They argued that there will be a reduction in waste and duplication, as well as better preventive services, which would lower costs in the long run.[56] Furthermore, CAP analyzed the expected benefits of the health care reforms for unmarried women. Liz Weiss stated that one quarter of unmarried females are uninsured, so this legislation would greatly affect this group. This bill could help unmarried women overcome a variety of obstacles, such as employers' failure to offer insurance and companies' refusing to allow them to purchase insurance because of preexisting conditions related to childbearing or domestic abuse. Additionally, the bill would allow unmarried children (both men and women) to remain on their parents' insurance until they reach the age of 26.[57] EPI similarly favored health care reforms, having published studies that show that dependence on employer-sponsored health care leaves too many Americans vulnerable.[58]

In 2007, Katie Donohue and David Kendall of the Progressive Policy Institute proposed a model of shared responsibility that rested on three pillars: an individual mandate requiring individuals to buy private insurance if they could afford it, financial assistance based on income, and choice and competition. Kendall also called for specialized health courts and a change in the way that the government dealt with malpractice. In 2005, Kendall wrote of the need for health care reform, prescribing a progressive plan that would cover all people and restrain costs.[59]

Meanwhile, the Center for Economic and Policy Research, while applauding the reforms of the bill, argued that it did not go far enough. Dean Baker, a macroeconomist and codirector of the Center for Economic and Policy Research in Washington, argued that health care would remain outrageously expensive even under the new legislation and that the way to bring down the price was to lower the costs of medications and medical supplies.[60] In a report written by the CBPP, Paul Van de Water and James Horeny argued in favor of the estimates and claims of the Congressional Budget Office and against the charges that state reform would not reduce federal budget deficits. They argued that these charges were unfounded and designed to disprove those who use economic reasons to oppose health care reforms.[61]

The Century Foundation had published works on the problems with Medicare, specifically the issue of seniors falling into this "donut hole" and being unable to get the coverage that they need.[62] The Century Foundation had also published a report examining the process of health care reforms and public opinion. The report explains that although initially the majority was against reform, once presented with some of the main provisions of the bill, the majority favored it.[63]

The Bipartisan Policy Center also played a significant role in health care reform by bringing together a variety of senators, notably Senators Howard Baker, Tom Daschle, and Bob Dole to reach agreements on certain health care issues.[64] The New America Foundation also made important strides in the health care debate. The New Health Dialogue, a blog on the various aspects of health care reforms in America, raised attention on important issues.[65]

These and other think tanks played an important role in defending the health care reforms that President Obama signed into law. They drew attention to the various benefits of the reforms, while working to disprove the various counterarguments presented by the bill's critics.

Meanwhile, on the opposing side of the reform argument, AEI raised numerous issues with the proposed reforms. In "The 'Individual Mandate' an Intrusion on Civil Society," AEI argued that Congress should not be allowed to control intrastate commerce and that only individual states can force everyone to buy health insurance.[66] Furthermore, in "Pricing Out Private Insurance," AEI asserted that "we can expect to face a scenario in which costs are relentlessly increasing, insurance profits are squeezed or eliminated and some of the most useful work of private insurance has been held in abeyance by misguided medical loss ratio limits. The entire system will be biased against for-profit firms, which will pay much higher fees and will often be held to stricter medical loss ratio standards."[67] AEI also called for a repeal of the bill and a need to mobilize Americans to vote for those who opposed it in the November 2010 elections. The Claremont Institute also called for a repeal of the bill, declaring that the bill was entirely partisan and that it degraded "health care's quality, raises taxes and insurance premiums while adding enormously to the deficit, and deliberately expands Americans' dependence on the federal government."[68]

The Heritage Foundation wrote extensively against the health care reforms. Heritage pointed to side effects of the law, such as job loss in the life sciences industry because of raised taxes.[69] This was especially bad timing, Heritage argued, and Congress should have prevented tax hikes if they were really seeking to stimulate the economy.

The Hudson Institute declared that the new bill violated the Constitution by forcing all Americans to buy health insurance whether they wished to or not.[70] The institute analyzed the expected outcomes of the bill with regard to income and taxes, declaring that "the new health care bill will add $1 trillion to the nation's $8 trillion debt."[71] It also voiced concern about tax rate increases for families that earn more than $250,000. The National Center for Policy Analysis echoed those complaints about the bill.[72]

Conclusion

The health care debate highlights the ability of think tanks to effectively disseminate information in both the public and private spheres. The independence of think tanks and the time and resources they have to devote to research allow them to offer information to an audience that ranges from the president to the average citizen. Their publications bring issues to the forefront of debate, focusing the attention of the American public on various aspects of the reforms and their potential outcomes, while providing policymakers with the knowledge that then serves as the foundation for policy development. Without think tanks, it is unclear whether the wealth and diversity of information would have surfaced against a backdrop of limited government resources and bureaucratic restrictions. Thanks to the efforts of think tanks, health care policy was not only developed and implemented but also continues to be evaluated, debated, and researched.

Case Study 5: Health Care Reform, the 2012 Election, and the Continuing Health Care Debate

The passage of PPACA and the Health Care and Education Reconciliation Act in March 2010 by no means ended the debate over health care in the United States. During the 2012 presidential election, Republican candidate Mitt Romney criticized the original act's provisions and made repealing both acts a campaign pledge. Criticism of the PPACA was supported by studies from a number of think tanks, which also questioned the act's effectiveness. Meanwhile, the Obama administration has continued to defend the viability of the reforms and has cited numerous studies by think tanks to support its claims.

PPACA or the Affordable Care Act (ACA) represents the most expansive health care reform in U.S. history. The Obama administration had made health care reform the primary target of its domestic policy. The administration claims that by consolidating the costs associated with health care, mandating that individuals buy health insurance, and providing tax credits, among many other measures, the act will extend coverage to uninsured Americans while simultaneously cutting costs.[73]

The administration has had to defend this claim vigorously from a host of criticisms across the political divide and to dissuade lingering public ambivalence about the reform. One example of the administration's defensive approach is its response in June 2011 to a widely circulated report by McKinsey & Company, a private consulting firm. The report claimed that the provisions of PPACA would force 30 percent of employers to stop offering health insurance to their employees.[74] This drew a response from Deputy White House Chief of Staff Nancy-Ann DeParle, who posted a short reply on the White House Blog entitled "Getting Insurance at Work." Citing studies by the Urban Institute and the RAND Corporation, she and the Obama administration argued that "employers will continue to seek out top talent: and the new law makes it easier for them to do so by tackling health costs and supporting small businesses." DeParle also pointed to a similar state law in Massachusetts as proof that public health care can be provided without sacrificing jobs in the private sector.[75]

The Democratic Party has been active in defending the legislation. The party's national website contains a page that asks visitors to find out "how health reform is helping you" by entering their information and finding out what benefits they will receive under ACA. The site also emphasizes the positive consequences of reform, namely, that ACA helps "stabilize the economy and reduce the deficit (by $100 billion in the next decade), cutting health care taxes for families and small business, and creating greater health care competition and accountability."[76]

Contenders for the 2012 Republican presidential nomination recognized that opposition to Obama's health care reforms was all but mandatory to gain the support of their rank-and-file voters. At the broadest level, their criticism was rooted in conservative philosophy, which views a national system of health care as a dangerous expansion of government bureaucracy, state power, and fiscal recklessness. There was also concern among Republicans that a government monopoly on health care coverage will delimit the options available for individual consumers in the health insurance market.

While there was some variance in the policy recommendations the Republican candidates presented as alternatives to ACA, there were certain common policies for which many of the would-be presidential candidates openly advocated. For the most part, the Republican contenders supported policies that they claimed would reduce the costs of health care and help individual consumers bear the costs of buying insurance, while keeping health care decidedly within the private sector. Michele Bachmann, Tim Pawlenty, Herman Cain, Ron Paul, and Newt Gingrich all called for health-related expenditures, including insurance premiums, to be made tax deductible to help private consumers bear the costs of health care. Bachmann, Paul, and Gingrich emphasized the benefits of encouraging market-driven competition among insurance companies, who would then be forced to offer attractive packages at affordable prices, while still leaving consumers a variety of options from which they might choose. To lower the costs of health care, Pawlenty, Cain, and Gingrich also argued in favor of tort law reform that is more difficult to enact. Under current tort law patients can engage in what Cain refers to as "frivolous lawsuits," thus driving costs up. Pawlenty was an advocate for forcing medical practitioners as well as insurance companies to increase the transparency of costs and benefits, thus making it easier for consumers to make rational, informed choices. Romney emerged from the mix with the nomination, in part because of his pledge to issue executive orders that would allow individual states to opt out of the new mandates should they wish to do so. Whatever the specific differences in their positions, all of the 2012 Republican candidates shared an opposition to the national system of health care and the elimination of the private health insurance sector. In addition, all of them were opposed to mandates that require individuals, whether employees or employers, to buy health insurance.

With Obamacare now constitutional, it became a major pivot on which both parties launched their attack in the 2012 presidential campaign. At the Republican National Convention in Tampa, Romney reaffirmed his intent to repeal Obamacare and "rein in the skyrocketing cost of health care" in order to help small businesses.[77] In response, at the Democratic National Convention in Charlotte, former president Bill Clinton refuted the Republican claims by focusing on the refunds guaranteed by Obamacare, as well as the extended coverage to include more people, especially the young and the seniors.[78]

The Input of Think Tanks

A number of think tanks have maintained the prudence of Obamacare's provisions. In a detailed study, the Urban Institute concluded that with the reforms, the costs of employer-sponsored insurance (ESI) would indeed be driven down. Moreover, this lowering of costs would be progressive, with small firms expecting to see the largest decrease in premium costs. Thus, lower costs of ESI would make it cheaper for employers to provide health insurance, and would, in turn, reduce the burden on consumers. Despite the fact that spending on health care by large firms would only marginally decrease (if it decreases at all), the Urban Institute still predicts that employer-sponsored health care coverage overall would not decrease.[79] The think tank also claims that, while tax measures under the new plan could result in job losses, these losses would be offset by the expansion of health services.[80] The Health Policy Center at the Urban Institute has claimed that "enactment of the ACA brings extraordinary opportunities for great security, affordability, adequacy, and equity in health insurance coverage." The center also acknowledges, however, that the political realities of enacting the sweeping reforms, which the legislation calls for, may present "substantial hurdles" to the implementation of the new legislation.[81]

In response to critics who claim that ACA would result in an expansion of Medicaid, which would take place at the expense of the states, CBPP has argued that this criticism is based on three false assumptions. First, CBPP claims that the policy's critics inflate the number of people likely to participate in Medicaid under ACA, which, in turn, results in an inflated estimation of Medicaid-related costs falling on the states. Second, it claims that critics have inflated the estimated costs of beneficiaries newly enrolled in Medicaid. Third, CBPP claims that critics have built costs into a reformed Medicaid, which "are not required under the Affordable Care Act."[82] Thus, CBPP concludes that critics who claim that ACA will result in an unsustainable and unfair expansion of Medicaid are overestimating how many people will participate in Medicaid, how much it will cost for them to participate, and what it is that will actually be required of Medicaid under the terms of the new legislation. CBPP also concurs with the Urban Institute's conclusion that ESI would not decrease under ACA.[83]

Brookings has not taken an official stance on Obama's health care reform (although it has stated a need for further reforms) but rather has generally conveyed a positive tone in its reports on the subject. In multiple publications, senior fellow Henry J. Aaron has been critical of opponents of the reform and those targeting it for repeal. He argues in "Multiple Fictions Drive Opposition to Health Care Law" that the reform legislation does in fact move the United States closer to a defined-contribution system as desired by the law's opponents; the subsidies received only cover a certain amount of recipients' plans and require them to cover the additional costs of more generous coverage.[84] He also claims that the government regulations prescribed under ACA would allow for more, not less, competitive insurance markets by providing information to consumers on the range of plans and their relative costs.

Similarly, an October 2010 study by researchers at the Engelberg Center for Health Care Reform concluded that ACA "include[s] a range of new payment and delivery system reforms designed to improve the overall performance of the health care system and contain the costs of expanding health insurance coverage."[85] In particular, the study notes that the law's initiatives to prevent wasteful spending on ineffective medical therapies and ensure long-term care delivery will help seniors with chronic health conditions. Senior fellow Alice M. Rivlin was positive in an opinion piece about the health insurance exchanges set up by ACA, noting that, if implemented properly, the exchanges will allow "market forces and consumer choice" to "improve quality and slow the growth of health care spending."[86]

EPI not only agrees with CBPP and the Urban Institute that ESI would not decrease, but it further predicts that subsidies and individual and employer mandates would actually result in its increase. Despite population growth, EPI claims that "the new law will reduce the number of uninsured by more than half over the next nine years."[87] Tax credits for individuals and families coupled with increased regulation of the insurance industry would drive down the costs to small businesses of providing insurance to employees. Thus, EPI's conclusions are in broad agreement with those reached by the Urban Institute.

CAP has been perhaps the most full-throated defender of reform. On June 10, 2011, it released the slideshow "Health Reform Works: A Presentation on Why We Needed Health Care Reform," which details what its authors view as the severity of the crisis before reform and the projected benefits of the new legislation.[88] Isabel Perera of CAP argued that ACA would be good for business, stating that small businesses will benefit from the increased competitiveness, which they will accrue because of tax credits and their ability to offer potential employees health care packages that they could not previously afford.[89] Tony Carrk, also from CAP, published a piece assessing the performance of ACA a year after its passage. He argued that, thus far, the act has assisted both business and individuals by lowering the cost of premiums and by making millions of businesses eligible to receive tax credits, and further notes that there is no evidence that employers are ceasing to provide health insurance for their workers.[90] This is a good example of a think tank acting as a public monitor of a recently enacted policy.

AEI is one of the think tanks critical of Obamacare. In several studies, AEI researchers have reached conclusions that aligned with the claims made by the 2012 Republican presidential contenders. David Hyman and William Sage argued that, because ACA failed to contain any tort reform, it fails to address the concern of critics that frivolous lawsuits are one of the main obstacles to lowering the cost of health care.[91] This lent weight to the need for malpractice reforms advocated by Pawlenty, Gingrich, and Cain. In another AEI study, researchers predicted that doctors and hospitals would be more likely to raise prices because of decreased compensation from Medicare.[92] Finally, Robert Kaestner and Anthony Lo Sasso argued that, as insurance coverage expands, so will the rate of hospitalization, thus driving up costs.[93] Overall, AEI findings indicated that the cost of health care will actually increase because of Obamacare, contrary to the claims of its proponents.

Diana Furchtgott-Roth of the Hudson Institute argued that new taxes on individuals making more than $200,000 dollars annually will result in lower rates of employment and investment, which will negate the increased revenues that such taxes aim to produce. Furthermore, Furchtgott-Roth argued that the revenue from these new taxes will not be used to support Medicare but, rather, will be diverted to covering the cost of health care for people who are too young to qualify for Medicare but who are guaranteed coverage under ACA. Furchtgott-Roth claimed that "$500 billion over the next decade is projected to be saved from Medicare and reallocated to the general health insurance scheme."[94] Hans Kuttner, also of the Hudson Institute, argued that ACA, by introducing concepts such as "essential health benefits," will politicize health care by empowering government officials—in particular the secretary of health and human services—to decide what benefits are to be considered "essential."[95] Thus, the Hudson Institute's findings, if accurate, could rightly be said to justify the Republican claims that Obamacare will result in an extension of state power that is nontransparent and susceptible to manipulation and corruption by interested parties at the expense of consumers.

Richard Epstein of the Hoover Institution has expressed concern about the constitutionality of the new health care laws. In particular, Epstein claimed that under the U.S. Constitution, individuals cannot be required to purchase health insurance, because the federal government is constitutionally barred from interference in intrastate commerce. Epstein also said that, contrary to claims by the Obama administration, the ability of the federal government to impose taxes to fund programs such as Obamacare will result in a de facto extension of federal power at the expense of the states.[96]

The Heritage Foundation has also been critical of the Affordable Care Act. Paul Winfree argued that the tax subsidies the act offers as incentives for purchasing insurance will be offset in the long term by a shrinking tax base. According to Winfree, when combined, these will result in larger budget deficits, which will in turn need to be offset by large tax increases that will slow economic growth.[97] Rita Numerof, also from the Heritage Foundation, argued that the "Accountable Care Organizations" that ACA establishes will stifle creativity in health care financing by creating a government-sponsored oligopoly of organizations that lack the dynamism and innovative power of private actors' competing against one another in the market.[98] Thus, the Heritage Foundation has provided studies that warn about the enlargement of the public sector and the expansion of the deficit, two themes the Republican presidential contenders emphasized in their criticisms of ACA.

The Cato Institute, which was one of the staunchest critics of Hillarycare in 1993, invariably has also opposed ACA. Robert A. Levy, chairman of the Cato Institute, has argued that the constitutionality of the individual mandate cannot be defended under the Taxing Power (its penalties are not taxes), the Commerce Clause (Congress cannot compel states to undertake certain activities in order to regulate them), or the Necessary and Proper Clause (the mandate is contrary to the founders' intentions for a limited government).[99] Michael D. Tanner focused more on effects in his report *Bad Medicine: A Guide to the Real Costs and Consequences of the New Health Care Law*. In this report, he stated that the ACA will cost "more than $2.7 trillion over 10 years of full implementation, and will add more than $823 billion to the national debt over the program's first 10 years."[100] He also contended that the new laws will increase taxes by $569 billion between now and 2019, and that millions of Americans will not be able to keep their current health care plans as costs rise. Tanner argued with Justin Owen in a later report that "as much as two-thirds of companies [will have] to change the coverage they offer to their employees."[101]

There are also other think tanks that have not drawn battle lines on either side, having neither advocated nor opposed the new laws, instead seeking to provide the public with balanced information. RAND is one such institution, partly because of its structure as a contract research think tank and partly because of its explicitly nonpartisan and objective approach. With regard to the effects of implementing an individual mandate, RAND claims a mandate "will have a negligible effect on aggregate national health spending but will increase government spending on *Medicaid* and *premium* subsidies." It also claims that, while an individual mandate will not make health care delivery more reliable, it will increase the life expectancy of the newly insured and increase the population's life expectancy by 1 to 4 million life years.[102] In a June 2010 study, Elizabeth A. McGlynn and other researchers concluded that ACA and the Health Care and Education Reconciliation Act together insured "the largest number of Americans while keeping federal costs as low as reasonably possible."[103] That analysis was based on a comparison of 2,000 different policy options and scenarios in which researchers found that Obamacare would insure 28 million more U.S. citizens while still being a politically and financially tenable option. Although other options could have saved more money, they argued that none of those alternatives would have survived the legislative process.

RAND has also conducted studies on the long-term effects of ACA's provisions on costs. In a May 2011 report, researchers looked at how new regulations would affect the number of employers who decide to "self-insure," or set aside funds in a trust to insure their employees.[104] Since self-insured plans are not subject to many of the new regulations under ACA (they do not have to provide "essential benefits," for example), it is widely assumed that a large number of employers will move to self-insurance plans that are more costly and less generous. The study, however, concluded that ACA would produce a disparity in neither benefits nor price between self-insurance and full-insurance plans. In another report RAND researchers noted that ACA's expanded Medicaid coverage and insurance exchanges would increase the number of citizens insured in California, Connecticut, Illinois, Montana, and Texas while increasing government health care spending in all the states except Connecticut, where it would decrease.[105]

Conclusion

Think tanks have provided both supporters of Obamacare and its critics with research and information that can be used to bolster their respective positions. As has been shown in this case study, some think tanks concluded that the Obama administration is correct in its claims about the financial and political efficacy of the new legislation, while others have lent credence to the criticisms leveled at Obamacare by, among others, the Republican contenders during the 2012 presidential elections. It is likely that as the new legislation begins to take effect, and as individuals and institutions debate its constitutionality in the courts and in the public sphere, the support of think tanks will continue to be solicited by both supporters and critics to further inform the discussion.

CASE STUDY 6: THE 2008 ECONOMIC STIMULUS PACKAGE

The subprime mortgage crisis, rising national debt, and a deteriorating overall economic situation resulted in various proposals for economic reform by U.S. think tanks. Although the difficulty in predicting economic outcomes complicates the ability of think tanks to affect the government's economic decisions, the ideas of think tanks were heavily incorporated into the 2008 presidential campaign and into the first acts of the Obama administration to stem the tides of the recession. Here, think tanks have produced an astounding array of research on controversial subjects that require immediate attention. This case study highlights think tanks as future-oriented institutions with bold and diverse policy proposals and the unique ability to effectively disseminate vast quantities of information to many key actors.

The U.S. economy cycles through regular intervals of expansion and contraction. Typically, the economy expands in periods of six to ten years, followed by recessions that last between six months to two years. According to the National Bureau of Economic Research (NBER) criterion, the United States has undergone thirty-two recessions since 1854, ten of which occurred between 1945 and 2001.

In the first decade of the twenty-first century, the U.S. financial system was in a perilous state. With the subprime mortgage crisis pulling the banking system into chaos, the United States plunged into a recession. Although GDP per capita (at $46,000), unemployment rates, and high capital investments were initially positive, these measures grew more somber, prompting fears that the recession might become a depression. In addition to the debilitating mortgage crisis, major concerns included national debt, a failing Social Security system, corporate debt, and a low savings rate. In addition to the volatile commodities markets, particularly oil and food markets, and changing exchange rates, U.S. external debt hit $12 trillion dollars, due in part to the war in Iraq.[106]

The tax burden in the United States remained a large issue to the taxpaying citizens within the nation. Compared with 1965, when the average household's tax burden was $10,800 (adjusted for inflation), the IRS reported that in the period 2007–08 the average American household paid $22,100 in federal taxes.[107] Throughout the 1990s and the years 2000–09, tax rates and policies mainly shifted along political lines, with hikes during the Clinton years and tax cuts during the Bush administrations.

Because of the dire lending situation and the instability of major banks, the Federal Reserve lowered the lending rate to historic lows in an attempt to stimulate the economy.[108] The initial rate reduction in January 2008 was the first since 9/11, and its sole purpose was to "jump-start the economy by stimulating borrowing, spurring new home construction, and encouraging consumer purchases of durable goods." Market trends continued to deteriorate, however, and in December 2008, the Fed slashed interest rates to 0.00 percent from 0.25 percent, a rate they retained through the fall of 2012, citing a slower-than-desired recovery.[109]

A first stimulus bill, which gave checks directly to those who paid income taxes, was proposed in the spring of 2008. A further stimulus package totaling almost $900 billion passed the House of Representatives on January 29, 2009. This package was a promising mix between tax cuts and investment projects. It narrowly passed without Republican support because Republicans advocated for tax cuts instead of infrastructure stimulus.

The Input of Think Tanks

The Hoover Institution supported the initial interest rate cut by the Federal Reserve, but cautioned that "the size and timing of the cuts are crucial."[110] John B. Taylor, a senior fellow at the Hoover Institution, noted that although the cut was earlier and more generous than expected, he believed that it would help the economy in predictable ways. Aligning with Taylor's comments, a week after the cuts were made, the Dow Jones Industrial Average appeared to show gains, which created the appearance that the administration's efforts had succeeded in stimulating the U.S. economy. However, the Hoover Institution was not universally in agreement with the Fed's interest rate cut. Robert E. Hall, another Hoover Institution senior fellow and chairman of the NBER's Business Cycle Dating Committee, noted, "Our ability to forecast [a U.S. economic recession] is extremely poor."[111] Similarly, John Makin, a visiting scholar at AEI, declared that the ability to predict the overall economic situation was difficult because of a "trio of uncertainties tied to credit markets, the economy, and the path of central bank policies in most of the industrial world."[112] In fact, the current U.S. economy had simply stopped growing as of December 2007.

While analysts initially disagreed on whether the United States was entering a recession, the NBER has since confirmed that peak economic activity was in December 2007.[113] Before this, the Congressional Budget Office had predicted that the interest rate cut would lessen the problems hanging over the housing markets and that the nation would avoid a recession. In hopes of avoiding a more severe financial crisis, Congress and the Bush administration approved a fiscal stimulus package worth around $145 billion in mid-January 2008 that provided rebate checks to many people. Although this package received bipartisan support within Washington, Russell Roberts, a research fellow at Hoover, was skeptical of the package, believing that injecting $145 billion into a $14 trillion economy was a fruitless effort, especially considering that such measures traditionally have "a poor track record of energizing the economy. Usually, the only thing that gets stimulated is a politician's approval rating."[114] Boskin instead argued that the Fed should gradually lower interest rates to combat a possible recession, an action that was taken by the Federal Reserve to no avail.

According to Martin Neil Baily, Douglas W. Elmendorf, and Robert E. Litan of Brookings, "The turmoil in the financial system is important primarily because of its impact on the overall economy." These three senior fellows proposed that the United States may well have been in recession and that further downward pressure on the economy was increasingly due to "expected declines in house prices, tighter lending standards and terms, and [2008]'s further rise in oil prices."[115] Baily, Elmendorf, and Litan noted that the dollar had risen as a result of the crisis and hoped that the interest rate cuts set in motion by the Federal Reserve in February 2008 would stall the recession. They did not disregard the possibility that an even graver economic downturn was entirely possible in the near future. On the basis of the fluctuations in the U.S. financial systems and economy in 2008, Brookings suggested a reform of the government's financial regulations and supervision.

Baily, Elmendorf, and Litan proposed a number of potential solutions to the economic crises befalling America. They suggested a more aggressive tightening of monetary policy early on in the crisis to constrain the housing boom but acknowledged that doing so would produce slower growth. Moreover, Brookings noted the lack of warning from policymakers with regard to the economic chaos. While citizens cannot expect policymakers to know when assets are overvalued or markets are going to collapse, policymakers should have greater responsibility to warn of "the growing risk of certain assets that might generate large rewards but could also lead to large losses."[116] Americans should have been warned that large increases in house prices were not a guarantee.

Moreover, several scholars at Brookings, while initially disagreeing with the first fiscal stimulus package, became proponents of such a strategy that is "timely, targeted, and temporary."[117] They were also supportive of the cuts made by the Fed. These economists admitted that many millions of households would default on their mortgages and that the government should take further efforts to reduce this number to try and prevent further economic recession.

Scott Lilly of CAP opposed the cut in the federal funding rate to zero percent. Lilly believed that after the slashing of these rates, it was up to tax and spending policy to deal with the crisis. He called for an appropriate mixture of new or increased expenditures and tax cuts to compose the stimulus package. With regard to the stimulus, Lilly stated, "A specific amount of money needs to flow into the economy within a specific time period . . . and that amount should not be compromised in order to meet other policy objectives."[118]

At the end of 2008, Will Straw and Michael Ettlinger, also from CAP, called for a stimulus package to tackle the immediate crisis and provide higher levels of confidence for better economic prospects. With regard to the housing crisis, according to Straw and Ettlinger, "CAP has long argued that at-risk mortgages should be modified and foreclosed properties should be returned to productive use to keep families in their homes, protect neighborhood housing values, and stabilize credit and housing markets."[119]

Analysts at the Hoover Institution speculated that oil prices would soon hit the record-high $150-a-barrel range, owing to in large part to the quick increases that had been characteristic of oil in the recent past. Their prediction was almost fulfilled on July 11, 2008, with oil prices hitting $147 a barrel. The Hoover Institution noted, "Almost every consumer product and service are affected by these increased costs: the food production, shipping, manufacturing, and transportation industries are just some of the nation's vital economic sectors that have increased consumer prices to offset increased fuel charges."[120] Unless the United States pushed for loosening its oil dependency, the economy would gravely suffer in the upcoming future.

According to Martin Neil Baily at Brookings, the economy and the war in Iraq were two separate policy issues. High oil prices are largely the result of strong demand, notably from China and India, and limited supply. Fear of turmoil in Iraq may have boosted oil prices but not nearly enough to account for the huge price surge and the current rate of inflation. Baily disparaged Washington's habit of borrowing money to pay for the war and the Fed's low interest rates, which accounted for the high inflation rates and economic woes facing the country. Moreover, Baily named the "mortgage mess and the big slump in residential construction" as primary causes of the U.S. economic fumbles. Although Baily castigated the Fed for its policies since 2005 during the mortgage crisis, he applauded their recent tactics to gain control over the financial situation. While Baily did agree with much of what fellows at Hoover wrote, he noted that although it was tempting to "wrap it into a single package with our current economic crisis and the policy mistakes that contributed to it . . . muddling the messes does not help."[121]

Robert E. Hall and Alvin Rabushka, both senior fellows at the Hoover Institution, built on the work of Hoover fellow Milton Friedman by proposing a flat income tax of 19 percent. A flat income rate tax would tax all income at one rate and eliminate all deductions, resulting in a much simpler tax code and tax return form. Although the 19 percent tax has not been adopted by the United States, the push for such an act culminated in President Reagan's Tax Reform Act of 1986, which replaced multiple rates with 15 percent and 28 percent. Hoover senior fellows John F. Cogan and R. Glenn Hubbard warned that the increased government spending and taxes proposed by some presidential candidates would "drive the personal income tax burden up by 25 percent to its highest point relative to GDP in history."[122] Cogan and Hubbard offered a three-pronged solution to the economic slowdown without raising taxes: reform entitlements to slow their cost growth, eliminate all nonessential spending in the remainder of the budget, and adopt policies that promote economic growth.

During their campaigns, Barack Obama and Hillary Clinton both outlined plans to increase exemptions and tax cuts to alleviate the tax burden of poor and middle-class families. Obama and Clinton endorsed plans to let the tax cuts enacted during the Bush administration in 2001 and 2003 expire. By contrast, Senator John McCain advocated a reduction in corporate taxes and a repeal of the alternative minimum tax.[123] Hall and Rabushka pointed out that regardless of who was elected, disagreements would be inevitable.

To alleviate the economic crisis Obama would roll back the Bush tax cuts for those making more than between $200,000 and $250,000; conversely, McCain proposed to permanently extend all of the Bush tax cuts. McCain followed the suggestions of those at Hoover who advocated not increasing the tax burden while maintaining the Bush tax cuts. Obama and McCain also pushed for a simplified tax return filing process, a suggestion similar to Hall and Rabushka's work at the Hoover Institution.[124] Obama also supported investment into clean energy, a venture that McCain pursued under the label of "post carbon." Both presidential nominees appeared to have heeded the warning of the energy crisis mentioned by the Hoover Institution. When it came to the economic recession, the high gas prices, and the Iraq War, Obama was much more closely aligned to positions taken by Brookings scholars.

Conclusion

Brookings, the Hoover Institution, and CAP, as well as numerous other think tanks, have played an essential role in the recent discussions on economic policy. President Bush remained steadfast in his economic policies during his two terms in office, and the current state of the economy reflects his unwavering policy decisions. Although increasing the national debt, creating housing and Social Security crises, decreasing the value of the American dollar, and vastly increasing gas prices may not have been Bush's immediate aims, they became corollaries of his fiscal policy. Now, however, politicians are taking a more advice-friendly approach to the making of economic policy in the wake of such failed policies. Even though McCain, the Republican presidential candidate in 2008, continued to advocate the tax cuts initially proposed by Bush during his campaign, he placed greater focus on "post carbon" energies. By doing so, he followed the policy suggestions of the Hoover Institution. Meanwhile, the 2008 Democratic presidential candidates followed the policy suggestions of Brookings, with a little overlap with the Hoover Institution. Analysts from both Brookings and Hoover wrote similar policy reports on a diverse group of issues, and both candidates were likely to select an economic policy that would, in some capacity, reflect the ideas and proposals of the two organizations. CAP also influenced Obama's policies, advocating a mix of expenditures and tax cuts to ensure that the stimulus package would boost the stability of the economy.

Think tanks are not the only institutions that provided research and advice regarding the declining economy. University scholars have changed their focus from purely academic research to policy advice. Highly regarded professors of economics have written for major newspapers and conducted interviews for radio and television stations as a way to disseminate their advice on how best to ameliorate the economic situation. Many professors have even begun to take a partisan approach to their research. For example, Jeffery Miron of Harvard University's Economics Department has written articles advocating his libertarian approach to the economy, mainly characterized by tax cuts over government spending.[125] In fact, Harvard has been relishing the opportunity to contribute policy advice, even adding a link to the economics home page and articles written by professors giving their recommendations and analysis. Their involvement has not gone unnoticed. Professor Martin Feldstein was appointed to President Obama's Economic Recovery Advisory Board in February 2009. Thus, individuals in the social sciences, but not necessarily involved with think tanks, are contributing to the expert analysis on which Obama has relied on for advice.

Harvard is not the only academic institution that has been offering advice. The University of California at Berkeley, another university with a highly ranked economics program, has also been at the forefront of economic advice. Not only have professors Carl Shapiro and Joseph Farrell been picked to work for government organizations such as the Department of Justice and the Federal Trade Commission, but Berkeley has also been holding seminars and roundtable discussions to discuss the economic crisis. In these discussions, professors have considered the global impact of the U.S. economic problems as well as specific problems that President Obama will continue to face throughout his presidency.

However, it is still important to consider that in the face of a true crisis, think tanks are serving two of their primary functions as researchers and advocates, helping policymakers to feel if not entirely sure about the best path to take at least fairly well-informed. Whatever the outcome of Obama's first steps have been to combat the economic crisis, think tanks have continued to bring new ideas and perspectives to the table.

CASE STUDY 7: RESOURCES FOR THE FUTURE AND DOMESTIC CLIMATE CHANGE POLICY

Resources for the Future (RFF) made climate change a crucial topic on the U.S. political agenda. RFF provided significant research, and, in doing so, paved the way for scholarship on climate change. Working in the public and private spheres, RFF embodied many of the aims of modern think tanks, including raising public awareness of issues, providing unbiased research, advocating for policy, and influencing the decisions of policymakers.

RFF has been a leader in current climate change policy analysis. RFF's legacy in natural resource management and policy stretches back to the 1950s, when it was the first think tank to specialize in energy and environmental economics. In the late 1960s, John Krutilla and Allen Kneese led RFF's influence in academics and policy through their prized social science research. Krutilla's classic article, "Conservation Reconsidered," developed the pillars of resource economics: the "existence value" of wilderness areas, the "option value" of preservation, and the irreversible nature of some economic development. Kneese, along with Robert Ayers and Ralph d'Arge, linked environment, engineering, economic, and eco-logical models to industrial production. These historic achievements set RFF's reputation for unbiased, original research in the environmental field that contin-ues to the present day.

The Input of Think Tanks

In 1997, Raymond Kopp, Richard Morgenstern, William Pizer, and Michael Toman unveiled a plan for a cost-effective reduction in U.S. greenhouse gas emission, creating a feasible approach of carbon reductions that would ensure both environmental benefits and economic predictability. This research was ahead of its time, proving RFF's lead on now-popular climate change issues. Both sides of the aisle routinely look to RFF's research findings as an objective baseline for their political discourse. For example, in March 2009 RFF con-ducted private briefings for six U.S. senators on climate change design issues be-fore comprehensive energy legislation came to the Senate floor. RFF scholars also participated in regular briefings for Senate staff on issues ranging from cost-containment options, policies to address leakage and competitiveness issues, and the distributional impacts of different climate policies on U.S. households.

Internationally, Lord Nicholas Stern, author of the *Stern Review*, held a pri-vate lunch at RFF in 2009 to discuss U.S. and international climate policy de-velopments with Obama administration officials and RFF staff. Recently, in fact, senior fellow Richard Morgenstern was invited to assist the World Bank in developing a cap-and-trade system to help the government of Mexico regulate its greenhouse gas emissions.

RFF researchers often provide expert analysis to NGOs, government agencies, and Congress on climate change issues. In 2010 senior fellow Dallas Burtraw and fellow Joe Aldy, former special assistant for energy and environment to President Obama, contributed to a Government Accountability Office study that extracted lessons from climate change regulation in Europe. In 2009 RFF scholars provided testimony more than seven times on climate change issues before the Senate Committee on Energy and Natural Resources, the Senate Subcommittee on Energy, Natural Resources and Infrastructure, the Senate Finance Committee, the House Ways and Means Committee, and the House Energy and Commerce Subcommittee. These expert testimonies covered issues such as the effects of eliminating tax preferences for oil and gas companies, the effects of a carbon dioxide cap-and-trade program on households, market flexibility in climate change legislation, policy options to address the potential for leakage, distributional impacts of federal climate policy, and energy research and development. RFF experts have influenced House legislation such as the American Clean Energy and Security Act of 2009, also known as the Waxman-Markey Bill, and the Clean Energy Jobs and American Power Act, the Kerry-Boxer Bill, in the Senate.

Conclusion

In 1991 China established its first environmental think tank organization modeled on RFF. This imitation demonstrates RFF's continued influence on the scholarship of domestic and current international climate and environmental issues, as well as its success in many areas of think tank activity. RFF not only gave testimony before Congress and provided briefs to the legislative and executive branches but also generated high-profile and persuasive articles for the public. As an independent organization, RFF was able to sidestep the political biases, bureaucratic formalities, lack of specific funding, and rigid general procedures that slowed government research on the subject. This independent nature and policy-oriented research—defining characteristics of think tanks in general—allowed RFF to produce forward-thinking and innovative research that demanded government action.

CHAPTER FOUR

Think Tanks in Action

FOREIGN POLICY CASE STUDIES

THE FOLLOWING CASE studies illustrate the vital role that think tanks assume in the formation of U.S. foreign policy. Foreign policy is addressed through an examination of the North Korean nuclear talks, the "surge" strategy during the Iraq war, the 9/11 Commission, the atrocities in Darfur, Sudan, and the "Buy America" provision in 2009 stimulus bill that one think tank regarded as outright "protectionism." Within these case studies are examples of the revolving door phenomenon, the process through which each new administration draws analysts from think tanks, particularly from those with a shared political ideology, and members of the outgoing administration likewise resume their places at various think tanks. This revolving door ensures that these policy experts and analysts are never far from the action in Washington. They intermittently serve within the government or within think tanks, where they generate new ideas or provide opposing viewpoints for the administration in place.

CASE STUDY 1: NUCLEAR WEAPONS IN NORTH KOREA

Since North Korea threatened to withdraw from the Treaty on the Non-Proliferation of Nuclear Weapons and began developing nuclear weapons in the 1990s, nuclear negotiations with North Korea have been a contentious subject.

Several U.S. administrations have called on a wide variety of considerations and views from think tanks to make the most prudent decisions concerning North Korea. This case study demonstrates the importance of think tanks in proposing alternative views to the administration and fostering a continuous debate.

In 1994 U.S. president Bill Clinton and North Korean leader Kim Il-Sung signed the Agreed Framework, in which North Korea promised to freeze and ultimately dismantle its burgeoning nuclear weapons program.[1] In turn, the United States and other countries would help build two power-producing nuclear reactors for the North Koreans. In 2000 North Korea threatened to restart its nuclear weapons program if the United States did not pay restitution for lost electricity due to ongoing delays during the construction of the civilian nuclear reactors. In his January 2002 State of the Union address, President George W. Bush labeled North Korea as part of the "Axis of Evil," along with Iran and Iraq, and went on to say that "by seeking weapons of mass destruction, these regimes pose a grave and growing danger."[2]

In October 2002, the United States revealed that North Korea had admitted to restarting its nuclear weapons program.[3] By the end of the year, the United States and South Korea suspended their compliance with the Agreed Framework, and the North Koreans removed the International Atomic Energy Agency (IAEA) seals and cameras from their nuclear facilities and expelled weapons inspectors. In early 2003, North Korea withdrew from the Nuclear Non-Proliferation Treaty.[4] North Korea demanded one-on-one talks with the United States in April 2003 after announcing it had nuclear weapons and would test, export, or use them.[5] In August, the first round of six-party talks between the United States, North Korea, China, Japan, Russia, and South Korea took place. Two subsequent rounds of talks were held in February and June 2004 looking for a resolution to the tensions, which resulted in an impasse and indefinite postponement.[6]

Talks resumed in 2005, at which point North Korea offered to relinquish its weapons program if the United States and the four other nations involved in the negotiations allowed North Korea to run a civilian nuclear power program and provided a light water reactor. The United States and Russia refused. By November of that year, the talks hit yet another impasse after the United States levied financial restrictions against North Korean banks and corporations for alleged involvement in currency counterfeiting and other illegal activities.[7] In December, a senior U.S. diplomat branded North Korea a criminal regime, involved in "arms sales, drug trafficking, and currency forgery."[8]

In April 2006 North Korea refused to rejoin the six-party talks without the U.S. release of funds frozen in Macau. North Korea test-fired six missiles in

July and detonated a nuclear device in October. The United Nations Security Council then imposed wide-reaching sanctions on the North Korean regime. In early 2007, envoys prepared for six-party talks to resume. They reached a breakthrough in February, when North Korea agreed to take steps toward dismantling its weapons program and shutting down its civilian nuclear reactors in exchange for access to North Korean bank accounts that had been frozen overseas. In June 2007 the United States released $25 million worth of North Korean assets held in Macau. On September 30, North Korea signed an agreement to allow U.S. experts to take the lead in dismantling its nuclear weapons program. In December 2007 U.S. envoy Christopher Hill declared that progress on disabling the Yongbyon nuclear reactor was going well.[9]

In January 2008 the United States criticized North Korea for failing to meet its deadline at the end of 2007 for declaring its nuclear activities. Following the election of conservative leader Lee Myung-bak, South Korea then declared all aid to the North conditional on complete nuclear disarmament and human rights progress. Despite North Korea's long-awaited declaration of its nuclear assets in June 2008, relations between the two Koreas deteriorated rapidly. In October 2008 the United States removed North Korea from its list of countries that sponsor terrorism in return for full access to its nuclear sites. However, North-South relations continued to decline, and in November 2008 North Korea threatened to cut off all overland travel between the two states as a result of South Korea's "confrontational policies." By December 2008 six-party talks were again stalled as North Korea refused to agree in writing to a verification protocol presented by the other countries, which included verifying past nuclear activities and the current extent of their nuclear arsenal.[10]

In January 2009 North Korea announced it was no longer honoring political deals nor maintaining diplomatic relations with South Korea, accusing Seoul of "hostile intent."[11] The following month, North Korea announced preparations for the launching of a rocket carrying a communications satellite, a move similar to the rocket launches in 2006. This prompted a response from the six countries involved in the talks as well as from the United Nations. Additionally, President Obama stated on April 3, 2009, while in a conference with President Nicolas Sarkozy of France, "We will work with all interested partners in the international community to take appropriate steps to let North Korea know that they cannot threaten the safety and stability of other countries with impunity."[12] North Korea ultimately failed to fully launch their missiles, but nevertheless it took the initiative to set a deliberate date for missile deployment for 11:30 a.m. on April 4, 2009. The explicit scheduling of the missile launch, despite previous launch failures, was seen as defying the international community with adverse political as well as technological motives.[13]

On April 11, 2009, the UN Security Council issued a presidential statement, a move only one step away in gravity from a resolution, condemning North Korea for the event and warning against any similar action in the future. The statement also tightened existing sanctions, which was an attempt "to send a very clear message to North Korea that what they have done under the guise of a satellite launch is in fact a violation of their obligations and indeed that there are consequences for such actions," Susan Rice, ambassador to the United Nations, elucidated.[14] Five days later, on April 16, North Korea expelled inspectors from the IAEA, instructing agents to remove seals from equipment, to switch off surveillance cameras, and to leave the country. North Korea also ordered the U.S. experts monitoring the Yongbyon plant to leave the country.

Pyongyang subsequently left the six-party talks and responded to the United States' threats of "consequences for 'kicking these personnel out,'" with its own assertions to "reactivate all of its nuclear facilities and go ahead with reprocessing spent fuel."[15] The reprocessing of spent fuel separates plutonium from nuclear waste, which could be used to fuel reactors and make nuclear weapons. Following North Korea's departure from the talks, the UN Security Council imposed tougher sanctions on North Korea in June 2009.

In a visit to Pyongyang in December 2009, U.S. envoy Stephen Bosworth said he and North Korean officials had reached "common understanding" on the need to revive the six-party talks. Despite this apparent diplomatic victory, relations collapsed once again in March 2010, when a South Korean warship, the *Cheonan*, was sunk near the North Korean border. South Korea responded in May by breaking off all trade relations with North Korea, explaining that they had come across evidence of North Korea's responsibility in the sinking of the *Cheonan*. North Korea responded by calling this evidence, the finding of a North Korean torpedo, a "fabrication" and cut all diplomatic relations with the South.[16] In a further escalation, North Korean forces proceeded to shell the island of Yeonpyeong following a South Korean artillery drill that November, in what secretary-general of the UN Ban Ki-moon referred to as "one of the gravest incidents since the end of the Korean War."[17] After the death of Kim Jong Il in December 2011, Kim Jong Un succeeded his father and within six months conducted what "most observers think . . . was a long-range missile test," further straining relations with the United States.[18]

The Input of Think Tanks

Given the Heritage Foundation's long-standing advocacy for missile defense, it should serve as no surprise that it was not happy with the Agreed Framework of 1994 negotiated by President Clinton and that it spent considerable time throughout the 1990s arguing for tougher action on the North Korean conundrum. As early as July 1994, Richard D. Fisher, a senior fellow at Heritage, argued that agreeing to a weapons program freeze as opposed to full disarmament was unwise and caused the United States to "lose the initiative" against North Korea. Fisher was also an early advocate of multiparty talks concerning the weapons issues and insisted that the United States engage South Korea and Japan by pushing for them to guarantee full diplomatic relations in exchange for dismantling their nuclear program. Additionally, he called for an effort to secure China's involvement in the issue, namely, by connecting its cooperation on negotiations with North Korea to the fact that it holds the "most favored nation" trade status with the United States.[19]

The Heritage Foundation also incorporated the North Korean problem into its successful missile defense advocacy program. In a 1998 "Backgrounder" report, Baker Spring and James Anderson cited the findings of the Rumsfeld Commission, chaired by former secretary of defense Donald Rumsfeld, which concluded that the United States "might well have little or no warning before operational deployment" of missiles. Spring and Anderson cited North Korea's growing missile program, noting that the gravest threat to the United States in 1998 was missiles armed with nuclear, biological, or chemical warheads.[20] They implied that given the events in 1998—missile tests and U.S. demands for weapons inspectors to verify North Korean compliance—the Agreed Framework was ineffective.[21]

When George W. Bush took office in 2001, Georgetown professor William Taylor, writing for the Nautilus Institute, encouraged Bush to continue the Clinton-era policy of diplomacy despite the "painfully slow reciprocity" from North Korea.[22] The new president most likely was disinclined to follow such a course of action, because important players in his administration came from the Heritage Foundation. A notable example was Bush's speechwriter, Michael Gerson, who was a senior policy adviser at Heritage.[23] In 2002 when North Korea's nuclear weapons program was revealed, President Bush promptly labeled the nation as a member of the "Axis of Evil" in his State of the Union Address, which was authored by Gerson.[24] This speech demonstrated the change in policy toward North Korea from Clinton's to Bush's. It directly shows the influence that different think tanks had over each administration, and because Gerson, an adviser from Heritage, wrote the speech, it logically explains the Bush administration's tougher stance on the North Korean disarmament problem and its missile defense policy that the Heritage Foundation advocated.

Bush's policy followed the general outline of long-standing recommendations by Heritage Foundation scholars: a dismissal of bilateral talks with Pyongyang in favor of multilateral, six-party talks and an insistence on having the North Korea dismantle its nuclear weapons program. President Bush never acceded to North Korea's request for one-on-one talks, despite the incentives offered by Pyongyang to do so in April 2003. This approach was applauded and encouraged during the 2004 U.S. presidential election by the Heritage Foundation's Dr. Balbina Y. Hwang in light of John Kerry's promise to engage North Korea bilaterally.[25] Some scholars at Heritage had called for versions of the Bush approach as early as 1994.[26] During George W. Bush's first term, Heritage scholars such as Larry Wortzel, Baker Spring, and Balbina Hwang encouraged the multiparty framework of talks and the continued demands for total nuclear disarmament.[27] As early as April 2003, former Secretary of State George P. Shultz said publicly, "We should get the Chinese, South Korea, Russia and Japan involved in diplomacy."[28] Given Shultz's close academic relationship with former Secretary of State Condoleezza Rice, it is a testament to the revolving door effect that the multilateral approach on the North Korea issue flourished during Rice's tenure at Foggy Bottom.[29]

Nevertheless, the Bush administration still received criticism from right-wing think tanks for not adopting a hard-line approach during the six-party negotiations. At the announcement in February 2007 that Pyongyang had pledged to begin steps toward shutting down its nuclear reactor in exchange for the U.S. release of frozen North Korean assets, *National Review* blogger Andy McCarthy remarked that the situation resembled "1994 all over again: [The United States makes] energy aid and other concessions to them in exchange for their mere promise to take initial steps toward denuclearization."[30] For his part, John Bolton, former U.S. ambassador to the United Nations and current senior fellow at the American Enterprise Institute (AEI), criticized the North Korean deal as contradicting the "fundamental premises of the president's policy he's been following for the past six years."[31] These right-wing think tanks demonstrate another important role that think tanks play in the development of foreign policy: they draw attention to varying opinions and different ideas by openly castigating the president when he does not follow the strategies they advocate.

Bush's policies at the end of his administration even drew criticism from Heritage analysts. Following the election of conservative Lee Myung-Bak in

December 2007, Heritage senior fellow Bruce Klingner argued for a unification of South Korean and U.S. interests to "enhance negotiating leverage" and increase the conditionality of engagements with North Korea.[32] The United States effectively ignored this approach and agreed in October 2008 to remove North Korea from its list of states sponsoring terrorism in return for a pledge to accept the verification protocol negotiated during the six-party talks. Klingner denounced this policy as "trading a tangible benefit for an intangible promise"; he argued further that the move alienated South Korea and Japan by ignoring their security and economic concerns.[33]

More recently, with the launching of test missiles and reports of Kim Jong Il having suffered a stroke, the Obama administration was in a perfect place to consider a range of think tank policy proposals. The Heritage Foundation continued to advocate for the aggressive use of military and economic sanctions through the six-party prism to support the implementation of a "rigorous and intrusive verification mechanism."[34] Since the North Korean missile launch of April 16, 2009, Heritage has criticized the actions, or perceived inactions, of the Obama administration on their blog *The Foundry*. Fellows writing on the blog warned that the missiles were technologically more successful than supposed had been predicted and that North Korea's efforts in this area should not be underestimated. Additionally, fellow Paul Stares at the Council on Foreign Relations urged President Obama to consider various contingency strategies in the likely event of an upcoming leadership change in North Korea—a change that ultimately took place following Kim Jong Il's death in 2011. In particular, he recommended supplementing increased commitment to six-party talks with a quiet bilateral dialogue with China to discuss solutions regarding mutual security and political concerns.[35] Since the death of Kim Jong Il and the apparent instability of the new regime, the Heritage Foundation has continued to stand firm in its advocacy of robust defensive measures to prepare for any potential crises.[36]

AEI has been pushing for the Obama administration to avoid reliance on soft power, warning that without the ability to respond militarily, all negotiations are empty talk. AEI fellow Dan Blumenthal has deeply criticized the defense cuts in the national budget, stating that only through maintenance of "its role as 'Asia's security guarantor' the United States can hope to secure an enduring peace in this dynamic region."[37] AEI has emphasized military power and ally seeking, specifically that Japan and the United States "should explore all missile-defense options, including airborne lasers."[38] The United States is consistently regarded as helpless in face of the actions of North Korea because of certain diplomatic and military capacities particularly given its close ties to South Korea, while Japan is seen as "not bound by an alliance with South Korea and has more freedom of action to defend itself, with less risk of escalation."[39]

Brookings has published many pieces with categorically different opinions from those presented by either the Heritage Foundation or AEI. Brookings scholars have promoted and supported efforts to maintain the soft power stance favored by the Obama administration. On March 23, 2009, visiting fellow Sun-Won wrote a fifteen-page paper, before the 2009 missile launch, in which he stated that "the United States needs to indirectly inform North Korea of the possible U.S. responses if North Korea goes ahead with the planned launch . . . the best course is to resolve the issue through dialogue."[40] Obama did just that, with subsequent actions at diplomacy, including a call for other nations to leave North Korea in "an isolated position" that would hopefully lead to eventual concessions.[41] The launch was also seen as a failure technologically as well as strategically for North Korea as it "cannot proclaim that it is now a militarily credible nuclear state with the requisite technology for warhead miniaturization and a delivery vehicle."[42]

The Carnegie Endowment for International Peace has argued the same line as Brookings, publishing supportive analysis of the Obama administration's actions. It has further advocated flexibility and understanding from Washington in conversations with Asian countries. For instance, a report published in the early days of President Obama's administration asserts that "most Chinese scholars would like the new U.S. administration to show more flexibility in the talks. . . . They firmly believe that flexibility on the American side would ease North Korea's stance and help achieve settlement expeditiously."[43] Following similar calls for soft power, the report advocated for soft power through diplomacy, stating, "There is a consensus among those in foreign policy circles in China that America should open direct dialogue with North Korea."[44] These policy proposals have been influential in the Obama administration. In January 2009 Secretary of State Hillary Clinton declared that the six-party talks "have merit as a negotiating vehicle," and State Department spokesman Sean McCormack added that "Pyongyang will have to meet its six-party commitments before realizing diplomatic benefits."[45]

However, Susan E. Rice, current national security adviser, former Brookings senior fellow, and former ambassador to the United Nations, has argued that bilateral talks offered the best opportunity for achieving verifiable disarmament in North Korea. In a 2005 piece published in the *Washington Post*, she lambasted the Bush administration's refusal to negotiate directly with Kim

Jong Il and argued that even if such negotiations failed, the talks would give the United States a greater reason to persuade China and others to support punitive actions.[46] Such bilateral talks have since been stalled, and President Obama has consequently stated that the actions of North Korea merited a "strong international response." He also called for a "stronger global regime" to put more effective pressure on the North Koreans.[47] Obama has appealed for support from the UN Security Council and pushed for stronger punitive measures against violators of the Non-Proliferation Treaty, looking for collective action against North Korea specifically. Regarding the new threats posed by the ascent of Kim Jung Un, think tanks have advocated the strengthening of existing security measures, but policy prescriptions have been stymied by the overall lack of knowledge about the form and behavior of the new regime.[48]

Conclusion

In this case study, various think tanks have contributed to both the creation of foreign policy toward North Korea and have levied criticism against the policy measures implemented during the last two administrations. Each think tank advanced a specific opinion by issuing reports and criticizing the actions of presidents when official policy and their own recommendations diverged. The Heritage Foundation's consistent attack on the Agreed Framework with North Korea helped keep skepticism of the deal alive throughout the Clinton administration and helped prepare scholars and future policymakers for the prospect of the agreement's eventual unraveling. During the Bush administration, the Heritage Foundation contributed substantially to the formulation of a North Korean foreign strategy, while at the same time remaining critical of the extent and manner in which it was actualized.

Brookings scholars have provided constant criticism of the Bush administration, and subsequently, its policies maintained a separate dialogue on the same topic. This conversation has come into play as many of the leading minds in the current administration, such as National Security Adviser Susan Rice, were former fellows at Brookings. Regardless, the drumbeat of opposition from think tanks representing the full political spectrum has provided a wealth of sound information on the North Korea issue for both policymaker and citizen alike to digest and draw conclusions. The work of think tanks generating reports and garnering media attention on North Korea's nuclear ambitions will ensure that the U.S. government's decisions will not be undertaken in a vacuum devoid of public debate and advice.

CASE STUDY 2: THE AMERICAN ENTERPRISE INSTITUTE
AND GEORGE W. BUSH'S "SURGE" STRATEGY IN IRAQ

The Iraq War and the ensuing occupation of Iraq was one of the defining foreign policy initiatives of George W. Bush's presidency. It has been labeled a serious blunder, a setback in Middle East relations, and a budgetary black hole by critics in Congress, the media, and the general public. Yet despite the critics and their concerns, the Bush administration pushed onward, seeking to lay the seeds of stability in a post-Saddam Iraq. Even in face of low public opinion of the war and contrarian advice from congressional research groups, President Bush was able to legitimize an increase in troops with the help of think tanks. This case study highlights the influence of think tanks in shaping U.S. foreign policy in Iraq, which was at times in opposition to governmental advisers.

In March 2006, Congress created the Iraq Study Group (ISG) in response to increased public concern over U.S. actions and continued presence in Iraq. The ISG lacked a specific statutory mandate, but it quickly assumed responsibility for providing a "forward-looking assessment of the current and prospective situation in Iraq, including policy suggestions and advice." Its investigation was facilitated by the Congress-funded United States Institute of Peace (USIP) with the support of the Center for the Study of the Presidency, the Center for Strategic and International Studies (CSIS) and the James A. Baker Institute for Public Policy at Rice University. ISG is a notable example of the revolving door phenomenon that is manifested in policy formation; when personnel from ISG were replaced, their replacements were often drawn from think tanks. In turn, bureaucrats from the previous administration that were replaced returned to the think tank sphere, at least until a new administration brought them back into the government.

ISG was a ten-person bipartisan panel cochaired by revolving door luminaries such as James A. Baker, a Republican (R), former secretary of state 1989–92, and current chair of the James A. Baker Institute for Public Policy at Rice University, and Lee Hamilton, previously a Democratic (D) congressman from Indiana and former president of the Woodrow Wilson International Center for Scholars.[49] ISG members also included former secretary of state Lawrence S. Eagleburger (R), former Bill Clinton adviser Vernon Jordan (D), former chief of staff to President Clinton Leon Panetta (D), former defense secretary William Perry (D), former senator Charles S. Robb of Virginia (D), former senator Alan Simpson of Wyoming (R), and former Supreme Court associate justice Sandra Day O'Connor (R).[50] Former CIA director Robert Gates (R) and former New

York mayor Rudy Giuliani (R) were also members, although both left the ISG to pursue other interests—Gates to become secretary of defense and Giuliani to concentrate on running for president.

Congressional support for the creation of the ISG was strongly bipartisan, led primarily by Representative Frank Wolf (R-Va.) who had been advocating for an external reassessment of the situation in Iraq since the summer of 2005.[51] Despite its lack of involvement in the creation of ISG, the Bush administration supported the formation of the group and provided it with access to White House information and resources including funding for a trip to Iraq.[52] The group made its findings public in a published report on December 6, 2006. The report found that violence in Iraq was underreported and provided seventy-nine recommendations.[53] Recommendations included the significant downsizing of U.S. combat forces in Iraq to levels below 70,000 troops; increased embedding of U.S. forces within the Iraqi military and police units to assist with their training; a system of further assistance to the Iraqi government conditional on the achievement of certain security and political benchmarks; and the inclusion of diplomats from neighboring states, including Iran and Syria, in discussions on stability.[54]

The Input of Think Tanks

On December 27, 2006, three weeks after the release of the ISG report, retired army brigadier general Jack Keane and AEI analyst Frederick Kagan published a brief article in the *Washington Post* disagreeing with the ISG's recommendations. According to Keane and Kagan, a troop *increase* of 20,000 to 30,000 in Iraq for approximately eighteen months, with an emphasis placed on the city of Baghdad, was necessary to stabilize the country sufficiently so that a functional Iraqi government could be established.[55] This "surge" would bring security, which was necessary politically and economically for Iraq. Kagan and Keane, however, warned against a short surge that would last only three to six months. They argued that it took soldiers about that long to become familiar with their environment and that a short surge would redeploy troops back home at a time when they would start to become effective in Iraq. Kagan presented this strategy formally on January 6, 2007, in a forty-seven-page AEI report entitled *Choosing Victory: A Plan for Success in Iraq.*[56]

On January 20, 2007, President Bush unveiled his new plan for U.S. operations in Iraq.[57] Consistent with the Baker-Hamilton report that ISG released, Bush emphasized joint operations between U.S. and Iraqi forces and promised diplomatic outreach efforts on Iraq's behalf to neighboring Middle East nations such as Saudi Arabia, Egypt, Jordan, and the Gulf States. Iran and Syria were conspicuously absent from this list, despite the ISG's recommendation of their inclusion. More contradictory, however, was President Bush's response to the fundamental question of U.S. troop involvement. Rather than supporting a downsizing of U.S. forces, President Bush favored the advice of Keane and Kagan, calling for the deployment of 20,000 additional U.S. troops to Iraq with the vast majority—five combat brigades total—going to Baghdad.[58]

Conclusion

President Bush's decision to adopt the recommendations of the Kagan report achieved two key objectives. First, through association with such names as retired general Jack Keane, a decorated U.S. Army officer with thirty-seven years of service, and Fred Kagan, a reputable military historian who had taught at the U.S. Military Academy, the Bush administration gained much-needed credibility in support of its policy on Iraq.[59] At the time of the report's release in December 2006, 52 percent of the U.S. public thought the United States was losing the Iraq War and only 25 percent of respondents believed Bush had a clear solution to the Iraq problem.[60] As a result, President Bush was reluctant to try any plan that was seen as originating solely from the White House.

Second, by acknowledging the political importance of independent think tanks such as AEI, President Bush bolstered the position of the White House relative to Congress. After the ISG released its report, former secretary of state Baker stressed that it was "probably the only bipartisan report [Bush] is going to get," and it was "vital not to treat it like a fruit salad, taking a bit here and a bit there."[61] Despite this advice, President Bush noted repeatedly in the run-up to announcing the new surge strategy that while the Baker-Hamilton report was "important," the White House would be drawing information from a number of reports.[62] The Bush administration also relied on reports from the Pentagon, the U.S. State Department, and the National Security Council. This tactic effectively limited the influence of the congressionally appointed ISG and gave the White House freedom to consult partisan institutions that reflected its own ideology. Ultimately, President Bush's lip service to the ISG in the form of increased diplomatic efforts did little to hide the truth; the new surge strategy was a clear refutation of a bipartisan solution in favor of Keane, Kagan, and AEI, a prominent conservative think tank.

CASE STUDY 3: THE CENTER FOR AMERICAN
PROGRESS AND STRATEGIC REDEPLOYMENT

This case study demonstrates the ability of think tanks to influence U.S. presidents when they disagree on their foreign policy. The Center for American Progress (CAP), and specifically its use of the media and political debates, shows how strongly think tanks can pressure the executive branch. Indeed, while criticizing the Bush administration, CAP simultaneously issued and promoted its own updated, alternative strategies for Iraq.

Following the September 11 attacks on the World Trade Center in 2001, President Bush declared a "war on terror." In his State of the Union Address to Congress on January 29, 2002, he listed Iraq, Iran, and North Korea as composing an "Axis of Evil," thereby changing a major focus of U.S. national foreign policy from terrorist groups to governments. In spring 2002, Iraq refused UN demands that International Atomic Energy Agency (IAEA) inspectors be permitted to enter the country. In September of that year, President Bush addressed a special session of Congress, asking for approval of multilateral action against Iraq. Iraq responded that it would allow inspections if action was withheld but quickly retracted that offer. In early 2003, Secretary of State Colin Powell made a case to the UN Security Council that, regardless of international opposition, the United States had a strategic imperative to invade Iraq and depose Saddam Hussein. In March the United States, accompanied by a "coalition of the willing," invaded the country and brought down Hussein's government. Soon after the fall of the dictator, violence and chaos ensued that eventually led to a massive and prolonged insurgency. The U.S. invasion was blamed for catalyzing the insurgency, and violence against U.S. troops continued even after President Bush declared an end to the war in May 2003. In December of that year, U.S. troops captured Saddam. By June 2004, sovereignty had been officially transferred to the Iraqi people, amid an increasingly bloody insurgency and a growing sectarian conflict. The killing continued into January 2005, when Iraq held its first multiparty elections in fifty years.

Although the United States declared the Iraq War a victory, its violent aftermath made U.S. troops' continued presence unpopular on the home front. In the 2006 elections, the Democratic Party won a congressional majority, largely a result of increasing domestic frustration with the war. The next day, Secretary of Defense Donald Rumsfeld, immensely unpopular and widely blamed for what now seemed like a botched invasion, resigned. This did not, however, slow the pace of the war. Though Bush's handling of the war had leveled his approval rating, certain right-leaning organizations such as the Heritage Foundation maintained that keeping up a strong military presence in Iraq was indispensable to the security of Americans and Iraqis alike.[63] In 2007, contrary to the advice of the bipartisan ISG, President Bush called for a surge in U.S. troops to Iraq, increasing the number of soldiers to 170,000 by deploying more than 20,000 additional soldiers.

Keeping in line with his campaign promises, President Barack Obama, newly sworn in, announced in February 2009 that all combat troops in Iraq would be removed by August 2010, with all other forces gone by December 2011—a goal that was ultimately met. In June 2009, Iraq Prime Minister Nuri Kamal al-Maliki declared himself the leader of an independent country, although Brookings labeled the situation as "a kind of violent semi-peace."[64] Amid a touchy peace in Iraq, the decision to implement a withdrawal program gained support across party lines in the United States. Senator John McCain, a former presidential candidate, said he was optimistic that the drawdown would lead to success.[65]

Today, under the Obama administration, the United States has shifted its national security strategy, dedicating more attention and resources to Afghanistan. In 2005, however, after two years of enduring a war with no clear strategy, the United States lacked a definitive consensus opinion on Iraq, and the policy debate grew increasingly contentious. Progressives struggled to find a coherent strategy on Iraq that allowed for orderly disengagement while managing possible negative consequences. The notion of a timeline for U.S. troop withdrawals was considered outside the mainstream debate.

The Input of Think Tanks

The initial report on Iraq released by CAP, *Strategic Redeployment*, evolved from a number of policy recommendations CAP made from 2003 to 2005. Settling on the strategy of redeployment at the organization's first major conference in fall 2003 helped set the framework for much of CAP's policy work. Throughout 2004 and early 2005, CAP introduced a number of proposals on Iraq that shaped the debate. One key idea in these early proposals was that U.S. policy should focus more on efforts of development assistance to improve the quality of life for Iraqis. This idea was ultimately put into practice with the introduction of provincial reconstruction teams in Iraq, and the program was expanded from 2006 to 2008.

In July 2005, under the leadership of John Podesta of CAP and Dick Leone at the Century Foundation, CAP convened a high-level group of national security experts to discuss alternatives for Iraq. Different voices were presented in "options memos," and there was a constructive exchange of ideas. In the end, a consensus was reached that progressives should make the Bush administration "own the Iraq War." Experts agreed that everything should be done to hold conservatives accountable for what was becoming one of the worst national security blunders in the country's history.

With that objective in mind, CAP released a memorandum in late August 2005 that outlined the mistakes and costs of the war. At this stage, however, there was no consensus on what a progressive Iraq alternative might look like. Some participants actually argued against developing an alternative strategy out of fear that progressives would end up painting themselves as "weak on defense." This accountability memo in August 2005 did not have a substantial influence on the policy debate, and some observers criticized CAP for not offering a clear policy alternative.

CAP staff conducted numerous briefings with key Capitol Hill staff members to build the case for an alternative plan and to address concerns over the plan's political implications. In particular, CAP believed that successfully framing this Iraq alternative was crucial. Rather than presenting it as a withdrawal for the sake of getting troops out of harm's way, CAP tried to demonstrate that pulling troops out would strengthen U.S. security.

In September 2005, CAP's national security policy team issued *Strategic Redeployment*, a policy prescription centered on three pillars: (1) that a troop drawdown was necessary to deal with problems of troop preparedness, especially among ground forces, (2) that the Iraq War was drawing resources and attention away from completing the mission in Afghanistan, and (3) that staying in Iraq without a clear endgame was providing fodder for terrorist propaganda.

In fall 2005, Senators Joe Biden, Jack Reed, Russ Feingold, Carl Levin, John Edwards, John Kerry, and Chuck Hagel joined the growing chorus of critics (including the House Out of Iraq Caucus) in not only issuing criticisms but also in presenting novel strategies for the war. Some proposed a specific date for U.S. troop withdrawals. Others simply argued that it was necessary to begin redeployments to put pressure on the Iraqi leadership and to signal that assistance from the United States was not inexhaustible.

One pivotal moment in this debate was the so-called Murthquake, an incident in which Representative John Murtha (D-Pa.) blasted Bush's Iraq policy in November 2005 and called for a redeployment of U.S. troops. Murtha made this public call shortly after reading the *Strategic Redeployment* report and meeting with its authors. Murtha's call for troop redeployments coupled with

CAP's continued policy work and external relations strategies helped the policy idea garner broader public attention.

The organization's policy and communications teams worked together to criticize the "National Strategy for Victory in Iraq" tour, a major public relations campaign to boost support for Bush's Iraq policy from December 2005 through the spring. CAP issued a series of memos and briefed journalists on questions they should ask and points they should raise about the president's statements on the war. In 2006 CAP also began hosting an annual foreign policy conference on the anniversary of the commencement of the war with prominent keynote speakers such as former National Security Adviser Zbigniew Brzezinski and ISG cochairman Lee Hamilton.

At the outset, members of CAP's team continued to brief congressional leaders on Iraq as the 2006 midterm elections loomed. The organization developed some unique policy and communications products in an effort to capture attention while Congress was introducing legislation aimed at changing war policy. One example was a series of quarterly "report cards" on the Bush administration's handling of the war. These were released at media events on Capitol Hill throughout 2006, with prominent leaders such as Senators Joe Biden and Jack Reed in attendance. In summer 2006, CAP offered advice to progressive leaders in Congress as they prepared for extended floor debates over the Iraq policy. CAP's policy team also tried to develop a consensus position among congressmen in 2006. These efforts bore fruit when a letter from progressive congressional leaders, which embraced most of the policy recommendations of *Strategic Redeployment*, was presented to the ISG.

The 2006 midterm elections were a turning point in the country's Iraq debate, with conservatives losing ground and more progressive voices entering Congress in a wave of public opposition to Bush's course in Iraq. In December 2006, the bipartisan ISG presented its recommendations, many of which resembled some of the initial ideas in *Strategic Redeployment*, including increased regional diplomacy with all of Iraq's neighbors and a phased drawdown of combat troops.

In early 2007, when President Bush proposed to increase U.S. troop levels, CAP led the progressive fight for a "diplomatic surge," issuing an influential memo to the incoming Congress that advocated an aggressive posture on war policy. This was the first in a series of memos to Congress in spring and summer 2007 offering recommendations on legislative approaches for forcing the Bush administration to change course.

CAP had also quietly coordinated with a number of Iraqi activist groups throughout 2005 and 2006. Until 2007, however, no formal coalition could be created, in large part because a consensus had not formed among progressive groups on key issues related to Iraq. The 2006 midterm elections and the Bush administration's rejection of the ISG's advice removed this impasse. The refusal of the administration to listen to the group's recommendations and its insistence on a troop surge convinced many that Bush was ignoring voters' messages in 2006. The Bush administration's actions inspired efforts to develop a formal coalition in 2007 to push for change in policy on Iraq. At the same time, CAP continued its multitiered strategy of working to shape the debate through congressional leaders, opinion formers, media outreach, and cooperative work with activist groups.

CAP staff also offered advice to several candidates for office at the state and national levels, which helped amplify its message and increase support for its plan. For example, "Strategic Reset," a policy that CAP advocated, helped inform Barack Obama's decision to withhold the training of Iraq's security forces until the Iraqi government made progress toward political accommodation. The report sought to define the forward edge of the progressive debate in the same way *Strategic Redeployment* had a year earlier. It recommended a quicker withdrawal of U.S. troops—one year, compared with the eighteen-month timeline recommended in the initial *Strategic Redeployment* report—while presenting a more comprehensive plan for regional diplomatic initiatives aimed at stabilizing Iraq and the region. This and other stances President Obama took on the war were modeled after CAP's work.

While engaged on all of these fronts, CAP continued to update its proposals and policy ideas in light of the dynamic situation on the ground in Iraq, issuing further policy reports throughout 2006 to 2008. As conditions worsened and Iraq's political transition moved forward, CAP produced the "Strategic Reset." In summer 2007, when some conservatives and journalists questioned whether a troop withdrawal could be implemented in less than one year, the policy team issued a separate document, a military-focused report, "How to Redeploy," which offered more details on the military logistics of withdrawing troops. Through such proposals and policy ideas, CAP has remained an influential party in the policymaking process.

Conclusion

By fall 2007, repeated attempts by Congress to persuade the Bush administration to begin a phased redeployment of U.S. troops had failed while the surge of U.S. troops in Iraq coincided with declines in violence in the country. CAP's team continued to criticize the conservative message on Iraq and to present a progressive strategy to the media and in policy debates. At the same time, CAP engaged in a number of debates addressing the more centrist alternatives presented for Iraq, including the Iraq strategy entitled "conditional engagement" that Center for a New American Security offered. The "conditional engagement" strategy envisioned a lengthy U.S. troop presence in Iraq to provide training and support to Iraq's security forces, but it offered few new ideas for the Iraq policy debate and largely restated many of the earlier ideas on regional diplomacy, economic reconstruction, and political engagement in Iraq.

CAP's Iraq strategies eventually became the consensus position on Iraq among progressives. Furthermore, the initial ideas presented in *Strategic Redeployment*, which were updated in subsequent policy reports, garnered increased support in Iraq. By 2008, Iraqi leadership demanded a clear timeline for U.S. troop withdrawals from the Bush administration as it negotiated a "status of forces" agreement. What had been an outlier policy recommendation in 2005—a clear timeline with an end date for U.S. troop withdrawals in Iraq— had become official U.S. policy (see case study 7 for further discussion of think tanks and the final withdrawal of U.S. troops from Iraq).

CASE STUDY 4: THE 9/11 COMMISSION— AN AD HOC ISSUE NETWORK

After the terrorist attacks on the World Trade Center and Pentagon, the 9/11 Commission was created and given the task of explaining the underlying causes of 9/11 and what measures could be taken to prevent further terrorist attacks. The U.S. government entrusted this important task not to a commission of bureaucrats but to a bipartisan commission of think tank scholars and former government officials. The commission and its reports show the trust and confidence that the government has in think tank scholars, as well as the influence their policy advice can have on presidential elections. This case study also demonstrates the ability of think tanks to act as an intermediary between citizens of the general public and the government.

In November 2002 Congress and President George W. Bush created the National Commission on Terrorist Attacks upon the United States, commonly known as the 9/11 Commission. The commission was charged with providing a "full and complete" accounting of the attacks of September 11, 2001, and with recommendations as to how to prevent such attacks in the future.[66] The 9/11 Commission consisted of the following individuals:

- Thomas H. Kean, chair: Kean was a former governor of New Jersey and formerly the chair of the Carnegie Corporation of New York, Educate America, and the National Environmental Education and Training Foundation. He had also served on the boards of the National Endowment for Democracy, the Robert Wood Johnson Foundation, and the National Council of the World Wildlife Fund.[67]
- Lee H. Hamilton, vice chair: Hamilton was president and director of the Woodrow Wilson International Center for Scholars. Before that, Hamilton served for thirty-four years as a Democratic congressman, representing Indiana. He later served on the ISG in 2006.[68]
- Richard Ben-Veniste, attorney: Ben-Veniste served as chief of the Watergate Task Force in the Watergate Special Prosecutors Office from 1973 to 1975 and special outside counsel of the Senate Committee on Government Operations from 1976 to 1977. Also he was a presidential appointee to the Nazi War Crimes and Japanese Imperial Government Records Interagency Working Group, which reviewed and declassified secret documents relating to war crimes from World War II.[69]
- Fred F. Fielding: Fielding served as White House counsel for President George W. Bush from 2007 to 2009. Fielding was previously counsel to President Reagan from 1981 to 1986.[70]
- Jamie Gorelick: Gorelick served as deputy attorney general in the Clinton administration from 1994 to 1997 and also served as vice chair of Fannie Mae, a government-sponsored mortgage company.[71]
- Slade Gorton: Gorton, a former Republican Senator from the state of Washington from 1982 to 2000, served on the Appropriations; Budget; Energy and Commerce; Science, Space, and Technology; Transportation and Infrastructure; and Natural Resources committees.[72]
- Bob Kerrey: Kerrey served as a Democratic senator from Nebraska for twelve years. Before that, he served a term as governor of Nebraska. He later served as president of New School University in New York City and now serves as cochair for the advisory board of Issue One.[73]
- John F. Lehman: Lehman served as secretary of the navy in the Reagan administration from 1981 to 1987 and served as a deputy to Henry Kissinger on the National Security Council during the Nixon years. Today he is, among other things, on the board of trustees at the Foreign Policy Research Institute and chair of its Program on National Security.[74]
- Timothy Roemer: Roemer served as U.S. ambassador to India. Previously Roemer was the president of the Center for National Policy and a

distinguished scholar at George Mason University's Mercatus Center, a nonprofit research and educational institution. From 1991 to 2003, he represented Indiana as a Democrat in the House of Representatives.[75]

• James R. Thompson: Thompson was the governor of Illinois from 1977 to 1991. He also served on the American Bar Association Commission on Separation of Powers and Judicial Independence from 1996 to 1997.[76]

This list highlights the large number of think tank scholars that composed the 9/11 Commission and were appointed to the important task of assessing one of the worst attacks on U.S. soil since Pearl Harbor. Also of interest was the decision of the president and Congress to bring in scholars from both sides of the political spectrum. Although this decision may have sacrificed political influence over the 9/11 Commission, it added objectivity and legitimacy to its report's findings.

Notably, while the 9/11 Commission drew personnel from many of the largest U.S. think tanks, the commission also sought out the work of scholars from smaller think tanks, such as the Foreign Policy Research Institute (FPRI). One of the commissioners, John Lehman, got his start as a staff member at FPRI in the 1960s and later served on Henry Kissinger's staff and as secretary of the navy (1981–87), in which capacity he built the 600-ship navy and laid out what came to be called the "Lehman Doctrine" (a land-sea stategy to confront the Soviet Union should war break out). His experience as a scholar and government official equipped him with the critical thinking, innovative tools, and knowledge of the policy process, all skills necessary to serve on the 9/11 Commission. He was coeditor of an FPRI book, *America the Vulnerable: Our Military Problems and How to Fix Them*, which was completed just before 9/11 and published just after. As this example demonstrates, it is not just the largest research organizations that are influencing Washington; smaller think tanks also can have a strong impact on policy.

On July 22, 2004, two years and ten months after the attacks, the 9/11 Commission released its report. It was received with great fanfare, and within seven days, 50 million people had visited the commission's website, which provided a free copy of the report.[77] Publisher W. W. Norton sold its initial printing of 600,000 copies and printed an additional 200,000.[78] Among the recommendations it made were the following:

• Creating a National Center for Counterterrorism to coordinate the counterterrorism operations of the CIA, FBI, Department of Defense, and the Department of Homeland Security

- Creating the post of director of national intelligence (DNI) to oversee and coordinate the efforts of all U.S. intelligence agencies
- Developing a comprehensive screening system at U.S. borders, including a biometric entry and exit system
- Creating one permanent standing committee for homeland security in each house of Congress
- Establishing a specialized national security work force at the FBI
- Strengthening the intelligence collection capabilities of the CIA's clandestine service[79]

The Input of Think Tanks

The 9/11 Commission released its report in the middle of the 2004 presidential election. This put the commission and its recommendations, in the words of analyst Stuart Rothenberg, at the "front and center" of the presidential race.[80] In the days following the report's publication, Congress pledged to hold fifteen hearings to examine the commission's work during its August recess. Democratic presidential candidate John Kerry promised to adopt all of the 9/11 Commission's recommendations and vowed to extend its work mandate for an additional eighteen months.[81]

The most important measure of the 9/11 Commission's impact was the impact it had on President Bush's decisionmaking. In the beginning, Bush opposed the commission. However, many 9/11 victims' families undertook a strong lobbying effort that attracted the attention of influential senators, such as Joe Lieberman and John McCain. This effort, coupled with congressional concessions that gave Bush the power to name the commission's chair, compelled the president to agree to the proposal.[82] Amid the fanfare that greeted the 9/11 report's release in 2004 and the pressure from electoral opponent Senator John Kerry, Bush's spokesmen declared he was actively studying the commission's recommendations and deciding which could be quickly enacted by executive order.[83]

By December 2005 the White House had issued a press release trumpeting its progress on adopting the 9/11 Commission's recommendations. Of the six major recommendations detailed above, the Bush administration claimed to be making progress on four of them. The government created the National Counterterrorism Center and named Michael Leider its first director in July 2005. The post of DNI was created with the Intelligence Reform and Terrorism Prevention Act of 2004, with John Negroponte, former ambassador to the United

Nations and Iraq, being the first to serve in the position. The Bush administration also championed the creation of the U.S.-VISIT entry-exit system, a biometric security system that claims to ensure that legitimate travelers have access to the United States while U.S. borders remain closed to terrorists. Last, without providing specifics, the press release claimed that President Bush "has led the effort to transform the FBI into an agency focused on preventing terrorist attacks through intelligence collection and other key efforts, while improving its ability to perform its traditional role as a world-class law-enforcement agency."[84]

Conclusion

The 9/11 Commission was formed and charged with investigating the terrorist attacks of September 11, 2001, because of advocacy efforts from the informal issue network that was composed of the families of many 9/11 victims. Influenced by the informal issue network, Congress demanded action from President Bush. A key factor in the 9/11 Commission's success was that its members were part of the revolving door, many of whom had experience in government positions and think tank research. The commission had great influence because the members' credentials, due to their revolving door status and the trust that Americans place in ex officio bodies outside the government, gave it credibility. The high citizen interest coupled with the debate in 2004 over government reform was a testament to the 9/11 Commission's power. The resulting debate forced President Bush to make a public show of considering the recommendations of a body whose creation he initially opposed. To underscore this point further, President Bush publicly trumpeted his adoption of four of six major recommendations by the panel at the end of 2005. In short, informal issue networks can and often do influence debates concerning U.S. policy.

CASE STUDY 5: DARFUR—SCHOLARS, POLICYMAKERS, AND ISSUE NETWORKS WORKING TOGETHER

Darfur, a region that before 2004 was both foreign and obscure to U.S. ears, has now become almost synonymous with mass murder and genocide. This region might well have remained obscure without various activist groups drawing attention to the situation there. The cooperation of think tanks, advocacy groups, religious leaders, and celebrities serving as goodwill ambassadors increased public awareness about the conflict in Darfur. While their push for government action may not have been successful, their drive for U.S. intervention demonstrated the ability of far-reaching coalitions to influence public opinion despite government opposition.

In early 2003 rebels in the Sudanese region of Darfur began attacking government targets and invoked the ire of the Sudanese government. Initially the conflict was limited to two main rebel groups, the Sudan Liberation Army (SLA) and the Justice and Equality Movement (JEM), but both groups quickly split into a multitude of smaller factions divided along ethnic lines. In response, the government mobilized "self-defense" militias to battle the groups and funded violent gangs known as the Janjaweed—militias allegedly responsible for a campaign of mass murder and genocide that claimed the lives of roughly 300,000 Sudanese citizens.[85]

In 2006, the first Darfur Peace Agreement was signed between the Sudanese government and a faction of the SLA, led by Minni Minawi. However, the conflict between the government, other rebel groups, and the Janjaweed militias continued to escalate between 2003 and 2006, leading to a United Nations Security Council resolution on August 31, 2006, to send 17,300 UN peacekeepers to Darfur.[86] The UN force was intended to replace 7,000 existing African Union (AU) peacekeepers, whose mandate ended in September 2006. However, the Sudanese Government in Khartoum protested the resolution, resulting in its indefinite suspension in October.

In the same month, the Bush administration passed the Darfur Peace and Accountability Act of 2006, which acknowledged the occurrence of genocide in Sudan, expanded support for the African Union Mission in Sudan, and agreed to assist the International Criminal Court (ICC) in prosecuting those guilty of war crimes in Sudan. Conflict continued through early 2007 amid allegations that Russia and China were providing arms to Sudan in contravention of UN- and U.S.-enforced trade embargos. In July 2007, the Sudanese government resumed bombing in Darfur, leading to UN Security Council Resolution 1769, which finally authorized a hybrid UN-AU force (United Nations–African Union Mission in Darfur, UNAMID).

Peace talks began in October 2007 between the leaders of the smaller rebel groups and led to their reunification into the two large rebel groups in December 2007—the JEM and the SLA. Despite this progress, the JEM launched an attack on the Sudanese government in the cities of Omdurman and Khartoum in May 2008 and faced a violent response from the Sudanese government. Overall, the fighting between the government and the rebel groups as well as the atrocities committed by the Janjaweed displaced 2.5 million Darfuris, and in April 2008 the death toll was believed by some to have reached more than

300,000.[87] At the time these crimes were being perpetrated, only 60 percent of the UNAMID forces had been deployed in Darfur, which still experiences daily violence and infighting between the various rebel factions.

In addition, in July 2008 the ICC released an indictment against President Bashir in the early months of the Obama presidency citing murder, genocide, and several counts of crimes against humanity. This sparked a new debate about the possible implications of an ICC-issued arrest warrant on the nation's stability. President Bashir responded by threatening to block both humanitarian aid and the UNAMID peacekeeping forces from entering Sudan. Since then, three counts of genocide have been added to the list of charges, making Bashir the first sitting leader ever to be indicted by the ICC. Despite the charges, Bashir continues to travel freely to many African nations—including Kenya and Chad—nations that have signed obligations to arrest those wanted by the ICC. President Obama has continued the United States' policy of using soft power in the conflict and has simply expressed disappointment verbally toward these African nations.

The Input of Think Tanks

Think tanks have played a critical role in the formation of U.S. foreign policy toward the Darfur crisis. Indeed, one of the initial advocates for U.S. intervention in Sudan was Hudson Institute senior fellow and former Reagan administration official Michael Horowitz.[88] With a background as a champion of human rights, Horowitz lobbied Congress to implement tough sanctions against Sudan—reminiscent of those levied against apartheid-era South Africa. This lobby, although unsuccessful, generated significant public awareness about Sudanese issues. It also helped push Congress to the Sudan Peace Act in 2002, which made significant progress in facilitating the end of the Sudanese North-South civil war.[89]

Bush's stalwart refusal throughout presidency to send U.S. troops into Darfur reflected the long-standing position of major conservative think tanks such as the Cato Institute, which emphasized a "regional solution [that did] not include any U.S. troops."[90] As early as 2004, Cato's foreign policy director Christopher Preble argued that the United States should "encourage [Egypt, Chad, and Kenya] to clean up their own backyard, which they can and should do," and he also pointed out that "Sudan is much closer to the European Union than the United States and consequently more of a strategic concern" for the European Union.[91] The Heritage Foundation was more supportive of the United States imposing bilateral economic sanctions and blocking financial aid

to Sudan from international monetary institutions such as the International
Monetary Fund, but similarly urged the Bush administration to "rule out the
deployment of U.S. ground troops, which are already stretched thin."[92]

The continued failure and slow-moving progress of UN and AU initiatives
have increased pressure from both liberal think tanks and grassroots public interest groups for new and effective U.S.-led strategies. Initiatives such as the
Enough Project launched by the Center for American Progress offer detailed
policy proposals for U.S. decisionmakers.[93] Moreover, groups such as the Save
Darfur Coalition, which represents more than 180 faith-based advocacy and
human rights organizations, focus more on increasing public awareness and generating political will. In November 2008, the Enough Project, the Save Darfur
Coalition, and the Genocide Intervention Network published a joint letter to
the Obama administration arguing for U.S. enforcement of a no-fly zone over
Darfur, expanded economic sanctions, enforcement of the arms embargo, and
reduced Sudanese influence over the UNAMID forces in Sudan.[94]

Together these organizations are a significant political force and have the potential to directly influence Obama's foreign policy as much as their respective
counterparts did with the Bush administration.[95] In 2007, while a senior fellow
at Brookings, Susan E. Rice personally testified before the Senate Foreign Relations Committee in favor of U.S. military enforcement of a no-fly zone.[96] Similarly, Vice President Joe Biden stated in April 2007 that he thought "it was time
to put force on the table and use it," arguing that "2,500 U.S. troops could radically change the situation on the ground right now."[97] Both President Obama
and former Secretary of State Clinton did not openly support direct military
intervention. However, in May 2008 during the presidential campaign, they, together with Senator McCain, issued a joint statement pledging to pursue "peace
and security for the people of Sudan" with "unstinting resolve."[98] Thus far for the
Obama administration, this pledge has meant a continuation of the Bush-era
policies toward Sudan. The Obama administration's comprehensive policy on
Sudan was released in October 2009 and promised "frank dialogue" and an insistence on preventing the region from becoming a haven for international terrorists. Experts have called the policy "anticlimactic," especially after Obama's
open criticism toward President Bush's policy on the Darfur issue.[99]

In December 2007 Brookings senior fellow Roberta Cohen observed, "Darfur is not a national security priority for any Western state. . . . The U.S. military is overstretched in Iraq, NATO is engaged in Afghanistan, and Sudan can
rely upon China, Russia, and the Arab League to shield it from robust international
action."[100] At the time, it certainly appeared that way for those advocating

strong U.S. military and diplomatic intervention. President Bush's refusal to consider military sanctions reflected the influence of major conservative think tanks, especially since, in another example of the revolving door concept, the Bush administration was composed of many former employees of these conservative think tanks. However, over time aggressive new think tanks, such as CAP, together with grassroots advocacy groups, such as Save Darfur, came to dominate the debate on Darfur with policy proposals heavy on U.S. involvement, resulting in an unprecedented level of public involvement in the national security policy-making process. Given that many high-ranking Obama officials already hold similarly divergent views on the future of U.S. involvement in Darfur, it was initially speculated that this pressure would result in an abrupt shift in foreign policy strategy. At the same time, the politicians and analysts who remain supportive of the strategies that were historically employed by the Bush administration continue to play an important role in providing alternative perspectives through their respective think tanks and providing broader opposition within the public debate.

At the same time, conservative Christians have composed one end of the informal issue network helping drive debate on the Darfur debacle. A broad left-right coalition made up of activists such as Kenneth Roderick of Christian Solidarity International, Freedom House's Nina Shea, and Faith McDonald of the Institute of Religion and Democracy undertook a civil disobedience campaign in front of the Sudanese embassy in the United States during the summer of 2004. In October 2006 evangelical activists such as Ted Haggard and Rich Cizik of the National Association of Evangelical, the Reverend Samuel Rodriguez of the National Hispanic Christian Leadership Conference, and the Reverend Geoff Tunnicliffe of the World Evangelical Alliance took out print ads in major U.S. newspapers, organized letter-writing campaigns, and requested to meet with President Bush to discuss the Darfur situation.[101]

At the opposite end of the political spectrum, liberal Hollywood celebrities such as George Clooney have also worked to keep public attention focused on Darfur. In April 2006 Clooney appeared at a National Press Club talk with former Republican presidential candidate Senator Sam Brownback of Kansas and then Democratic presidential candidate Senator Barack Obama of Illinois to generate publicity for an upcoming public rally on the issue. At the conference, Clooney stated that Darfur was the "first genocide of the 21st century. What [Darfuris] need now is the American people and the world's population to help them."[102] It is worth noting that Senator Brownback, a longtime champion of action to stop the conflict, said after the event that he had never received as much media attention for any of his own public events concerning Darfur in the previous two years.[103]

In September 2006 George Clooney and Nobel Peace Prize laureate, Holocaust survivor, and author Elie Wiesel spoke with members of the UN Security Council, urging them to take action against the Sudanese government. Then in December Clooney led a delegation to visit China and Egypt to discuss the Darfur crisis. It included Kenyan Olympian Tegla Loroupe, who serves as a United Nations ambassador of sport; U.S. Olympic athlete Joey Cheek; fellow actor Don Cheadle; and David Pressman, a human rights lawyer and former aide to Secretary of State Madeleine Albright.[104] As noted earlier, China has been instrumental in protecting Sudan from United Nations pressure.

The Left and Right have come together to plan events and raise awareness of the Darfur issue among the public and policymakers alike. On April 28, 2006, thousands of people descended on Washington, D.C., to urge stronger actions by policymakers to end the genocide in Darfur. Attendees included 240 busloads of activists from forty-one states and notables such as Clooney and Wiesel, and Michael Steele, Maryland's then lieutenant governor.[105] The rally prompted President Bush to issue a statement declaring that those attending the demonstration "represent the best of our country." Bush went on to say to the activists that "every life is precious, every human being is important. And the signal you send to the world is a strong signal, and I welcome your participation."[106] Another joint event occurred in December 2007. Crowds that included the evangelical Christian activist Richard Cizik and actress Mia Farrow staged a rally outside the Chinese embassy in Washington on International Human Rights Day to pressure China to use its leverage in Sudan to bring resolution to the Darfur crisis.[107] Farrow has been active on the issue in her own right, publishing two editorials in national newspapers demanding that China take a leading role in stopping Darfuri violence.[108]

Conclusion

The alliance of think tank scholars, politicians, evangelical Christians, and entertainers demanding action on Darfur has brought considerable attention to an issue that might not have received attention otherwise. However, despite all their activism, they have not been able to significantly alter the status quo on action in Sudan. Despite Cohen's and others' assessment that military action by any of the Western superpowers or coalition of other states is unlikely, the diverse group of Darfur activists continues to keep the issue alive in the public consciousness. At the very least, they ensure that U.S. policymakers ignore Darfur at the risk of losing political support from evangelical Christians, liberal activists, and those that follow them.

CASE STUDY 6: THE "BUY AMERICA" PROVISION OF THE 2009 STIMULUS PACKAGE

After the downward spiral of banks and stock markets in 2008 led to one of the largest economic crises in U.S. history, fiscal stimulus and rejuvenation of the national economy became watchwords for politicians. The fiscal stimulus reform, while having foreign policy implications because of the modern globalized economy, still generally remained a domestic issue until a "Buy America" provision was added. The shock waves and fears of protectionism this measure sent to U.S. foreign trade partners made it imperative to address the issues of the "Buy American" provision swiftly before such a measure set off a vicious cycle of protectionism across the globe. The following event analysis is an example of the ability of think tanks to respond rapidly and precisely to a national agenda item and to exert their influence on such decisions.

On January 27, 2009, the House of Representatives voted to include a Buy American provision requiring that all public projects using iron and steel funded by the fiscal stimulus program be processed in the United States. This tactic is not new, as Congress has passed virtually the same bill during each of the past seven decades. The bill intended to make the United States independent of foreign suppliers as well as to reinvest money that would potentially be spent abroad into the national economy. Although popular with many policymakers, the provision proposed to be added to the 2009 stimulus package soon created intense discussion, both at home and abroad.

Trade partners abroad were highly displeased with the provision. BBC news called it "a threat to UK defense jobs" and quoted Parliamentary Under-Secretary of State Lord Bach, saying that the UK government "would very much regret if this gets through Congress unchanged."[109] Many considered it a violation of World Trade Organization guidelines; others feared it would provoke other states to adopt similar protectionist measures, creating a trade war. Vice President Biden, along with many other policymakers, disagreed: "I don't think there's anything anticompetitive or antitrade in saying when we are stimulating the U.S. economy that the purpose is to create U.S. jobs. The same thing is happening in Britain, the same thing is happening in Europe, the same thing is happening in China, and they're not worrying about U.S. jobs."[110]

As the opposition escalated, Senator John McCain tried to eliminate the provision from the bill altogether, and President Obama conveyed to Congress that he did not want the bill to pass without any changes. He told a reporter for Fox News, "We can't send a protectionist message" in the stimulus bill or send the false message to trading partners "that somehow we're just looking after ourselves and not concerned with world trade."[111] The stimulus plan passed on Friday, February 13, 2009, with the Buy America provision still in place, though with modified language. Added clauses stipulated that the provision followed World Trade Organization rules and allowed for imports from the thirty-eight countries with which the United States has trade agreements, leaving Brazil, India, and China as the only major trading partners that could be subject to the restriction. Loopholes have been created, however, such as "what they ship to America would not be turned away if doing so 'would be inconsistent with the public interest.'"[112]

The Input of Think Tanks

The Heritage Foundation published a memo in June 2005 asserting that, despite widespread support for the provision, "protectionism undermines homeland security and national defense."[113] Reasons cited included worries that innovation would be reduced and that prices would increase since labor is more expensive in the United States. Such legislation was also said to damage relations the United States has with other countries. Brookings then fellow Christopher S. Robinson presented a different front two years later, stating, "Targeted protection of critical technologies and industrial capabilities will be absolutely essential in the future." He was cognizant of the reasons to keep trading free, recognizing that "the current bureaucratic apparatus and entrenchment of prescriptive protectionist legislation has dampened America's ability to adjust to the global market and adaptively protect and compete."[114]

The Buy American provision sparked further controversy, with experts from many think tanks weighing in on the debate. The Peterson Institute for International Economics could arguably be given credit for starting the debate and bringing the provision into the public eye. C. Fred Bergsten, director, immediately mobilized the trade team at the institute after the House of Representatives voted to include a Buy America provision. He understood that the Senate was "considering a much more sweeping prohibition of foreign procurement."[115] After informing key members of the administration that Peterson was performing the analysis, and "after some high-level intermediation by Bob Rubin and Carla Hills, the National Economic Council in the White House asked if [the Peterson

Institute] could get [its] results by Saturday, January 30th, [2009,] so they could use it to prepare for the Senate debate starting on Monday, February 1."[116] President Obama was observed making comments to Fox News the day afterward, hopeful that Congress would work with the language of the provision so as to not be as protectionist and to work within the World Trade Organization framework.

The Peterson Institute then published the analysis as an eleven-page policy brief on February 2, posted it to their website, and reached out to media outlets. This created an active debate with other think tanks quickly weighing in, including Jagdish Bhagwati, an economist then at the Council on Foreign Relations, who remarked, "To argue that we are now free to terminate access to our procurement in areas we previously agreed to open to bids from the Europeans is to unravel that bargain unilaterally and in violation to the concessions we made." Richard Scott from the Economic Policy Institute countered, figuring that countries such as China and Russia that had not signed procurement codes "simply want something for nothing. Giving them access to stimulus spending will dilute the impact of the recovery bill and eliminate all incentives for them to sign the codes."[117] The policy brief, however, which stated that "the Buy American provisions would violate U.S. trade obligations and damage the United States' reputation, with very little impact on U.S. jobs," dominated the tone of the conversation.[118]

The Senate drastically toned down its Buy American language by indicating that the provision should be implemented in a manner fully consistent with the international obligations of the United States. This was the second preferred option (to eliminating the amendment altogether) in the policy brief that the Peterson Institute put forward.

Conclusion

As Bergsten noted in his letter, "The causality from our analysis of the situation and policy recommendation to the sharp changes in the attitudes of both the President and the Congress" cannot be traced. He added, "We can observe, however, that no one else even attempted to prepare and publicize an analytically grounded response to the protectionist threat in the very short time available. We can also note that, since the White House asked for our work on a much expedited schedule, it is reasonable to assume that they used it."[119] As the language in the final bill was much diluted from the original and the issue of strengthening protectionism was entirely evaded, it is evident that the debate greatly affected the outcome of the policy. The Peterson Institute succeeded in setting the tone and influencing the direction of the conversation. Bergsten views this event as a nearly prototypical example of how a think tank should try to operate since Peterson was able to apply its data and models to the specific case very quickly and develop a highly credible presentation in response to the proposed legislation. Bergsten concluded, "At the same time, we were able to utilize our ongoing relationships with both officials of the new Administration (as noted above) and the media to inject our message effectively into the policy debate."[120] A relationship of input and results made the Peterson Institute "feel that [it] at least helped move matters in a constructive direction."[121]

In this instance, the Peterson Institute was able to at least dilute some of the language of the Buy American provision. Even though its policy brief, along with input from other think tanks such as the Council on Foreign Relations, could not completely reverse the policy decision, its position is now recognized and may steer future debates along the lines of its advocated policies. This case study shows that think tanks play an important role, even when they do not initially reverse policy opinions on specific topics. Rather, they can influence future decisions and vocalize differing opinions.

CASE STUDY 7: STRATEGIC RESET AND DIPLOMACY TO END THE IRAQ WAR

Leading up to the 2008 presidential election, Senator Barack Obama's frustration with the Iraq War was one of the principal issues on which his campaign focused. He promised the American people that his administration would end the United States' engagement in Iraq. This case study builds on the discussion in case study 3 and examines President Obama's foreign policy decisions surrounding Iraq and exhibits the role that think tanks play in policy formation. From policy briefings to the revolving door concept, think tanks have affected the decisions of the Obama administration regarding U.S. presence in Iraq.

Since the outset of the 2003 invasion of Iraq, a large U.S. constituency denounced the government's decision to insert a military presence in Iraq. In fact, many continue to view the decision to topple Saddam Hussein's regime as the principle foreign policy error during the Bush administration. The outcome of this unpopular decision, a seemingly endless war, enabled Barack Obama to secure the presidency in 2008. His standing was boosted by a wave of public disapproval toward those who supported the war. It remains to be seen, however, if Barack Obama's promises of change and his diplomatic decisions in Iraq will succeed or fail.

Since 2009 President Obama has straddled a fine line between the left-wing call for an immediate and widespread withdrawal of U.S. armed forces and the more moderate view favored by the majority of center-leaning Republicans. Senator Obama's policy proposed during his campaign in 2008 was denigrated as a "basic vision of withdrawal with muddy particulars that, if he is elected, is destined to meet an even muddier reality on the ground."[122] His February 2009 postelection statement, in which he outlined a more specific policy on the Iraq War, contained details for Iraq diplomacy that included a complete removal of U.S. "combat forces" by August 2010, but the retention of a "transitional force" of 35,000 to 50,000 personnel."[123] This number, although a drastic reduction from the 140,000 troops that were stationed in Iraq at the time, postsurge, was still seen as a moderate number by left-wing Democrats such as Speaker of the House Nancy Pelosi. In accordance with this policy, President Obama announced the end to combat operations in Iraq in August 2010: "So tonight, I am announcing that the American combat mission in Iraq has ended. Operation Iraqi Freedom is over, and the Iraqi people now have lead responsibility for the security of their country. Having drawn down 100,000 troops since taking office, a much smaller force will stay to train and assist the Iraqi forces during the transition period."[124]

The Obama strategy, conceived in 2008 and 2009, was carefully worded and was an important component of his campaign. It appeared unique but in practice has turned out to be similar to the plan laid out by the U.S.-Iraq Status of Forces Agreement that the Bush administration signed in 2008.[125] In the end, while President Obama based a large part of his 2008 campaign on the call to end the Iraq War and reduce U.S. troop presence, his final policy decision was considerably more nuanced, influenced by an understanding of the intricacies in leaving Iraq and the ramifications of troop withdrawal in the Middle East. We must therefore further examine the inner workings of the Obama policy on Iraq to better understand the role that policy experts who work in U.S. think tanks, specifically CAP, the Center for New American Security (CNAS), and CSIS, have had on the administration.

The Input of Think Tanks

From the swath of voices offering advice on what course the war should take, the current administration has turned to several prominent think tanks for counsel. Three think tanks in particular—CAP, CNAS, and CSIS—have advised both the Bush and Obama administrations, and their contributions have varied, ranging from criticism to forecasting to policy recommendations. Regarding the Obama administration, theses think tanks have mostly provided advice on how to best transfer authority to Iraqis and move away from war. Many of the reports focus on the best way to withdraw from the theater; others simply analyze Obama's present and future challenges, both in Iraq and the region as a whole.

CAP has published several reports on "strategic reset" in Iraq, a reset that started in the Bush era and has continued into the Obama presidency. Lawrence J. Korb, a senior fellow at CAP, has been outspoken in suggesting that disengagement should be the prime objective in Iraq. Three of the reports that Korb and his colleagues published included detailed plans on how to draw down U.S. troops. Their publications included *How to Redeploy: Implementing a Responsible Drawdown of U.S. Forces from Iraq*, updated in August 2008, preceded by *Strategic Reset: Reclaiming Control of U.S. Security in the Middle East* in June 2007, and a shorter report titled *Strategic Redeployment: A Progressive Plan for Iraq and the Struggle against Violent Extremists*. Korb then traveled to Iraq in 2009 and wrote a commentary titled "Impressions from Iraq." In his first statement, he referred to clashes with the Bush administration and criticized Obama's strategy to withdraw rapidly, stating how later, "after his election, President Obama began implementing the strategic agreement and began to fulfill his campaign promise by agreeing to withdraw all combat troops by August 31, 2010 and all the troops by the end of 2011."[126] Later that year, Korb also wrote an article on Obama's progress that appeared to support Obama's policy. Korb wrote, "Obama developed a plan to wait until after the Iraqi elections in January to begin to withdraw the bulk of our combat troops and the Iraqi elections in January.... The plan has worked so well that Odierno has actually accelerated the withdrawal pace because our setting out a plan to leave has convinced the Iraqis that we are in fact leaving."[127]

Brian Katulis, also a senior fellow at CAP, is another consistent analyst of the Iraq policy and has published several additional shorter articles critiquing and reporting on the state of Iraq during the Obama era. Katulis, with Korb, has authored several reports on strategic reset and wrote a report entitled *Iraq's Political Transition after the Surge: Five Enduring Tensions and Ten Key Challenges*, which outlines the primary policy challenges in Iraq. In 2009, he wrote an report on lingering political tensions in Iraq entitled *Attacks Highlight Uneven Progress in Iraq*, in which he asserted that "the surge of U.S. forces in Iraq did not achieve its stated purpose of bridging enduring divisions among Iraqis" and that "the United States and others outside can play a role, but Iraqis must ultimately take the lead in addressing the challenges of how to bridge divisions over sharing power."[128] Korb and Katulis, among others, appear to have heavily influenced the Status of Forces Agreement, demonstrating the influence of their reports on the redeployment of troops from Iraq. Korb's impressions during his trip to Iraq in 2009 were part of a report that was written as an "assessment of the country's security situation" for the Iraqi ambassador, Christopher Hill, and General Ray Odierno, demonstrating further CAP's input in strategic reset in Iraq.[129] As CNAS stated in one of its articles in 2008 analyzing Obama's policies in Iraq, "Closest to the Obama camp are the determined withdrawal advocates at the Center for American Progress, which is home to McDonough, as well as Iraq specialists and campaign advisers Larry Korb and Brian Katulis. Korb and Katulis co-authored CAP's signature Iraq plan, which they call 'strategic reset' and which calls for a swift exit accompanied by intensified diplomacy."[130]

CSIS has generally sounded a cautious note, with senior expert Anthony Cordesman, CSIS's leading voice on the Iraq War, serving as a strong advocate of a gradual, conditions-based withdrawal that would not jeopardize U.S. security gains or Iraqi stability. Cordesman repeatedly suggested that a focus on "responsible withdrawal" was insufficient to manage the difficult transition of responsibility to the Iraqi government and military. In a memo to the commander of U.S. forces in Iraq, General Odierno, Cordesman declared that it was "critical to avoid focusing too much on managing the withdrawal of our forces, and the tasks we face if everything goes according to plan. We must have a good set of contingency plans and options for dealing with serious crises."[131] A couple of weeks later, he again advised against a precipitous withdrawal, asserting that "an exit is not an exit strategy. U.S. policy has to look at other considerations than simply when and how quickly it should remove its troops."[132] Overall, CSIS sounded a warning about the U.S. withdrawal from Iraq that would prove later to be prescient.

CNAS has produced a variety of publications that criticized U.S. policy in Iraq. In particular, its authors were skeptical of Obama's plan for withdrawal. In the beginning of his presidency, CNAS—specifically journalist Michael Crowley—criticized Obama's intentions in Crowley's article "Barack in Iraq— Can He Really End the War?" The article, written in 2008 shortly after Obama took office, went so far as to claim "that a total U.S. withdrawal isn't achievable and Obama knows it." It dissected Obama's claims and assertions about immediate withdrawal, his response to tensions and violence within the country, and the ongoing training of Iraqi security forces. The article also emphasized CNAS's overall influence on Obama's policy in Iraq, asserting, "Obama also draws expertise from a more centrist Washington policy shop, the Center for a New American Security (CNAS), which has issued a plan envisioning up to 60,000 troops in Iraq for several years."[133] Additionally, CNAS came out with a report in 2010 that assessed Obama's engagement strategy in Iraq. The piece focused on the administration's foreign policy as a whole but honed in on the Iraq issue.

Conclusion

In his attempt to prepare Iraq for an independent future, Obama found himself under fire for what some saw as an unspecific and unrealistic plan. Moreover, think tanks advising Obama analyzed the issue from multiple angles, provided mixed reviews on the issue, and offered an inconsistent perspective on strategic reset. CAP, however, appears to have pulled considerable weight in the decision-making process, publishing strategy reports on troop withdrawal that led to the Status of Forces Agreement in 2008. CNAS and CSIS also offered prescriptive briefs and insisted that troops remain in Iraq for an indefinite period of time. As the war ground on, Obama continued to consult think tanks to determine the best methods to stabilize the country and bring U.S. troops home for good.[134]

CHAPTER FIVE

New Challenges and Trends Facing U.S. Think Tanks

TODAY, THE EFFECTS of globalization, and the increasing demand for public policy responses to the world's array of political, economic, and social issues, have placed think tanks in a critical position as advocates, researchers, and policy advisers. The overall effect of globalization has made U.S. think tanks even more critical to Washington's policymaking process and has further solidified the unique position of public policy research institutions in the United States.

But with increased visibility, higher demands for research, and transnational influences, the Fifth Estate must grapple with both new research expansions and challenging transitions. As was noted in the introduction, the term *think tank* is widely accepted around the globe to describe organizations that I define in the following way: "public policy research analysis and engagement organizations that generate policy-oriented research, analysis, and advice on domestic and international issues, which enable policymakers and the public to make informed decisions about public policy issues." Think tanks have become a global phenomenon because they are playing a critical role for governments and civil societies around the world by acting as bridges between knowledge (academia) and power (politicians and policymakers).

In the United States, the government and individual policymakers use the expert knowledge of think tank scholars to tackle the challenges and trends and make informed policy decisions. Policymakers need understandable, reliable, accessible, and useful information about the societies they govern. They also need to know how current policies are working as well as possible alternatives and their likely costs and consequences. This expanding need has fostered the growth of independent public policy research organizations.

Given the expanding role of think tanks, they also face critical threats and opportunities. These challenges fall into four broad categories:

1. Competitive
2. Resource
3. Technological
4. Policy

These four challenges can be summarized by the "four mores": more issues, more actors, more competition, and more conflict. There are also the "four Ms," requiring continual focus: mission, market, manpower, and, of course, money. Beyond the institutional challenges are other overarching trends in think tanks and their research. The following sections highlight some of the critical trends and challenges confronting think tanks and policymakers around the world. Table 5-1 outlines these trends.

CURRENT MEGA-TRENDS IN THINK TANKS AND POLICY ADVICE

Beginning in the 1970s, public policy research institutions experienced explosive growth, with representation in virtually every country. The boom was driven and defined by globalization, the growth of civil society, increasingly complex policy issues, and new demands for timely and concise analysis. In recent years, however, the surge has subsided and the pace of think tank establishment has slowed. The drivers of this change are redefining think tanks and policy advice as we know it.

Globalization

Globalization is unquestionably one of the most profound and powerful trends that continually shapes and drives the flow of technology, resources, knowledge, people, values, and ideas. Globalization and the growth of the knowledge-based economy have led to competition among knowledge-based institutions

TABLE 5-1. Current and Emerging Trends Confronting Think Tanks

Current issues
    Globalization
    Growth of international actors
    Democratization
    Demands for independent information and analysis
    Big data and supercomputers
    Increased complexity of policy issues
    The Information Age and the rate of technological change
    Increasingly open debate about government decisionmaking
    Global "hacktivist," anarchist, and populist movements
    Global structural adjustment
    Economic crisis and political paralysis
    Policy tsunamis
    Increasing political polarization
    Short-termism

Emerging issues
    Dramatic shifts in funding patterns
    Increased specialization
    Increased competition
    Influence and independence
    Outputs versus inputs
    Phantom NGO think tanks
    Hybrid organizations
    Impact of the Internet, new media, social networking, and the cloud
    Action versus ideas
    Greater emphasis on external relations and marketing strategies
    Going global
    Leadership and managing tensions
    Decentralization of power
    Blurring of the lines between think tanks and journalism
    Global gridlock
    Crisis fatigue

worldwide for the best ideas and people. New technologies have leveled the global playing field in a way that challenges established powers and elite institutions around the world. There are now 2 billion people who have access to the Internet in every region of the world, and the number of Internet users and mobile phone subscribers is growing steadily.[1] While the Internet facilitates the dissemination of information and allows for more competition between think tanks, the sheer increase in volume of knowledge available as a result of globalization renders it more difficult to find verified, quality information. Additionally, while globalization has increased competition, it has also broken down cultural barriers. As University of Sussex professor Luke Martell notes, "National differences have become less marked as people consume culture from around the world rather than being so dependent on that of their own nation. This is facilitated . . . by global electronic communications such as the internet, globalized TV broadcasts, migration, and tourism."[2]

Another feature of the transnationalization of think tanks is the manipulation of these organizations to project national interests abroad. U.S. foundations and development agencies have "exported" U.S. think tank models abroad, and it has become objective of development policy to promote progress in a U.S. or Western style.[3] While this trend shows an obvious Western tilt, the think tank network is not simply a Western phenomenon. Indeed, the think tank network around the world seems to represent one group of actors in a greater global civil society. Think tanks have established their own transnational networks and use these links to collaborate, share, and open dialogues about policy solutions.[4] Through these networks, think tanks are able to create cross-national policy transfers that extend beyond detached policy analysis. Thus, with these new networks, scholars advocate for the spread of policy ideas and practices in a broader scope.[5] The globalization of think tanks is forging bridges across national borders, developing a consistent exchange of ideas between scholars, and influencing the spread of policy ideas.

Growth of International Actors

The proliferation of state and nonstate actors, such as nongovernmental organizations (NGOs) and international government organizations (IGOs), has created a demand and provided the support and space for the global expansion of think tanks. The Union of International Organizations reports that there are as many as 66,000 international organizations worldwide, with 1,200 added to its database annually.[6] "The formation of an organized actor indicates strength and stability, and therefore a basis for power. The potency of an actor is reflected in a number of characteristics, such as unity, level of institutionalization, legitimacy, media control and others."[7]

While think tanks qualify as nonstate actors, they have less clout compared with IGOs. As we have seen, there is some dispute about how to properly measure the impact of think tanks in promoting policy. This challenge is certainly not unique to think tanks. However, it is easier to link an IGO resolution than the recommendation of an individual think tank to domestic legislation because many other nonstate actors supply information in tandem. Hence, the agglomeration of the work of these various suppliers is more likely to produce actual results.

Democratization and Decentralization of Power

Democratic movements around the world have helped fuel the demand for independent analysis of public policies and the creation of a new set of nongovernmental think tanks. According to Freedom House, the number of electoral democracies worldwide has risen from 69 in 1989 to 118 in 2012, accounting for 61 percent of today's states.[8] As *New York Times* columnist and Pulitzer Prize–winning author Thomas Friedman relates, this trend toward increased political participation is closely tied to globalization: "countries that are globalizing sensibly but steadily are also the ones that are becoming politically more open, with more opportunities for their people, and with a young generation more interested in joining the world system."[9]

However, many countries that have recently made the transition from dictatorship to democracy are still facing poverty and underdeveloped economies. Think tanks in such countries must contend with those issues, in addition to such issues as a public that is generally skeptical toward civil engagement, underdeveloped philanthropic traditions, and difficulty recruiting expert staff members. Richard Rose, director of the Center for the Study of Public Policy, notes that "the longer a regime uses free elections as a facade while those inside government use elected office to enrich themselves, the greater the divergence will become between those countries making progress toward the completion of democracy and those going nowhere. Moreover, the longer corruption persists at the elite level, the greater the likelihood that the mass of the electorate will become indifferent to dishonesty."[10] Think tanks also must deal with political environments that lack transparency and therefore play an important role by disseminating information and serving the public's growing appetite for accurate information and analysis.

Demands for Independent Information and Analysis

Over the past fifteen years, the state's monopoly and control of information has rapidly diminished because of technological advances and democratic movements. With the emergence of the "data revolution," there is a new need for governments, NGOs, and research institutes to collaborate in sharing data and closing data gaps.[11] These trends have created a space for knowledge-based institutions like think tanks to provide independent information and analysis. "Big data is the oil of the information economy that needs to be treated as an economic asset. If not, actors are doomed to the old witticism of knowing the price of everything and the value of nothing."[12]

The World Bank has called for a Global Partnership for Data Revolution for Sustainable Development to help think tanks collaborate in sharing data. Involving a plethora of agencies, the collaboration would focus on developing and sharing relevant information. Think tanks will play a crucial role in the process, which could further efforts for more independent analysis and information. However, the large number of think tanks and other institutions working to meet the demand for information means that the quality of information could potentially suffer.

Big data involves the collection and analysis of massive amounts of information to pinpoint critical data points and trends. This new analytic capability is made possible by supercomputers, which may become the think tanks of the near future, rendering traditional think tanks and their staffs superfluous. To draw in the discussion of the increasing influence of economically developing nations, in 1997 none of the world's fastest 100 supercomputers was found in a BRIC country (Brazil, Russia, India, and China). Today, six from that list are in use in China, including the Tianhe-2, the world's fastest computer, and six others can be found in the remaining BRIC nations.[13] The technological development of the BRIC countries is indicative of other developing countries beginning to adopt their own technological revolutions. These tech adjustments are often made in an environment without privacy laws or regulations systems in place to check big data gathering. "As of 2013, 101 countries had data privacy laws or bills in place. Only 40 developing economies have such laws or bills."[14] This remarkably impressive development highlights not only the rise of the BRICs but also the importance of big data and high-level technology in an increasingly interconnected world.

Think tanks can carve a niche in these environments and thereby stave off their potential extinction. As developing countries adopt these technological practices, think tanks can provide the necessary consulting and policy advice to recommend adequate privacy laws and regulations to accompany these advancements. They can also inform unsuspecting publics about the data potential behind supercomputers.

The Tech Revolution and the Rate of Technological Change

Better, cheaper, and faster technology has made it much easier for individuals and small organizations to operate and publicize their work. Internet, social networks, the cloud, and handheld computers have made it much easier for individuals and organizations with limited financial resources to conduct research and disseminate findings globally.

Organizations use websites and social networks to share their agendas and findings. Many of these approaches operate outside the traditional academic review process, peer-reviewed publications, and communication channels. These changes have dramatically increased the timeliness, reach, and impact of research and commentary that is not associated with institutions but rather is conducted by individuals and social movements. The combination of globalization and continual technological innovation has empowered these individuals in a way that poses a major challenge to established knowledge-based institutions like universities and think tanks. Sociologist and globalization expert Manuel Castells has termed this force "the network society," a new social structure that utilizes the Information Age technologies to endlessly expand, reconfigure, and overcome limitations of traditional networks.[15]

Individuals, now empowered by the Internet and social networks, can create loose organizations and networks that can effectively challenge the state. For example, Twitter jumped from 1.6 million users in 2008 to 32.1 million a year later.[16] Twitter users currently number at an estimated 500 million today.[17] The accessibility and broad permeability of such social media allow individual users to wield enormous influence, particularly in creating movements with wide appeal at lightning speed.

Because of the tech revolution, advocacy think tanks are now facing competition from intellectual entrepreneurs who publish online publications and who aggregate content. Think tanks need to develop relationships with such aggregators to effectively communicate their advocacy efforts and promote research to a larger audience.

Increasingly Open Debate about Government Decisionmaking

Interest groups and public citizens are less likely to accept government information and rationales, which in turn creates a demand for more independent sources of analysis. Global policy and advocacy networks have increased the power and influence of these organizations. Perhaps the cause of this political opening is not so much technical but rather due to large events in the international system that have contributed to the following:

- The downfall of right-wing authoritarian regimes in southern Europe in the mid-1970s
- The replacement of military dictatorships by elected civilian governments across Latin America from the late 1970s through the late 1980s
- The decline of authoritarian rule in parts of East and South Asia starting in the mid-1980s
- The collapse of communist regimes in Eastern Europe at the end of the 1980s
- The breakup of the Soviet Union and the establishment of fifteen post-Soviet republics in 1991
- The decline of one-party regimes in many parts of sub-Saharan Africa in the first half of the 1990s

These events, termed by Samuel Huntington as "third wave democracy," could also be partly responsible for increasing open political debate.[18]

The public's distrust and skepticism of government decisionmaking has propelled the movement toward open debate. The public is increasingly likely to trust the ideas, advice, and scholarship of independent think tanks. Just 40 percent of the richest countries of the Organization for Economic Cooperation and Development expressed confidence in their national governments in 2012, 5 percent less than in 2007. The drop in confidence is most significant in countries hardest hit by recession, such as Greece.[19] The depleted faith in government around the world opens a crucial place for think tanks to influence policymaking and thus have a greater impact on society at large.

The digital revolution has allowed the public to voice its commitment to transparency, participation, and collaboration, and governments therefore are pressured to respond and adapt to the changing dynamics surrounding the decisionmaking process. The latest news about government security measures has also pushed firms in the private sector to call for more transparency regarding government decisionmaking. Tech giants like Google, Facebook, and Microsoft have all called for the government to reveal data requests made by security agencies.

Global "Hacktivist," Anarchist, and Populist Movements

During a span of eighteen months, a seemingly unrelated set of movements sprang up across the globe that had one thing in common: they were all antiestablishment at their core. The groups that emerged in countries as diverse as India, Greece, Egypt, Tunisia, China, Bahrain, Chile, the United States, and Turkey can be described as a wave of global populism. These movements have gathered the young, unemployed, underemployed, and disaffected into often-leaderless mass movements that are challenging the established political and economic order. Fueled by the economic crisis, political paralysis, and policy gridlock of many regional and national governments, these popular movements have surfaced to give voice to the public dissatisfaction with the corruption, the abuses of civil liberties, and the general ineffectiveness and indecisiveness of their leaders. It is also in response to a gap in creditability and representation where citizens feel that they have been marginalized and that elected leaders are out of touch with their needs and interests.

What WikiLeaks, the Arab Awakening, Take Back America, the Tea Party, the Jasmine Revolution, anti-immigrant groups in Europe, and anticorruption groups in China and India have in common is that they are enhanced and enabled by a brand of 1960s-style community-organizing techniques that are coupled with powerful new technologies such as social networks (Facebook, Twitter, YouTube), cell phones, handheld computers, and new media (Al Jazeera and the *Huffington Post*, for example). Such technologies have made spreading images or videos of police or government brutality unprecedentedly easy, so regimes may no longer be able to quell such protests by force without arousing further mobilization. In a world of such social mobilization, there are questions as to how activists, bound together by technology rather than clear leadership, will develop consensus and reconcile their diverse interests.[20] For example, antigovernment protestors in Ukraine who protested former pro-Russia Ukrainian president Viktor Yanukovych used Facebook and the Internet to gain information about the movement's developments. The protesters claimed that such sources provided more reliable information than state television. Therefore, social media and other websites play a major role in disseminating information and even motivating and framing citizens during national uprisings and protest movements.

The emergence of new platforms for channeling information, such as various social networking platforms and cloud computing, has led to information becoming much more accessible and convenient to attain for the public, further adding to the vast reservoir of available knowledge; however, such platforms also encourage "hacktivist" activities, such as Edward Snowden's leak of classified National Security Agency information in 2013. Coalfire, an independent firm specializing in information technology governance, risk, and compliance services, has predicted that there will be a "significant security breach" at a cloud service provider housing "sensitive information on tens if not hundreds of thousands of individuals."[21] With the rise of the "hacktivist" mentality, the dissemination of information, particularly sensitive information, will become more prominent. Moreover, with increased technological access and greater transnational criminal networks, operations are organized and result in greater information leakage.[22]

Global Structural Adjustment

There is a major global structural adjustment that is turning the world upside down. The economically developed countries are now in crisis, while many developing countries are experiencing real sustained economic growth. The main risks to the global economy, and in particular developed countries, are a stalling of progress on the euro area crisis, debt and fiscal issues in the United States due to the Great Recession, a disruption in global oil supplies, and a slowing of Chinese investment.[23] The emerging-market share of world GDP rose from approximately 37 percent in 2000 to 50 percent in 2012.[24] Intense competition from developing countries and emerging economies has placed intense competitive pressures in the manufacturing, service, and high-tech sectors that traditionally have been dominated by the North. This economic shift from global North to global South is due, in part, to "favorable demographic shifts, rising investments and increased productivity."[25] While emerging markets in the BRIC countries are progressing better than those in developed countries, they are stagnant in comparison to new emerging countries like Nigeria, the Philippines, and Mexico. In particular, East Asia benefited from this demographic shift after the 2007 financial crisis.[26] Growth in China was hindered by its trade partnership with the United States, but China kept impressive growth rates up throughout the crisis.

The current economic crisis also created challenges to the liberal economic order and plunged the traditional economic powers of the world into fiscal and monetary crisis. The crisis and associated fiscal constraints have brought into focus the deep-seated structural and fiscal problems that policymakers historically have deferred from one administration to the next. These problems have now begun to surface in the domestic political landscape, and failure to deal with them ten or fifteen years ago has left policymakers with a host of difficult choices. Making these tough decisions does not come easy for politicians who must face reelection. The reality is that the standard of living in the North will decline, entitlements will have to be cut, and taxes will have to be raised. No politician wants to bring this message to the electorate.

At the same time, institutions of global governance such as the G-20, UN Framework Convention on Climate Change, the World Bank, the International Monetary Fund, and the World Trade Organization are losing momentum in addition to credibility. "Where this trust deficit exists most notably, and most destructively, is between North and South. . . . Though the world is experiencing a profound transformation with more wealth and power being transferred to the South—especially to Asia—the North is still in control. However, the North now recognizes that it cannot properly address global challenges without the support and participation of the South."[27] Extreme partisanship, and thus the concomitant political paralysis, combined with the growth of developing nations, could also contribute to the United States' loss of clout in economic IGOs, such as the World Trade Organization.

Policy Tsunamis

An increasing number of political, natural, and social phenomena at the national level have a global impact. As globalization intensifies, these transnational events will grow in number and intensity and will create what I term *policy tsunamis*. I use the term *tsunami* because these policy problems will appear on the policy landscape in one country and then grow in size and complexity as they sweep across the globe with devastating consequences. Globalization, with the help of the Internet, enhances interdependence among nations and people, thereby allowing citizens to demand more from power authorities within and beyond their borders. Yet such interdependence can cause the spillover of policy problems that results in contagion across the globe.[28] Only those countries that are able to identify, track, and analyze these transnational shock waves will be able to respond to them effectively. The economic crisis of 2008, the Arab Spring, and WikiLeaks caught policymakers and the public off guard. John Bolton writes, "Several European governments which co-operated with the U.S. are now predictably running for the tall grass, endangering the continuity of existing programs and damaging prospects for future co-operation."[29] The

leaks by Bradley Manning and WikiLeaks of classified Pentagon and State Department cables caused Europe to lose its trust in Washington's ability to protect
and safeguard classified information. There have always been local events that
have had global implications, but what is new is the speed and intensity in which
these policy issues travel around the globe and rapidly reach a crisis stage.

Short Termism

Many politicians choose to focus on short-term issues and crises rather than
address the large looming crises that are just ahead. "Short termism" is, in part,
a result of the culture of Western society. Many politicians opt not to face major
policy issues (an aging or a declining population, climate change, sovereign
debt, to list a few) that put their nations at risk because they would rather dodge
and defer the issue to ensure their reelections. "Politics, technology and human
nature all militate in favour of kicking the can down the road. The most severe
financial and economic crisis in more than half a century has further discouraged
policymakers from raising their eyes from the present to the distant horizon."[30]
Indeed, George Papandreou, former prime minister of Greece, stated, "Citizens
feel alienated with conventional politics and frustrated by the absence of effective policies that serve societies' needs."[31] Think tanks are increasingly viewed as
being part of the problem because they do not force policymakers to address
these issues and fail to pressure elected leaders into necessary action.

However, think tanks can alter their tendencies toward short termism by
determining realistic measurable targets for combating long-term transnational
problems. In conjunction with NGOs, they can also function as watchdogs and
apply more pressure to governments to act in the long term by producing reports that discuss the grave consequences of inaction. IGOs, NGOs, and think
tanks can also begin the process of international cooperation by working
together to effectively address some of the large looming crises of today, such as
the world's aging population, sustainable growth, aging transport and energy
infrastructure, and a restructure of international institutions so that they better
represent the modern, globalized world.

EMERGING ISSUES FACING U.S. THINK TANKS

While many factors have contributed to the changing marketplace of ideas and
policy advice, several forces have emerged that are redefining think tanks and
the policymaking process, including changes in funding patterns and the

growth of an information-rich environment. Limited private and public funding for think tanks has resulted in more short-term, project-specific funding, rather than long-term institutional support. Think tanks also face competition from advocacy organizations, for-profit consulting groups, law firms, and electronic media for the attention of busy policymakers and an increasingly distracted public. In today's environment anyone can be a think tank, at least virtually.

Traditional measures of impact and policy research are less relevant than ever, and the best mediums for reaching policymakers and the public are in a constant state of flux. This poses an existential challenge for think tanks—but also an incredible opportunity to increase the quality of their output and their ability to reach a larger audience.

Dramatic Shifts in Funding Patterns

National, regional, and local governments have cut their funding for public policy research while corporations and private foundations have limited their grant making to project-specific support. The economic crisis of 2008 sparked a considerable shift in sources of think tank funding. According to Alejandro Chafuen's "Think Tanks for Freedom: A Snapshot of the U.S. Market," foundations served as the largest source of support to think tanks until 2011. Donations from individuals have replaced foundations as the most prominent source of funding for think tanks and this trend is likely continue to grow. On average, corporations contribute approximately 10 percent of the revenue granted to the institutes that participated within Chafuen's sample. This is down from 18 percent since 2000. Roughly half of the organizations reported that individual donors are the largest source of support: 48 percent of revenue bases come from individuals and 40 percent from foundations. Just 2 percent can be attributed to other sources, most of which are magazine subscriptions to think tank magazines, such as that published by the Reason Foundation.[32] Decreased funding and operating support has put think tanks at risk of supporting the status quo in policy debate, rather than providing alternatives.[33] Nobel laureate professor James Rothman of Yale University, Professor Randy Sheckman of the University of California at Berkeley, and Professor Thomas Suedhof of Stanford University say that government budget cuts threaten research and undermine the overall outcomes of the institutions' research.[34] Sub-Saharan African think tanks have been particularly hard-hit by the economic downturn, both for economic reasons and because many African countries lack the local funding options available to think tanks elsewhere because of a weaker culture of philanthropy.[35]

Yet although diminished funding may perhaps jeopardize innovation with respect to policy research and prescription, it is equally important to recognize that funding of any amount tends to influence the particular research agenda that a think tank pursues. It is, therefore, critical that policy institutes implement the systems and procedures necessary to safeguard the integrity and independence of the work they produce. In addition to such internal measures, it is suggested that think tanks maintain a wide variety and a large number of donors, so as to further avoid a situation in which those who make up these policy institutes feel beholden to government or other narrow special interests.[36] Think tanks are often viewed as nonpartisan, nonbiased sources; however, the sources of funding can influence a think tank's focus. Kathleen Clark, a professor at Washington University and political ethics expert, said, "If you're a lobbyist, whatever you say is heavily discounted. If a think tank is saying it, it obviously sounds a lot better. Maybe think tanks aren't aware of how useful that makes them to private interests. On the other hand, maybe it's part of their revenue model."[37]

Keeping donors happy is more important now than ever, for if an organization's backers do not see desired results, they have an increasingly vast array of alternative organizations to support. One particular negative outcome of this trend is the potential for pressure by a political donor to lead to self-censorship among both individual scholars and think tanks as institutions. A researcher is unlikely to write an essay or publish a study that she or he knows will upset a boss or donor. For instance, when he was a senior fellow at the American Security Project, Michael Cohen noted in June 2011 in the *New Republic* that the *Wonk Room* blog of the Center for American Progress (CAP) had not run a single story about the Afghanistan war in the prior five months. During the Bush years, CAP had frequently taken up the war and been an adamant critic of the administration's policies; once Obama more or less continued those policies, however, CAP grew silent.[38] Experiences such as the one at CAP demonstrate that funders have the capacity to shape and influence projects pursued and opinions espoused by the research institution and potentially harm the objectivity of the institution.

In response to the steady decrease in think tank funding, and the increasing politicization that this decrease has caused, On Think Tanks founder Enrique Mendizabal suggests transforming funding into organizational development grants, which would hypothetically support three specific areas: quality control of research products, increased communications and advocacy capacity, and internal institutional development and governance. This change, he argues, will "turn our core grants into development vehicles."[39]

Increased Specialization

Specialized institutions and programs are attractive to funders who want to target their dollars at specific problems or issues. In fact, the increasingly desperate demand for funding arguably may be the most prominent factor facilitating the specialization of think tanks. This trend toward increased specialization has had a direct impact on the programs, constituencies, and funding sources of multipurpose policy organizations, which in turn has increased competition among think tanks. It has become increasingly difficult for think tanks to convince prospective funders that their programs are worthy of support. Moreover, increased specialization discourages interdisciplinary responses to complex issues and limits creativity of scholars.[40] As think tanks become more specialized, they tend to focus their research according to topic. Organizations such as the National Taxpayers Union or the Health Care Cost Institute are single-focus think tanks that research only one topic. Others focus on a small number of issues, such as the Pacific Research Institute (education, technology, and health care) or the Employment Policies Institute (health insurance and labor compensation). Think tanks also demonstrate a regional focus. The Middle East Forum, the National Bureau of Asian Research, and the large number of state-based think tanks in the United States narrow their research scope according to issues pertinent to the geographic area of focus. Finally, a third way in which think tanks have become increasingly specialized is specialization according to guiding political ideologies: libertarian, left-liberal, conservative, and religion based are a few examples.[41] Notably, the increased specialization of think tanks often results in greater funding confidence that their money is directed toward issues that the funders support.

One negative outcome of specialization is a blindness to the interdisciplinary methods for solving issues from a multiplicity of angles. Think tanks are "embracing specialization as a means of distinguishing themselves from the competition"; however, specialization, while providing think tanks with an edge in particular areas and fields, discourages interdisciplinary responses.[42] Not only does globalization enhance interdependence between countries; it also intensifies interdisciplinary approaches to global issues. For example, the study of "South-South" cooperation and transfer is "an interdisciplinary undertaking."[43] Complex issues require the adoption of interdisciplinary approaches that can better address the multivaried nature of these issues. Specialization limits the exhaustion of possible policy suggestions of scholars and renders these suggestions less applicable and practical.

Increased Competition

Think tanks have embraced specialization as a means of distinguishing themselves from the competition. The increase in think tanks resulted in greater competition, and the influence of organizations such as consulting and law firms have heightened the competition. By distinguishing itself and developing a specific niche, a think tank proves its legitimacy in the policy dialogue. This branding has taken the form of functional, political, and issue specialization that helps market the institution to donors who are increasingly providing project-specific support, to policymakers, and to the public who is trying to make sense of the crowded marketplace of ideas and institutions. To really strengthen competitiveness, think tanks could diversify "across many specializations."[44] By diversifying and expanding their niches, they can provide suggestions from a more holistic and well-rounded approach. Approaching or employing fewer think tanks for policy advice and consultation would be more convenient and cost-efficient for policymakers who seek help in drafting policies. Moreover, most policies require interdisciplinary approaches, and there is a surplus of specialized think tanks.[45] The merging, acquisition, or collaboration of think tanks is one possible suggestion.

Despite the interdisciplinary nature of policy, the vast majority of the think tanks that have come into existence in the past thirty years have been focused on a single issue or area of policy research. More recently, think tanks have faced a new competitive threat from consulting firms, law firms, advocacy groups, and cable news networks that now directly compete with think tanks for gifts, grants, and contracts. Similarly, many colleges and universities are encouraging the growth of policy and research centers, which further heightens competition for conventional think tanks.[46]

Influence and Independence

As think tanks become more visible and influential, some organizations appear to be losing their voice and independence along the way. Managing the tensions associated with relevance, influence, and independence is a delicate balancing act that must be carefully managed if think tanks are to maintain their credibility with policymakers and the public. Of particular hindrance is the fact that they seldom publish critiques or objective studies on their own work.[47] Evaluating success and overall impact is another great challenge. Andrew Selee, executive vice president at the Wilson Center in Washington, D.C., notes that the evaluation of success using tracking data on the number of publications, media citations, and speeches is an essential component to directing and focusing research and policy initiatives. On the basis of this evidence, a think tank can determine whether it is following the original goals and mission of the project and of the organization. However, given the ever-shifting terrain of policymaking, it is crucial to be nimble and adapt to this changing landscape.[48] Thus, by consistently evaluating and reevaluating an organization's impact, scholars and leaders in the organization can develop an open dialogue about the organization's successes and failures and therefore can better anticipate the shifting tides of policymaking and advocacy.

Outputs vs. Impact

Historically, think tanks have placed a focus on output over impact. How do think tanks measure their impact? For many institutions, it is limited to the number of books and policy briefs produced rather than providing the impetus for new legislation or changes in policy.[49] This issue is further complicated by donors, who are increasingly interested in supporting "high-impact organizations" and want think tanks to demonstrate their impact on public policy. When the organizational goal is for "high impact," the consequence is often that high-pressure environments are created in which scholars feel that their success rests on the capacity to alter policy or seriously impact the policy decisionmaking process. Selee argues that think tanks, like corporations and nonprofits, need to develop methods of evaluating success that are constructive learning experiences for the scholars. He maintains that measurement is quite difficult given the desire to succeed in high-impact circumstances. It is crucial to view success through various lenses and to look at impact on relative, not absolute, grounds.[50] If the organization lessened the pressure to achieve "high impact" in all outcomes and evaluated impact through a variety of mechanisms and measurements, it would ultimately foster a more open research environment. Moreover, by mitigating pressure from donors, an organization allows think tank scholars more breadth and freedom to research and collaborate.

One effective measurement tool is to look at indicators of impact through a monitored "intermediate" lens, when intermediate measures are used to effectively measure impact in smaller, short-term circumstances. "Impact indicators" are focused more on intermediate outcomes such as the "number of citations" rather than on ultimate outcomes such as the "number of people helped by a new policy." A majority of potential readers prefer qualitative monitoring and evaluation (M&E) because it is a "practical translation of a focus on outcomes," while the quantitative M&E cannot capture "all the nuances of a policy effort."[51]

Phantom NGOs as Think Tanks

Governments are creating think tanks designed to appear to be NGOs but that are in fact arms of the government. Similarly, corporations and individuals have established think tanks to promote their special interests. This trend raises concerns about a lack of transparency and private interest that is masquerading as public interest. In Britain, the *Guardian*'s combative George Monbiot has written a number of pieces warning that "secretive think tanks are crushing our democracy" by engaging in "secret corporate lobbying."[52] The United States is not immune from such secretive organizations. In fact, Washington, D.C., is becoming a hotbed for such think tanks—those that act more like lobbying and public relations bodies than sources of independent ideas or policy critique.[53] Moreover, the overlap between think tanks and Washington demonstrates the pervasive influence of partisanship into scholarship. For example, the appointment of former Republican senator Jim DeMint as president of the Heritage Foundation in 2013 provoked questions about the foundation's overt politicization and its failure to "separate intellectual inquiry from raw partisan politics troubles conservatives."[54]

Many think tanks in the United States that are tax-exempt under their 501(c)(3) status now feature affiliated, non-tax-exempt lobbying arms.[55] It ought not to come as a surprise, then, that "calls for more think tank transparency grew louder in the U.S." in late 2013, echoing Nobel Prize winner Paul Krugman and "a broad range of other commentators from across the political spectrum" who "have long called on think tanks to reveal their funders."[56] Although this public criticism led Center for American Progress to release a list of its funders, other organizations such as the Heartland Institute (HI) argued for "continued opacity," and cited the "donors' right to privacy."[57] Yet these latter organizations are not to be perceived as the exception; Harvard University's Brooke Williams has recently found that one-third of the top fifty U.S. think tanks do not disclose their donors. More critics of think tanks question the motivations behind their policy research. Gerry Hassan, a research fellow at the University of the West of Scotland, argues that an outright analysis of the audience that think tanks serve would highlight that they have vested interest in catering to corporate interests, accountancy firms, and lobbyists. He examines the fact that few of the policies supported by think tanks have aided the general populace.[58] Hassan's criticism highlights a general skepticism about the objectivity of think tanks because of their donor's influence. However, given the vast array of donors, it would be impossible for a think tank to tailor research and advocacy to the demands of all donors.

Hybrid Organizations

As think tanks have faced new challenges in the societies in which they operate, they have adapted and created hybrid institutions. Think tanks inherently occupy "an intermediate structural position" among academic, political, and economic fields and media outlets, and this overlap has often made their precise definition difficult.[59] More and more think tanks are a blend of organizational types (academic research center, consulting group, marketing firm, and media outlet), and the roles of key staff have changed, as well. The staff of think tank institutions is "comprised of multifaceted individuals who are part scholar, journalist, marketing executive, and policy entrepreneur."[60] Think tank budgets and staffing patterns now place as much emphasis on policy research as they do on promoting it and the scholars who conduct it. In fact, the functions that think tanks now assume have become so multifaceted and heterogeneous that scholars Donald E. Abelson and Christine M. Carberry note that aside from "acknowledg[ing] that think tanks are nonprofit, nonpartisan organizations engaged in the study of public policy, few scholars have outlined other criteria which would allow them to distinguish think tanks from other types of nongovernmental organizations."[61]

The Impact of the Internet, New Media, Social Networking, and the Cloud

Information no longer translates into power unless it is in the right form at the right time, and this idea is redefining how think tanks operate. Most think tanks now have websites and conduct policy debates via the Internet. Yet this digital development has not been without challenges, described as "digital disruption."[62] Among the host of challenges now faced by think tanks is the pressure to increase the speed of searching for and disseminating information, the rising levels of global competition, and the elevated difficulty in sustaining internal communications.

A Pew Research Center poll found that 70 percent of people in the United States use the Internet for news.[63] The reality is that more and more people get their information from the Internet, traditional and new media, and through social networking sites. This reality requires that organizations reexamine how they create, disseminate, and discuss public policy issues. Organizations must also reconsider the methods they use to reach their constituents and the clients they serve as well as how they can produce academic-quality research that is understandable and accessible to policymakers and to the public. Enrique Mendizabal contends that devising a digital strategy is not only pertinent to communication but to research and management, as well. He notes that "Twitter can be used to find information (research), disseminate it (communication), and keep team members connected and informed of a project's activities (management)."[64] To maximize the potential that could be realized with respect to increased capacity, efficiency, and dissemination, Mendizabal adds that think tanks ought to tailor their engagement with contextually specific types of digital strategies.[65] The power of a well-constructed digital strategy, On Think Tanks contributor Nick Scott agrees, can "improve agility, buy time for under-resourced staff and provide additional opportunities for collaboration."[66]

This new reliance on the Internet also raises questions about the difference between visibility and influence for think tanks; often the popularity of a think tank on the Web does not translate into an ability to effect change.[67] These dramatic changes have transformed how public policies are analyzed and debated and have forced think tanks to keep pace with these changes or risk being buried by them. When considering how to increase the overall impact of an organization, the creation of accessible and comprehensible information is absolutely essential. Grupo FARO, a think tank in Ecuador, observes that the "gathering of evidence is not enough." Findings and arguments need "to be communicated in a way that speaks to politicians and policy advisers (the top-down view of policy process) as well as to journalists and ordinary citizens (the bottom-up view)."[68] Evidence and in-depth research must evolve into narratives that can captivate and relate to a broader audience on a personal level. Social media and technology married with succinct and accessible analyses will ultimately foster knowledge sharing.

Action vs. Ideas

Nonpartisan, multipurpose organizations are forced to abandon traditional methods of operation, such as dialogue and debate, and, as we have seen, now they must consider new methods as funders and other stakeholders in the policy process have grown impatient with conferences, forums, and seminars on public policy issues. This trend is a result of the influence of donors who now prefer operational, advocacy-oriented programs and institutions over conferences, forums, and seminars. Subrat Das, executive director of the India-based Centre for Budget and Governance Accountability, spoke of the need for advocacy in effecting change: "If we want to achieve results or some impact . . . for that we need to reach out to the relevant stakeholders. We might strive for excellent quality research, and we might disseminate our research finding through our publications . . . and yet those might not reach out to the relevant stakeholders."[69] One new method to reach out to these relevant stakeholders is by applying elements of games to another setting, such as funding. This process of "gamification," currently being employed in business models, could be an effective tool to increase the involvement of funding partners and other key stakeholders in the policy process.[70] New policy-oriented institutions have outmarketed traditional policy research establishments that fail to understand and respond to the fundamental changes that have taken place in Washington and other capitals around the world. Some scholars say that think tanks in the political process are best at capturing the imagination of the public. In other words, they are most likely to affect political thinking—through knowledge platforms, policy research, and learning/teaching.

Greater Emphasis on External Relations and Marketing Strategies

The rise of special interests and a need for a quick response to complex policy problems have created a greater demand for policy research and fostered the growth of specialized public policy think tanks. This has placed greater emphasis on marketing strategies and external relations that effectively target key constituencies and donors. Think tanks must now develop strategies for "flexible output," whereby they produce daily or weekly short-form content, such as blog posts and social media updates that are in addition to less frequent long-form reports.[71] Think tanks are forced to redesign their "products" so they can disseminate them to a number of strategically selected target audiences for the greatest impact.

In this new world, pithy, punchy policy briefs replace books, journals, and white papers to meet the time constraints of policymakers who need a quick response to policy issues and problems. A 400-page book or report now is reduced to a few pages or words if the material is disseminated as a text message or blog. These new realities pose immense challenges for think tanks that must adapt to these changes while not losing the quality and integrity of their research.

Additionally, some think tanks are becoming less involved in the creation of new knowledge and more concerned with "selling" their news.[72] For example, in 2008 CAP used about half of its budget for communication and public outreach—that is approximately eight times more than what similar policy organizations spent. With the creation of new knowledge becoming subordinated by the desire for think tanks to sell their "product," research and policy initiatives that benefit civil society become less important. Furthermore, as more think tanks emerge in civil society, CSOs must increasingly compete through marketing strategies to obtain funding and public support.[73]

Going Global

Think tanks, by necessity, are increasingly adopting a global presence, perspective, and audience. The economist Joseph Stiglitz commented that think tanks must "scan globally and reinvent locally" if they are to be effective in today's policy environment.[74] This trend is driven, in part, by transnational issues such as global warming and the proliferation of weapons of mass destruction, pandemics, and terrorism. In recent years, a number of global think tanks have emerged, for example, Carnegie Endowment for International Peace and the International Crisis Group, that are designed to address global issues and serve a global audience of policymakers.

Additionally, there is an ever-increasing presence of newly founded think tanks in emerging markets.[75] African think tanks are becoming more numerous, for example, although this is not to say that they are free of challenges. Many do not have a platform to set their own agendas. They are usually funded by foreign and international agencies and lack adequate funding to engage in long-term research programs, which effectively impinges on their capacity to provide long-term policy prescriptions. Scholar Hussein Elkamel underscores the difficulties experienced by African think tanks with respect to capacity building and independence, as well as the challenges that result from working within a fragile marketplace.[76] In light of these challenges, think tanks throughout Africa are advised to establish domestic funding as well as to invest in communication strategies such as social media to more efficiently articulate research findings to policymakers. It is also important, many scholars contend, that such think tanks collaborate and build alliances with other think tanks—both in the global North and South—to share "best practices." Digital communication strategies are likely to facilitate and proliferate this spirit of cooperation and partnership, and as such "can and do transcend national borders."[77]

Numerous think tanks are trying to cultivate stronger ties to counterpart organizations within their regions and across the world. The emergence of regional economic alliances as a result of global interdependence has created a new network of regionally oriented policy institutions. But these organizations tend to be the same ones that find it difficult to compete with the highly specialized organizations that have a clear market niche and constituency.

Leadership and Managing Tensions

An unprecedented number of think tank executives are retiring or stepping down. Many of these leaders founded or led the think tanks for many years, so the impact of these transitions is likely to be problematic. Leadership in a nonprofit think tank is different from ownership of a for-profit organization. There are no actual shares or stakeholders. When such a leader steps down, they become quasi-owners or "spiritual owners." The degree of ownership is in relation to the resources contributed. And that incurs the problem of how to retain the talents and resources through a leadership transition. Often high-profile, well-respected leaders "outperform their own organizations" in readership: Agustín Etchebarne, leader of an Argentinian think tank, has 33,000 Twitter followers, while his think tank has only 8,000.[78] The loss of such prolific leaders could reduce the audience that think tanks are able to reach. Key institutions such as RAND, the Peterson Institute for International Economics, the Urban Institute, and the Woodrow Wilson International Center for Scholars have all seen leadership changes in the recent past, and others like the Heritage Foundation and Brookings are planning for a transition to new leadership. The issue is more severe in Africa and Eastern and Central Europe, where the senior staffs are very small. Transitions there can have a far greater impact on an organization.

The successor generations of leadership—whether of governments or other institutions—are never easy, but nonetheless essential. One bad hire or a rocky transition can cripple an organization for years. Even when the search for an executive is successful, the institution will face a range of challenges that will require careful management by the governing board. New leaders will face new challenges. As scholar Andrea Moncada notes, "Increased competition, donor expectations, the 24-hour news cycle and the expectation to respond to politics" will place a strain on think tanks, particularly those with new directors who "do not have the same relationship with donors as their predecessors did."

In this situation, Moncada continues, research produced may be "in danger of being dictated by politics," as new leadership will not maintain the leverage necessary to resist donor requests.[79]

Thus, such think tanks will be required to deal with the continuing challenge of managing the tensions between influence and independence, rigor and relevance, degree of specialization and breadth and depth in the range of issues they seek to address, continuity and change in pursuing those issues, and ultimately what impact on policy and the lives of the people in the countries in which they operate think tanks will have.

LEAN, MEAN, POLICY MACHINES

The ongoing challenge for think tanks is to produce timely and accessible policy-oriented research that effectively engages policymakers, the press, and the public on the critical issues facing a country. Gone are the days when a think tank could operate with the motto "Research it, write it, and they will find it." Today, think tanks must be lean, mean policy machines. *The Economist* described "good think tanks" as those organizations that are able to combine "intellectual depth, political influence, and flair for publicity, comfortable surroundings, and a streak of eccentricity." New technologies are being created every day and at an accelerated pace that will continually force think tanks to identify new and faster ways to collect, sort, and analyze data and then communicate their findings to a highly segmented target audience using a variety of communication tools. Those who fail to organize and integrate these qualities into their think tank will become known for their "pedantry, irrelevance, obscurity, poverty, and conventionality."[80] Many think tanks have already successfully met this challenge and are now playing a critical role in bridging the divide between the academic and policy communities and policymakers and the public.

Clearly there is no shortage of policy challenges at the national, regional, and global levels, which means that the role and importance of independent think tanks will continue to grow. As mentioned earlier, the world we live in can be characterized by what has been described as the four mores: more issues, more actors, more competition, and more conflict. Over the past ten to fifteen years, governments and civil society groups have come to rely on think tanks for ideas and advice, and I am confident that this trend will continue well into the future.

CODA

From their embryonic beginnings in the eighteenth and nineteenth centuries, think tanks have grown into complex institutions permeating several political spheres and taking on several roles to supplement governmental and academic institutions. They, as an estate in their own right, have become a cohesive element in policymaking, filling in the gaps at all stages of policy formation. These chameleon-like organizations have evolved and adapted to a multitude of political climates, allowing them to weave their ideas all throughout Washington and the rest of the world.

Think tanks can act as insiders, serving as an integral part of the policy process, or they can act as outsiders, attempting to incorporate their ideas into policy by conducting research and analysis that are then aggressively marketed to policy elites and the public. These dual roles sometimes clash, only adding to the age-old tension between the world of theory and the world of policy. The academic-oriented school believes that think tanks should adhere to academic research standards and focus on big-picture issues, while the policy-oriented school believes that think tanks should concentrate on current political issues and the needs of policymakers.[81] The precise paths think tanks take and the possible ways in which they can balance these two roles remain to be seen.

In addition to serving these functions, think tanks have recently broadened their activities, making it more challenging to formulate a simple definition for the "brain boxes." Defining a think tank has become increasingly difficult since one must consider numerous factors, such as source of funding, strategy, and political orientation. The historical context and evolution of think tanks illustrate their increasingly intimate relationship with civil society and explain their heightened relevance and effectiveness in the political scene. Further, the "brain boxes," despite their variations, generally all seek to conduct broad public policy research, analyze trends, offer advice, evaluate government programs, exchange ideas, interpret policies for the media, and supply personnel to government agencies and offices.

The latter function, in particular, has gained prominence in recent years. The revolving door process is becoming more prevalent, and individuals have been rotating in and out of government positions and the think tank community according to the change in political ideology. Today, the trend that the revolving door embodies links the realms of policy formation and knowledge dissemination. As the highly academic scholars who typically inhabit think tanks obtain raw information and develop it into knowledge, retired political actors contribute their tangible experiences from working within the U.S. political system.

Through this increasingly popular phenomenon, the contemporary version of think tanks is born, generating a new, more interactive policymaking process.

Think tanks play the pivotal role of the Fifth Estate in civil society, influencing policy and generating new ideas. The history of think tanks, as well as their expanding presence throughout the world, attests to their heightening relevance and efficacy. Within the United States, an atmosphere conducive to the establishment and growth of think tanks has resulted in a strong relationship between policy formation and the input of experts beyond the governmental sphere, demonstrated by many case studies. More specifically, think tanks were influential in studies of Social Security and welfare reform during the Clinton and Bush terms, as well as in the study of other domestic issues. They ultimately informed foreign policy and became the foundation of decisionmaking bodies such as the 9/11 Commission.

These institutions act as more than just government counselors; they create a dialogue and generate knowledge for both academics and the general public. Despite the current financial strain on think tanks, which are in large part funded by private donors, their influence under the Obama administration remains evident and strong. Think tanks in the United States are aware of their many contributions, diverse duties, and immense influence, and they also look forward with anticipation to the possibilities and potential of the future. In addition, regional and global organizations such as the United Nations, World Bank, Asian Development Bank, and NATO have recently recognized the crucial role that think tanks play in the policymaking process.

Think tanks, by repeatedly offering insightful advice and analysis regarding policy, have established themselves as the vital Fifth Estate in the United States' political sphere. While other institutions may contend for this title, they simply do not possess the range and adaptability that think tanks have shown in the last decades. Think tanks certainly have no monopoly on policy advice, and the new challenges arising from unforeseen circumstances will always test their relevance. Nonetheless, they are also a dynamic cadre of institutions that have embraced new technology, new views on climate and energy, and a more global perspective.

Their continued tradition of excellence, resilience, and practicality is what will ensure their place as the Fifth Estate. Despite the current economic situation in the United States along with the other factors that work against the success of think tanks, if they can persist as they did in the winter of the Great Depression, after their great bloom during the American Progressive Era, their future looks bright.

The United States Think Tank Field Guide

As THINK TANKS have grown in number and influence, a handful of distinct breeds have emerged. Here's a guide to telling the wonks from the water carriers.

THE POLICYMAKERS

These organizations enjoy a competitive advantage over their rivals when it comes to government contracts and research. They have the know-how and PR skills that ministers, bean counters, and bureaucrats seek.

RAND Corporation   *Urban Institute*

THE PARTISANS

These ideology-driven organizations generate the leading ideas on the right and left, develop new political talent, and offer a home to out-of-power party leaders.

Center for American Progress   *Heritage Foundation*

THE PHANTOMS

Designed to look like NGOs, these organizations are, in fact, arms of the government. They have emerged as a favorite strategy for authoritarians to mask their diktats as flourishing civil society.

Institute for Political and   *Institute of International*
Military Analysis   *Law, Wuhan University*

THE SCHOLARS

The stars of the think tank world, these powerhouses of policy are regularly relied on to set agendas and craft new initiatives.

Brookings Institution   *Council on Foreign Relations*

Resources for the Future

THE ACTIVISTS

These do-gooders do not simply advocate for important causes. They have become top-notch policy and research hubs in their own right.

Amnesty International   *Human Rights Watch*

Source: James G. McGann, "The Think Tank Index," *Foreign Policy*, February 2009, pp. 82–84.

Categories of Think Tank Affiliations

AUTONOMOUS AND INDEPENDENT

Significant independence from any one interest group or donor and autonomous in its operation and funding from government.

Carnegie Endowment for   *Council on Foreign Relations*
American Enterprise Institute

Heritage Foundation

QUASI-INDEPENDENT

Autonomous from government but controlled by an interest group, donor, or contracting agency that provides a majority of the funding and has significant influence over operations of the think tank.

Center for Defense Information

UNIVERSITY AFFILIATED

Policy research center at a university.

Baker Institute for Public Policy, Rice University

POLITICAL PARTY AFFILIATED

Formally affiliated with a political party or political ideology.

Progressive Policy Institute

GOVERNMENT AFFILIATED

Part of the structure of government.

Congressional Research Service (U.S. legislative branch)

QUASI-GOVERNMENTAL

Funded exclusively by government grants and contracts but not a part of the formal structure of government.

Woodrow Wilson International Center for Scholars

Source: James G. McGann, "The Think Tank Index," *Foreign Policy*, February 2009, pp. 82–84.

Profiles of Leading U.S. Think Tanks, 2010–11

THE THINK TANK profiles are based on data collected in 2010–11 by the Think Tanks and Civil Societies Program (TTCSP) using a think tank survey instrument, the TTCSP Global Think Tank Database, and data collected from each institution's website and other web-based sources.

AMERICAN ENTERPRISE INSTITUTE

LOCATION: Washington, D.C.
BUDGET: $29 million
STAFF SIZE: 175
ESTABLISHED: 1943
WEBSITE: www.aei.org
SPECIALTIES: foreign policy, economic policy, social and political studies
HIGH-PROFILE SCHOLARS: Arthur C. Brooks, Martin Feldstein, Dick Cheney, Eliot A. Cohen, R. Glenn Hubbard, Christopher Galvin, Ayaan Hirsi Ali

ATLANTIC COUNCIL OF THE UNITED STATES

LOCATION: Washington, D.C.
BUDGET: $6 million
STAFF SIZE: 90
ESTABLISHED: 1961
WEBSITE: www.acus.org
SPECIALTIES: foreign policy, Asian studies, Africa studies, environmental policy
HIGH-PROFILE SCHOLARS: Henry Kissinger, Brent Scowcroft, Eric Shinseki, Susan Rice, Richard Holbrooke

BELFER CENTER FOR SCIENCE AND INTERNATIONAL AFFAIRS

LOCATION: Cambridge, Mass. (Harvard University)
BUDGET: N/A
STAFF SIZE: 261
ESTABLISHED: 1973
WEBSITE: http://belfercenter.ksg.harvard.edu
SPECIALTIES: international security, science and technology, environmental policy
HIGH-PROFILE SCHOLARS: Graham Allison, Niall Ferguson, Martin Feldstein, Joseph S. Nye

BROOKINGS INSTITUTION

LOCATION: Washington, D.C.
BUDGET: $90 million
STAFF SIZE: 450
ESTABLISHED: 1916
WEBSITE: www.brookings.edu
SPECIALTIES: foreign policy, Middle East studies, economic policy
HIGH-PROFILE SCHOLARS: Strobe Talbott, Kenneth Pollack, Alice Rivlin, Michael O'Hanlon

Carnegie Endowment for International Peace

LOCATION: Washington, D.C.
BUDGET: $23 million
STAFF SIZE: 160
ESTABLISHED: 1910
WEBSITE: http://carnegieendowment.org
SPECIALTIES: foreign policy, international security, Asian studies, democracy studies
HIGH-PROFILE SCHOLARS AND MANAGERS: Francis Fukuyama, Jessica Matthews

Cato Institute

LOCATION: Washington, D.C.
BUDGET: $22 million
STAFF SIZE: 120
ESTABLISHED: 1977
WEBSITE: www.cato.org
SPECIALTIES: constitutional studies, economic policy, social and political studies
HIGH-PROFILE SCHOLARS AND MANAGERS: Edward Crane, Michael Tanner

Center for American Progress

LOCATION: Washington, D.C.
BUDGET: $38 million
STAFF SIZE: 242
ESTABLISHED: 2003
WEBSITE: www.americanprogress.org
SPECIALTIES: defense policy, economic policy, health policy, education policy
HIGH-PROFILE SCHOLARS AND MANAGERS: John Podesta, John Prendergast, Tom Daschle

CENTER FOR GLOBAL DEVELOPMENT

LOCATION: Washington, D.C.
BUDGET: $27 million
STAFF SIZE: 76
ESTABLISHED: 2001
WEBSITE: www.cgdev.org
SPECIALTIES: globalization, international development, aid effectiveness
HIGH-PROFILE SCHOLARS AND MANAGERS: Nancy Birdsall, Steven Radelet, Todd Moss

CENTER FOR A NEW AMERICAN SECURITY

LOCATION: Washington, D.C.
BUDGET: $5 million
STAFF SIZE: 24
ESTABLISHED: 2007
WEBSITE: www.cnas.org
SPECIALTIES: foreign policy, international security, defense policy
HIGH-PROFILE SCHOLARS AND MANAGERS: Thomas E. Ricks, Robert Kaplan

CENTER FOR STRATEGIC AND INTERNATIONAL STUDIES

LOCATION: Washington, D.C.
BUDGET: $34 million
STAFF SIZE: 150
ESTABLISHED: 1962
WEBSITE: http://csis.org
SPECIALTIES: foreign policy, international security, defense policy
HIGH-PROFILE SCHOLARS: John Hamre, Richard Armitage, Zbigniew Brzezinski, Anthony Cordesman, Sam Nunn, Bill Cohen, Joseph S. Nye, Henry Kissinger, Brent Scowcroft

COUNCIL ON FOREIGN RELATIONS

LOCATION: Washington, D.C.
BUDGET: $48 million
STAFF SIZE: 293
ESTABLISHED: 1921
WEBSITE: www.cfr.org
SPECIALTIES: foreign policy, Asia studies, international security, international development
HIGH-PROFILE SCHOLARS AND MANAGERS: Madeleine Albright, Fareed Zakaria, Joseph S. Nye, Tom Brokaw, Colin Powell, Richard N. Haass

GERMAN MARSHALL FUND

LOCATION: Washington, D.C.
BUDGET: $38 million
STAFF SIZE: 110
ESTABLISHED: 1972
WEBSITE: www.gmfus.org
SPECIALTIES: foreign policy, environmental policy, energy policy, civil society studies
HIGH-PROFILE SCHOLARS AND MANAGERS: Craig Kennedy

HARVARD CENTER FOR INTERNATIONAL DEVELOPMENT

LOCATION: Cambridge, Mass. (Harvard University)
BUDGET: N/A
STAFF SIZE: 33
ESTABLISHED: 1998
WEBSITE: www.hks.harvard.edu/centers/cid
SPECIALTIES: international development, globalization, immigration and migratory studies
HIGH-PROFILE SCHOLARS: Daniel Putnam, Ricardo Hausmann, Kenneth Rogoff

Heritage Foundation

LOCATION: Washington, D.C.
BUDGET: $80 million
STAFF SIZE: 269
ESTABLISHED: 1973
WEBSITE: www.heritage.org
SPECIALTIES: defense policy, economic policy, social and political studies
HIGH-PROFILE SCHOLARS: Margaret Thatcher, Stuart Butler, Edwin J. Feulner

Hoover Institution

LOCATION: Stanford, Calif., and Washington, D.C.
BUDGET: $39 million
STAFF SIZE: 170
ESTABLISHED: 1919
WEBSITE: www.hoover.org
SPECIALTIES: constitutional studies, economic policy, social and political studies
HIGH-PROFILE SCHOLARS AND MANAGERS: Peter Robinson, Larry Diamond, Michael McFaul, Victor Davis Hanson

Hudson Institute

LOCATION: Washington, D.C.
BUDGET: $12 million
STAFF SIZE: 100
ESTABLISHED: 1961
WEBSITE: www.hudson.org
SPECIALTIES: economic policy, international security, Middle East studies, constitutional studies
BOLDFACE NAMES: Robert Bork, Michael Horowitz, Lewis Libby

NATIONAL BUREAU OF ECONOMIC RESEARCH

LOCATION: Washington, D.C.
BUDGET: N/A
STAFF SIZE: 45
ESTABLISHED: 1920
WEBSITE: www.nber.org
SPECIALTIES: economic policy
BOLDFACE NAMES: Martin Feldstein

NEW AMERICA FOUNDATION

LOCATION: Sacramento, Calif., and Washington, D.C.
BUDGET: $16 million
STAFF SIZE: 82
ESTABLISHED: 1999
WEBSITE: http://newamerica.net
SPECIALTIES: economic policy, science and technology, health policy
HIGH-PROFILE SCHOLARS: Eric Schmidt, Fareed Zakaria, Anna-Marie
   Slaughter, Francis Fukuyama, Bernard L. Schwartz, Walter Russell Mead,
   Douglas G. Bradley, Peter Bergen

OPEN SOCIETY INSTITUTE

LOCATION: New York, N.Y.
BUDGET: $450 million
STAFF SIZE: 800
ESTABLISHED: 1984
WEBSITE: www.soros.org
SPECIALTIES: democracy studies, civil society studies
BOLDFACE NAMES: George Soros

PETERSON INSTITUTE FOR INTERNATIONAL ECONOMICS

LOCATION: Washington, D.C.
BUDGET: $10 million
STAFF SIZE: 50
ESTABLISHED: 1981
WEBSITE: www.iie.com
SPECIALTIES: economic policy, international development, globalization
BOLDFACE NAMES: Larry Summers, Paul O'Neill, Indra K. Nooyi, Lee Kuan
   Yew, Donald F. McHenry, C. Fred Bergsten, Anders Åslund, William
   Cline, Aaron Posen

RAND CORPORATION

LOCATION: Arlington, Va.; Santa Monica, Calif.; and Pittsburgh, Pa.
BUDGET: $247 million
STAFF SIZE: 1,700
ESTABLISHED: 1946
WEBSITE: www.rand.org
SPECIALTIES: defense policy, economic policy, health policy, education policy
HIGH-PROFILE SCHOLARS: Gregory Treverton, Francis Fukuyama, Paul H.
   O'Neill, Richard J. Danzig

UNITED STATES INSTITUTE OF PEACE

LOCATION: Washington, D.C.
BUDGET: $34 million
STAFF SIZE: 325
ESTABLISHED: 1984
WEBSITE: www.usip.org
SPECIALTIES: foreign policy, democracy studies, international development
HIGH-PROFILE SCHOLARS: Stephen D. Krasner, Kerry Kennedy, Michael
   Posner

URBAN INSTITUTE

LOCATION: Washington, D.C.
BUDGET: $64 million
STAFF SIZE: 350
ESTABLISHED: 1968
WEBSITE: www.urban.org
SPECIALTIES: education policy, health policy, social and political studies, urban studies
HIGH-PROFILE SCHOLARS: Robert M. Solow

WOODROW WILSON CENTER FOR INTERNATIONAL SCHOLARS

LOCATION: Washington, D.C.
BUDGET: $35 million
STAFF SIZE: 160
ESTABLISHED: 1968
WEBSITE: www.wilsoncenter.org
SPECIALTIES: foreign policy, international security, environmental policy, democracy studies
HIGH-PROFILE SCHOLARS: Lee Hamilton, Haleh Esfandiari

Notes

Introduction

1. Craufurd D. Goodwin and Michael Nacht, *Beyond Government: Extending the Public Policy Debate in Emerging Democracies* (Boulder, Colo.: Westview Press, 1995), p. 12.

2. Ibid.

Chapter One

1. James McGann and Kent Weaver, eds., *Think Tanks and Civil Societies: Catalysts for Ideas and Action* (University Press of America, 2000), p. 4.

2. This is reflected in the following works: Donald Abelson, *Do Think Tanks Matter?* (McGill-Queens University Press, 2002), pp. 8–9; James Allen Smith, *The Idea Brokers: Think Tanks and the Rise of the New Policy Elite* (New York: Free Press, 1993), pp. xiii–xvi; James McGann, *Comparative Think Tanks, Politics, and Public Policy* (London and New York: Routledge, 2005), pp. 11–12; McGann and Weaver, *Think Tanks and Civil Societies*, pp. 4–5; Kent Weaver, "The Changing World of Think Tanks," *PS: Political Science and Politics* 22 (September 1989), pp. 563–64; Thomas Matthew Medvetz, "Think Tanks as an Emergent Field" (New York: Social Science Research Council, October 2008), pp. 9–10; Diane Stone, Andrew Denham, and Mark Garnett, eds., *Think Tanks across Nations: A Comparative Approach* (Manchester University Press, 1998), pp. 2–6; Andrew Rich, *Think Tanks, Public Policy, and the Politics of Expertise* (Cambridge University Press, 2004), pp. 11–12; Christopher DeMuth, "Thinking about Think Tanks, Part One of Two," *Think Tank with Ben Wattenberg*, PBS Think Tank series (October 2005), p. 2; Hartwig Pautz, "Think Tanks in Scotland," paper presented at the Fifty-Fifth Political Studies Association Annual Conference, Leeds, UK, April 4–7, 2005, pp. 2–5.

3. Medvetz, "Think Tanks as an Emergent Field," p. 9.

4. Rich, *Think Tanks, Public Policy, and the Politics of Expertise*, p. 11; Pautz, "Think Tanks in Scotland," p. 2.

5. McGann and Weaver, Think Tanks and Civil Societies, p. 4.

6. Stone, Denham, and Garnett, *Think Tanks across Nations*, p. 3.

7. Smith, *The Idea Brokers*, p. xiii.

8. Paul Dickson, *Think Tanks* (New York: Ballantine Books, 1972), pp. 26–31.

9. See Diane Stone and Heike Ullrich, *Policy Research Institutes and Thinktanks in Western Europe : Developments, Trends, and Perspectives* (Budapest : Open Society Institute, 2003), p. VII, and Hartwig Pautz, "Think Tanks in Scotland," paper delivered at the 55th Political Studies Association Annual Conference, April 4–7, 2005, p. 5.

10. Donald Abelson, *A Capitol Idea: Think Tanks and U.S. Foreign Policy* (McGill-Queen's University Press, 2006), p. 10.

11. Smith, *The Idea Brokers*, p. xiv.

12. Howard Wiarda, *Think Tanks and Foreign Policy: The Foreign Policy Research Institute and Presidential Politics* (Lanham, Md.: Lexington Books, 2010), pp. 30–31.

13. James McGann, "Think Tanks and the Transnationalization of Foreign Policy," *U.S. Foreign Policy Agenda* 7, no. 3 (November 2002), pp. 1–2 (http://usinfo.state.gov /journals).

14. Weaver, "The Changing World of Think Tanks."

15. DeMuth, "Thinking about Think Tanks," p. 2.

16. Weaver, "The Changing World of Think Tanks," p. 564.

17. Ibid.

18. Donald Abelson, "Think Tanks and U.S. Foreign Policy: A Historical Perspective," *U.S. Foreign Policy Agenda* 7, no. 3 (November 2002), p. 11.

19. James McGann, "Academics to Ideologues: A Brief History of the Public Policy Research Institute," *PS: Political Science and Politics* 25, no. 4 (December 1992), p. 734.

20. Ibid.

21. Ibid., p. 735.

22. Medvetz, "Think Tanks as an Emergent Field," p. 10.

23. Thomas Medvetz, "Hybrid Intellectuals: Toward a Theory of Think Tanks and Public Policy Experts in the United States" (December 2007), p. 1 (http://socialsciences .cornell.edu/wp-content/uploads/2013/06/Medvetz.hybrid.pdf).

24. Diane Stone and Andrew Denham, eds., *Think Tank Traditions: Policy Research and the Politics of Ideas* (Manchester University Press, 2004), pp. 3–4.

25. Ibid.

26. For an excellent discussion of the role of think tanks in Washington, D.C., see Richard N. Haass, "Think Tanks and U.S. Foreign Policy: A Policy-Maker's Perspective," *U.S. Foreign Policy Agenda* 7, no. 3 (November 2002), pp. 5–8. For an overview of the changing role of think tanks, see McGann, "Think Tanks and the Transnationalization of Foreign Policy."

27. Diane Stone, "Think Tank Transnationalisation and Non-Profit Analysis, Advice, and Advocacy," *Global Society: Journal of Interdisciplinary International Relations* 14, no. 2 (April 2000), p. 3.

28. McGann, "Think Tanks and the Transnationalization of Foreign Policy," pp. 13–18, 14.

29. Helle Dale and Robert O. Boorstin, "Influence of Think Tanks on U.S. Foreign Policy Formulation," Foreign Press Center Briefing (U.S. Department of State, February 28, 2006) (http://fpc.state.gov/fpc/64440.htm).

30. McGann, "Think Tanks and the Transnationalization of Foreign Policy," p. 14.

31. Tuğrul Keskingoren and Patrick R. Halpern, "Behind Closed Doors: Elite Politics, Think Tanks, and U.S. Foreign Policy," *Insight Turkey* 7, no. 2 (April–June 2005), pp. 99–113, 102.

32. McGann, "Think Tanks and the Transnationalization of Foreign Policy," p. 14.

33. Ibid., p. 15.

34. Ibid.

35. James G. McGann, "The Global 'Go-To Think Tanks,'" University of Pennsylvania (http://repository.upenn.edu/ttcsp/).

36. McGann, "Think Tanks and the Transnationalization of Foreign Policy," p. 15.

37. Ibid.

38. McGann, "Academics to Ideologues."

39. Weaver, "The Changing World of Think Tanks," p. 564.

40. McGann, "The Global 'Go-To Think Tanks.'"

41. A survey of U.S. policymakers a few years back found that members of the legislative and executive branches only have time to read thirty minutes a day.

42. Weaver, "The Changing World of Think Tanks," pp. 63–78, 563–78, 565–67.

43. David Ricci, *The Transformation of American Think Tanks: The New Washington and the Rise of Think Tanks* (Yale University Press, 1993).

44. Murray Weidenbaum, *The Competition of Ideas: The World of Washington Think Tanks* (New Brunswick, N.J.: Transaction Publishers), pp. 222–23.

45. James G. McGann, *Think Tanks and Policy Advice in the United States: Academic, Advisors, and Advocates* (London: Routledge, 2007).

46. James A. Thomson, Thomson at Twenty: Insights from the President of RAND, vol. 33, no. 3 (Winter 2009–10) (Santa Monica, Calif.: RAND Corporation, 2010).

47. Lee Michael Katz, "American Think Tanks—Their Influence Is on the Rise," *Carnegie Reporter* 5, no. 2 (Spring 2009), p. 4.

48. McGann, "Think Tanks and Policy Advice in the United States."

49. Rich, *Think Tanks, Public Policy, and the Politics of Expertise.*

50. Peter Singer, "Factories to Call Our Own: How to Understand Washington's Ideas Industry," *The Washingtonian*, August 2010, p. 44.

51. David Weigel, "Conservative Think Tanks Adjust to Tough Times," *Washington Independent*, March 13, 2009 (http://washingtonindependent.com/33697/conservative-thinktank-adjusts-to-tough-times).

52. Thomas B. Edsall, "Rich Liberals Vow to Fund Think Tanks," *Washington Post*, August 7, 2005, A01 (www.washingtonpost.com/wp-dyn/content/article/2005/08/06/AR2005080600848.html).

53. Democracy Alliance, "About the Alliance" (www.democracyalliance.org/about.php).

54. Silvia Montoya and Rachel Swanger, "Ideas for Policymakers: Enhancing the Impact of Think Tanks," *Policy Insight* 1, no. 2 (April 2007) (www.rand.org/pubs/corpo rate_pubs/2007/RAND_CP521-2007-04.pdf).

55. Stephen Boucher and others, *Europe and Its Think Tanks: A Promise to Be Fulfilled* (Paris: Notre Europe, 2004), p. 7 (www.notre-europe.asso.fr/article.php3?id _article=538).

56. Abelson, *A Capitol Idea*, p. 51.

57. Smith, *The Idea Brokers.*

58. Abelson, *A Capitol Idea*, p. 50.

59. Smith, *The Idea Brokers*, pp. 3, 10.

60. Rich, *Think Tanks, Public Policy, and the Politics of Expertise*, p. 36.

61. McGann, "Think Tanks and the Transnationalization of Foreign Policy," p. 14.

62. Katz, "American Think Tanks," p. 2.

63. Rich, Think Tanks, Public Policy, and the Politics of Expertise, p. 41.

64. Haass, "Think Tanks and U.S. Foreign Policy," pp. 5–8, 7.

65. Ibid., pp. 5–6.

66. Katz, "American Think Tanks," p. 2.

67. Stone, Denham, and Garnett, *Think Tanks across Nations*, pp. 110–11.

68. Smith, *The Idea Brokers*, p. 13.

69. Ibid., p. 12.

70. McGann, "Academics to Ideologues."

71. Resources for the Future, *Resources for the Future the First 25 Years 1952–1977* (Washington, 1977).

72. See Abelson, "Think Tanks and U.S. Foreign Policy," pp. 9–12, 11; also Abelson, *A Capitol Idea*, p. 76.

73. Katz, "American Think Tanks," p. 15.

74. Abelson, *A Capitol Idea*, pp. 78, 79.

75. Anuradha Mittal and Felicia Gustin, *Turning the Tide: Challenging the Right on Campus* (Oakland, Calif.: Institute for Democratic Education and Culture—Speak Out and the Oakland Institute, 2006), p. 12.

76. Jean Stefancic and Richard Delgado, *No Mercy: How Conservative Think Tanks and Foundations Changed America's Social Agenda* (Temple University Press, 1996), p. 3.

77. Smith, *The Idea Brokers*, p. 6.

78. Ibid., p. 7.

79. McGann and Weaver, *Think Tanks and Civil Societies.*

80. Abelson, "Think Tanks and U.S Foreign Policy," pp. 9–12, 11.

81. Ibid.

82. Katz, "American Think Tanks," p. 2.

83. IPS, "IPS History: 1963 to Today" (www.ips-dc.org/about/history).

84. Richard Haass and James McGann, "Edited Report" (January 6, 2008, personal e-mail).

85. Katz, "American Think Tanks," pp. 3, 1, 8.

86. Donald Abelson, "Mission Statement," Nixon Center for Peace and Freedom (www.nixoncenter.org/index.cfm?action=showpage&page=missionstatement).

87. James G. McGann, *The Competition for Dollars, Scholars and Influence* (University Press of America, 1994).

88. Stone, Denham, and Garnett, *Think Tanks across Nations*, p. 114.

89. Abelson, *A Capitol Idea*, p. 90.

90. Rich, *Think Tanks, Public Policy, and the Politics of Expertise*, pp. 7, 9, 10.

91. Ibid., pp. 4–5.

92. Ibid., p. 6.

93. James G. McGann, *Think Tank Impact Assessment Report* (Philadelphia: Foreign Policy Research Institute, 2008).

94. Rich, *Think Tanks, Public Policy, and the Politics of Expertise*, pp. 131–37.

95. McGann and Weaver, *Think Tanks and Civil Societies*, p. 14.

96. Ibid.

97. James McGann, "NGO Pushback: The Use of Legal and Extralegal Means to Constrain Think Tanks and Civil Society Organizations" (Philadelphia: Foreign Policy Research Institute, July 30, 2007).

98. James McGann, *2007 Survey of Think Tanks: A Summary Report* (Philadelphia: Foreign Policy Research Institute, 2007); James McGann and Stephen Boucher, "Think Tanks in Europe and America: Converging or Diverging?," Notre Europe, December 13, 2004 (www.notre-europe.eu/uploads/tx_publication/Semi22-en.pdf).

99. See James McGann and Erik Johnson, *Comparative Tanks, Politics and Public Policy* (London: Edward Elgar, March 2006); McGann and Weaver, *Think Tanks and Civil Societies*; Stone and Denham, *Think Tank Traditions*; Stephen Boucher, Martine Royo, and Pascal Lamy, *Les Think Tanks: Cerveaux de la Guerre des Idées* (Paris: Editions du Félin, 2006); Boucher and others, *Europe and Its Think Tanks*; Juliette Ebélé and Stephen Boucher, *Think Tanks in Central Europe: From the Soviet Legacy to the European Acquis* (New York: Freedom House, 2005) (www.freedomhouse.hu/pdfdocs/Think%20Tanks%20in%20Central%20Europe.pdf); Europe 2020, "What Common EU Policy toward North America by 2020?" (europe2020.org/spip/spip.php?article214&lang=en); EPIN, "Ideas, Influence and Transparency—What Could Think Tanks Learn and Contribute?," EPIN Think Tanks Task Force meeting, 2005.

100. McGann and Weaver, *Think Tanks and Civil Societies*.

101. Ibid.

102. McGann, "European Think Tanks," Working Paper (Philadelphia: Foreign Policy Research Institute, Spring 2006), p. 13.

103. Stone and Denham, *Think Tank Traditions*.

104. Open Europe, "The Hard Sell: EU Communication Policy and the Campaign for Hearts and Minds," December 27, 2008 (www.openeurope.org.uk/research/hardsell.pdf).

105. Boucher, Royo, and Lamy, *Les Think Tanks*.

106. EPIN, "Ideas, Influence and Transparency," p. 2.

107. McGann and Weaver, *Think Tanks and Civil Society*, p. 14.

108. McGann, *Think Tanks and Policy Advice in the United States*, p. 17.

109. Katz, "American Think Tanks."

110. Richard Haass in McGann, *Think Tanks and Policy Advice in the United States*, p. 92.

111. Katz, "American Think Tanks," p. 1.

112. Ibid., p. 6.

113. Joseph Nye, "Bridging the Gap between Theory and Policy," *Political Psychology* 29, no. 4 (2008), p. 600.

114. Notre Europe, "Think Tanks in Europe and America," 2006, pp. 3–4.

115. Ibid.

116. Matt Bai, "Notion Building," *New York Times*, October 12, 2003.

117. McGann, *Think Tanks and Policy Advice in the United States*, p. 30.

118. Ibid., pp. 26–28.

119. McGann and Weaver, *Think Tanks and Civil Societies*, p. 15.

120. Ibid., p. 16

121. McGann, "Think Tanks and the Transnationalization of Foreign Policy," pp. 16–17.

122. Dale and Boorstin, "Influence of Think Tanks on U.S. Foreign Policy Formulation."

123. Haass, "Think Tanks and U.S. Foreign Policy," p. 6.

124. Abelson, *Do Think Tanks Matter?*, p. 60.

125. Ibid.

126. McGann, *Think Tanks and Policy Advice in the United States*.

127. James G. McGann, "Think Tanks and Governments Bridging the Gap," presented at U.S. State Department Speakers Program, Rome, Naples, and Milan, November 19–22, 2012.

128. McGann, *Think Tanks and Policy Advice in the United States*, pp. 26–28.

129. Stone, "Think Tank Transnationalisation and Non-Profit Analysis, Advice, and Advocacy," pp. 153–72, 154.

130. Kathleen McNutt and Gregory Marchildon, "Think Tanks and the Web: Measuring Visibility and Influence," *Canadian Public Policy* 35, no. 2 (2009), p. 6.

131. Ibid., p. 3.

132. McGann and Weaver, *Think Tanks and Civil Societies*, p. 568.

133. McGann, "Think Tanks and the Transnationalization of Foreign Policy," p. 16.

134. Haass, "Think Tanks and U.S. Foreign Policy," p. 5.

135. RAND, "Core Research Areas" (http://rand.org/research_areas/).

136. RAND, "Thomson at Twenty: Insights from the President of RAND," *Rand Review* (Winter 2009–10).

137. Dale and Boorstin, "Influence of Think Tanks on U.S. Foreign Policy Formulation."

138. Hugh Gusterson, "The Sixth Branch: Think Tanks as Auditors," Social Science Research Council, March 2009 (www.ssrc.org/workspace/images/crm/new_publication _3/%7B12246172-7d36-de11-afac-001cc477ec70%7D.pdf).

139. Anthony M. Bertelli and Jeffrey Wenger, "Demanding Information: Think Tanks and the U.S. Congress," *British Journal of Political Science* 39 (2009), p. 250.

140. Ibid., p. 228.

141. Ibid.

142. Haass and McGann, "Edited Report."

143. Dale and Boorstin, "Influence of Think Tanks on U.S. Foreign Policy Formulation."

144. Haass and McGann, "Edited Report."

145. McGann, "Think Tanks and the Transnationalization of Foreign Policy," p. 16.

146. Robert Ranquet, *Think Tanks and the National Security Strategy Formulation Process: A Comparison of Current American and French Patterns* (National Defense University, 1995), p. 17.

147. Haass, "Think Tanks and U.S. Foreign Policy," p. 7.

148. Ibid.

149. Weaver, "The Changing World of Think Tanks," p. 569.

Chapter Two

1. Lee Michael Katz, "American Think Tanks—Their Influence Is on the Rise," *Carnegie Reporter* 5, no. 2 (Spring 2009), p. 13; Richard N. Haass, "Think Tanks and U.S. Foreign Policy: A Policy-Maker's Perspective," *U.S. Foreign Policy Agenda* 7, no. 3 (November 2002), p. 7.

2. See Diane Stone and others, "Bridging Research and Policy," paper presented at the Bridging Research and Policy International Workshop, Warwick University Coventry, UK, July 16–17 2001.

3. See Strobe Talbott in Katz, "American Think Tanks," p. 13.

4. Howard J. Wiarda, *Think Tanks and Foreign Policy: The Foreign Policy Research Institute and Presidential Politics* (Lanham, Md.: Lexington Books, 2010), p. 31; Katz, "American Think Tanks," p. 13.

5. Haass, "Think Tanks and U.S. Foreign Policy," p. 5; Stone concurs on a number of these points (civic education, broad output, conveners, marketing, and advocacy pursuits).

6. Diane Stone, "Think Tank Transnationalisation and Non-Profit Analysis, Advice, and Advocacy," *Global Society: Journal of Interdisciplinary International Relations* 14, no. 2 (2000), p. 3.

7. Haass, "Think Tanks and U.S. Foreign Policy," p. 8.

8. See Representative Jane Harman in Katz, "American Think Tanks," for example, who shares this notion; Donald Abelson, *Do Think Tanks Matter? Assessing the Impact of Public Policy Institutes* (McGill-Queen's University Press, 2002); Lindquist, "Three Decades of Canadian Think Tanks," in *Think Tank Traditions: Policy Research and the Politics of Ideas*, edited by Diane Stone and Andrew Denham (Manchester University Press, 2004); and Stone, "Think Tank Transnationalisation and Non-Profit Analysis, Advice, and Advocacy."

9. Hartwig Pautz, "Think Tanks in Scotland," paper presented at the Fifty-Fifth Political Studies Association Annual Conference, Leeds, UK, April 4–7 2005.

10. Wiarda, *Think Tanks and Foreign Policy*, p. 29.

11. Haass, "Think Tanks and U.S. Foreign Policy," p. 8.

12. Diane Stone, *Capturing the Political Imagination: Think Tanks and the Policy Process* (London, Frank Cass, 1996), p. 23.

13. Richard N. Haass, "Think Tanks and U.S. Foreign Policy: A Policy-Makers Perspective," November 1, 2002 (http://2001-2009.state.gov/s/p/rem/15506.htm).

14. Katz, "American Think Tanks."

15. Ibid., p. 6.

16. Ibid.

17. Ibid., p. 1.

18. Joseph Nye, "Scholars on the Sidelines," *Washington Post*, April 13, 2009, A15.

19. Helle Dale and Robert O. Boorstin, "Influence of Think Tanks on U.S. Foreign Policy Formulation," Foreign Press Center Briefing. U.S. Department of State, Washington, D.C., February 28, 2006 (http://fpc.state.gov/fpc/64440.htm).

20. Donald E. Abelson and Christine M. Carberry, "Policy Experts in Presidential Campaigns: A Model of Think Tank Recruitment," *Presidential Studies Quarterly* 27, no. 4 (Fall 1997), pp. 679–98.

21. Dale and Boorstin, "Influence of Think Tanks on U.S. Foreign Policy Formulation."

22. Abelson and Carberry, "Policy Experts in Presidential Campaigns."

23. Council on Foreign Relations, Richard N. Haass webpage (www.cfr.org/bios /3350/richard_haass.html); Mike Huckabee, interview on *Late Edition with Wolf Blitzer*, YouTube, December 16, 2007 (http://youtube.com/watch?v=YEEDs35vEYw).

24. Deborah Solomon, "Questions for David Frum: Right Hand Man," *New York Times Magazine*, January 6, 2008 (www.nytimes.com/2008/01/06/magazine/06wwln-Q4 -t.html?ex=1357275600&en=790838f3acd552d2&ei=5088&partner=rssnyt&emc=rss).

25. "The War over the Wonks," *Washington Post*, October 2, 2007 (www.washing tonpost.com/wp-srv/opinions/documents/the-war-over-the-wonks.html).

26. Ibid.

27. Hudson Institute, Charles Horner webpage (www.hudson.org/learn/index .cfm?fuseaction=staff_bio&eid=CharHorner); James McGann, "Think Tanks and Foreign Policy," January 2, 2008.

28. Barack Obama, "Strengthening Our Common Security by Investing in Our Common Humanity" (www.cgdev.org/doc/blog/obama_strengthen_security.pdf).

29. "The War over the Wonks."

30. Hillary Rodham Clinton, "Security and Opportunity for the Twenty-first Century," *Foreign Affairs*, November–December 2007.

31. Ibid.

32. See Haass in James G. McGann, *Think Tanks and Policy Advice in the United States: Academic, Advisors and Advocate* (London: Routledge, 2007), p. 92.

33. Haass, "Think Tanks and U.S. Foreign Policy," p. 7.

34. Donald Abelson, *A Capitol Idea: Think Tanks and U.S. Foreign Policy* (McGill-Queen's University Press, 2006), pp. 14–15.

35. Haass, "Think Tanks and U.S. Foreign Policy," p. 7.

36. Katz, "American Think Tanks," p. 3.

Chapter Three

1. Alex J. Pollock, *A New Approach to Personal Social Security Accounts* (Washington: American Enterprise Institute) (www.aei.org/).

2. Social Security Administration, "Social Security Basic Facts" (www.ssa.gov/news /press/basicfact.html).

3. President's Commission to Strengthen Social Security, "Strengthening Social Security and Creating Personal Wealth for All Americans," December 21, 2001 (www .csss.gov/reports/Final_report.pdf).

4. Lori Montgomery, "Deficit Panel Leaders Propose Curbs on Social Security, Major Cuts in Spending, Tax Breaks," *Washington Post*, November 11, 2010 (www .washingtonpost.com/wp-dyn/content/article/2010/11/10/AR2010111004029.html?sid =ST2010111606900).

5. Fiscal Commission, *Statement of Senator Max Baucus* (Washington: National Commission on Fiscal Responsibility and Reform, 2010) (www.fiscalcommission.gov /sites/fiscalcommission.gov/files/documents/MemberStatements.pdf).

6. *Saving Social Security: Which Way to Reform* (Brookings, 2003) (www.brookings .edu/events/2003/12/10community-development). Michael D. Tanner, "Take Advantage of Private Accounts' High Return Rate," *Indianapolis Star*, August 31, 2008 (www.cato.org/publications/commentary/take-advantage-private-accounts-high -return-rate).

7. President's Commission to Strengthen Social Security, "Strengthening Social Security and Creating Personal Wealth for All Americans."

8. Campaign for America's Future, "Bush Social Security Commission Members: Who Are They?," May 10, 2001 (www.ourfuture.org/news-releases/bush-social-security -commission-members-who-are-they).

9. Peter A. Diamond and Peter R. Orszag, *Saving Social Security: A Balanced Approach* (Washington: Brookings, 2004), p. xxiv.

10. George C. Edwards, *Governing by Campaigning: the Politics of the Bush Presidency* (New York: Pearson Longman, 2008), pp. 425–26. Brian M. Riedl and Alison Acosta Fraser, *How to Reform Entitlement Spending* (Washington: Heritage Foundation, 2009), p. 4 (www.heritage.org/research/reports/2009/01/how-to-reform-entitlement-spending -a-memo-to-president-elect-obama).

11. John McCain, "On Social Security" (www.ontheissues.org/2008/John_McCain _Social_Security.htm).

12. Jason Furman, *An Analysis of Using 'Progressive Price Indexing' to Set Social Security Benefits* (Washington: CBPP, 2005) (www.cbpp.org/cms/index.cfm?fa=view&id =48).

13. Christian E. Weller and Jeffrey B Wenger, *Let Us Count the Ways: The Costs of Social Security Privatization Are in the Details* (Washington: CAP, 2004) (www .americanprogress.org/issues/economy/news/2004/11/18/1207/let-us-count-the-ways -the-costs-of-social-security-privatization-are-in-the-details/).

14. Radha Chaurushiya and Christian Weller, "Social Security Privatization: Abandoning Family Values," CAP, April 2005 (www.americanprogress.org/issues /economy/news/2005/04/27/1440/social-security-privatization-abandoning-family -values/).

15. Weller and Wenger, *Let Us Count the Ways*.

16. Lawrence Mishel, *Lifting Cap on Social Security Taxes Would Rescue Retirement Program* (Washington: EPI, 2005) (www.epi.org/publications/entry/webfeatures _viewpoints_lifting_cap_on_SS_taxes/). John Irons, *Raising Cap on Social Security*

Tax Best Way to Fix Shortfall (Washington: EPI, 2009) (www.epi.org/analysis
_and_opinion/entry/raising_cap_on_social_security_tax_best_way_to_fix
_shortfall/).

17. Diamond and Orszag, *Saving Social Security*, pp. 3–5.

18. Perry Bacon Jr., "Candidates Diverge on How to Save Social Security," *Washington Post*, July 8, 2008 (www.washingtonpost.com/wp-dyn/content/article/2008/07/07/AR2008070702773.html).

19. Thomas E. MaCurdy and Eugene Smolensky, "Farewell, Welfare," video (Palo Alto, Calif.: Hoover Institution, 1997) (www.hoover.org/research/farewell-welfare).

20. Steve Hayward, The Shocking Success of Welfare Reform (Palo Alto, Calif.: Hoover Institution, 1998) (www.hoover.org/research/shocking-success-welfare-reform).

21. Isabel V. Sawhill, *Welfare Reform: An Analysis of the Issues* (Washington: Urban Institute, 1995) (http://webarchive.urban.org/publications/306620.html).

22. Hoover Institution, "Going for Broke? Welfare Reform" (www.hoover.org/research/going-broke-welfare-reform).

23. Ron Haskins, "Testimony of Ron Haskins, Senior Fellow, Brookings Institution, Washington DC, Senior Consultant, Annie E. Casey Foundation, Baltimore, Before the Committee on Finance, U.S. Senate," Brookings, February 2, 2003 (www.brookings.edu/~/media/Files/rc/testimonies/2003/0220welfare_haskins/2003 0220.pdf).

24. Kay S. Hymowitz, "Endangered Welfare Reform," *City Journal*, July 22, 2012 (www.city-journal.org/2012/eon0722kh.html).

25. Robert E. Rector, *Why Expanding Welfare Will Not Help the Poor* (Washington: Heritage Foundation, 1993) (www.heritage.org/research/lecture/why-expanding-welfare-will-not-help-the-poor).

26. Haskins, "Testimony of Ron Haskins." Michael Tanner, *Michael Tanner's Testimony on Social Security Reform before the House Ways and Means Committee* (Washington: Cato Institute, 2005) (www.cato.org/publications/congressional-testimony/michael-tanners-testimony-social-security-reformbefore-house-ways-means-committee).

27. Sawhill, *Welfare Reform*.

28. David A. Super and others, *The New Welfare Law—Summary* (Washington: CBPP, 1996) (www.cbpp.org/WCNSUM.HTM).

29. *Urban Institute Study Confirms that Welfare Bills Would Increase Child Poverty* (Washington: CBPP). See www.cbpp.org/URBAN726.HTM.

30. Tanner, *Michael Tanner's Testimony on Social Security Reform*.

31. Robert E. Rector, "Why Congress Must Reform Welfare" (www.heritage.org/Research/Welfare/BG1063.cfm).

32. Alan Weil and Kenneth Finegold, *Welfare Reform: The Next Act* (Washington: Urban Institute Press, 2003); Haskins, "Testimony of Ron Haskins"; Robert Rector and Patrick F. Fagan, *The Continuing Good News about Welfare Reform* (Washington: Heritage Foundation, 2003) (www.heritage.org/research/reports/2003/02/the-continuing-good-news).

33. National Health Expenditure Data, Baltimore, Md., Centers for Medicare and Medicaid Services (www.cms.hhs.gov/); Institute of Medicine, *Insuring America's*

Health: Principles and Recommendations (Washington: National Academies of Science, 2004) (http://iom.nationalacademies.org/Reports/2004/Insuring-Americas -Health-Principles-and-Recommendations.aspx).

34. "Timeline of the Health Care Debate," *PBS Newshour* (www.democraticunder ground.com/discuss/duboard.php?az=view_all&address=389x4633336).

35. Ibid.

36. Suzanne Garment, "Starting Over: Domestic Issues: Is Lack of Focus the Problem?" *Los Angeles Times*, July 3, 1994 (http://articles.latimes.com/1994-07-03/opinion /op-11340_1_health-care-reform).

37. Bob Woodward, *The Agenda: Inside the Clinton White House* (New York: Simon & Schuster, 1994), p. 316.

38. Adam Clymer and others, "The Health Care Debate: What Went Wrong? How the Health Care Campaign Collapse," *New York Times*, August 19, 1994.

39. Judith Rodin and Stephen P. Steinberg, *Public Discourse in America* (University of Pennsylvania Press, 2011), p. 100.

40. Brink Lindsey, "Patient Power: The Cato Institute's Plan for Health Care Reform," Briefing Paper no. 19 (Cato Institute, October 4, 1993) (www.cato.org/publications /briefing-paper/patient-power-cato-institutes-plan-health-care-reform).

41. John Goodman, National Center for Policy Analysis (www.ncpa.org/abo/staff /jcgoodman.html).

42. Robert E. Moffit, Heritage Foundation (www.heritage.org/about/staff/m /robert-moffit).

43. James Atlas, "The Counter Counterculture," *New York Times*, February 12, 1995 (www.nytimes.com/1995/02/12/magazine/the-counter-counterculture.html).

44. William Kristol, "How to Oppose the Clinton Healthcare Plan—and Why," Ashbrook Center, Ashland University, January 1994 (http://ashbrook.org/publications /onprin-v2n1-kristol/).

45. Jon Meacham, "The GOP's Master Strategist," *Washington Monthly*, September 1, 1994 (http://findarticles.com/p/articles/mi_m1316/is_n9_v26/ai_15856832/pg_6 ?tag=artBody;col1).

46. Ibid.

47. Peter Flaherty and Timothy Flaherty, "Chapter Nine: Healthcare," in *The First Lady: A Comprehensive View of Hillary Rodham Clinton*, edited by Peter Flaherty and Timothy Flaherty (Lafayette, La.: Vital Issues Press, 1996) (http://nlpc.org/sites /default/files/The%20First%20Lady-%20Health%20Care.pdf).

48. Ibid.

49. *Clinton Health Care Task Force Working Groups/Participants* (Tucson, Ariz.: Association of American Physicians and Surgeons, 1993) (www.aapsonline.org/clinton /AAPS/WORKING.PDF).

50. "The War over the Wonks," *Washington Post*, October 2, 2007 (www.washington post.com/wp-srv/opinions/documents/the-war-over-the-wonks.html).

51. Richard Brown (www.healthpolicy.ucla.edu/bio.asp?staffID=4).

52. "The First Presidential Debate," *New York Times*, September 26, 2008 (http:// elections.nytimes.com/2008/president/debates/transcripts/first-presidential-debate

.html); "Timeline: Milestones in Obama's Health Care Reform," Reuters, March 22, 2010 (www.reuters.com/article/idU.S.TRE62L0JA20100322).

53. Liz Goodwin, "Supreme Court Upholds Obamacare Individual Mandate as a Tax," *ABC News*, June 28, 2012 (http://abcnews.go.com/Politics/OTUS/supreme -court-upholds-obamacare-individual-mandate-tax/story?id=16669186).

54. "Obamacare Upheld by the U.S. Supreme Court," *National Post*, June 28, 2012 (http://news.nationalpost.com/2012/06/28/obamacare-upheld-by-the-u-s-supreme -court/).

55. Marc B. McClellan, *Show Me the Money: Options for Financing Health Reform* (Brookings, 2009) (www.brookings.edu/speeches/2009/0731_healthreform_mcclellan .aspx); Joseph Antos and others, "Bending the Curve: Effective Steps to Address Long- Term Health Care Spending Growth" (Brookings Institution, September 2009) (www .brookings.edu/research/reports/2009/09/01-bending-the-curve-to-address-long-term- health-care-spending-growth).

56. Ellen-Marie Whelan and Lesley Russell, *Better Health Care at Lower Costs* (Washington: CAP, 2010) (www.americanprogress.org/wp-content/uploads/issues /2010/03/pdf/health_delivery.pdf).

57. Liz Weiss, *Unmarried Women Will Greatly Benefit from Health Care Reform* (Washington: CAP, 2010) (www.americanprogress.org/issues/healthcare/news/2010 /03/26/7415/unmarried-women-will-greatly-benefit-from-health-reform/).

58. Elise Gould, "The Erosion of Employer-Sponsored Health Insurance," Briefing Paper no. 223 (Washington: EPI, October 8, 2008) (www.epi.org/publications/bp223/).

59. Katie Donohue and David Kendall, *Health Coverage for All* (Washington: Progres- sive Policy Institute, 2007) (www.ppionline.org/ppi_ci.cfm?knlgAreaID=111&subsecid =137&contentid=254475); David Kendall, *Health Care Costs and Malpractice Reform* (Washington: Progressive Policy Institute, 2008) (www.ppionline.org/ppi_ci.cfm?knlg AreaID=111&subsecID=138&contentID=254574); David B. Kendall, *Fixing America's Health Care System* (Washington: Progressive Policy Institute, 2005) (www.ppionline.org /ppi_ci.cfm?kaid=111&subid=138&contentid=253538).

60. Dean Baker, *The Passage of Health Care Reform: Time to Talk Seriously about Health Care* (Washington: Center for Economic and Policy Research, 2010) (www .cepr.net/index.php/op-eds-&-columns/op-eds-&-columns/time-to-talk-seriously -about-health-care/).

61. Paul N. Van de Water and James R. Horney, *Health Reform Will Reduce the Deficit* (Washington: CBPP, 2010) (www.cbpp.org/cms/index.cfm?fa=view&id =3134).

62. Beverly Goldberg, *Help, I've Fallen into the Doughnut Hole and I Can't Get Up: The Problems with Medicare* (Washington: Century Foundation, 2008) (www .healthpolicywatch.org/publications.asp?pubid=664).

63. Ruy Teixeira, *The Snapshot: Time for Comprehensive Health Care Reform* (Wash- ington: Century Foundation, 2010) (www.healthpolicywatch.org/commentary.asp ?opedid=2583). Alternatively, see "Public Opinion Snapshot: Time for Comprehensive Health Care Reform" (www.americanprogress.org/issues/public-opinion/news/2010 /03/01/7387/public-opinion-snapshot-time-for-comprehensive-health-care-reform/).

64. Senator Howard Baker, Senator Tom Daschle, and Senator Bob Dole, *Crossing Our Lines: Working Together to Reform the U.S. Health System* (Washington: Bipartisan Policy Center, 2009) (http://bipartisanpolicy.org/wp-content/uploads/sites/default/files/BPC_Crossing_Our_Lines_Report.pdf).

65. New America's Health Policy Program, *The New Health Dialogue* (Washington: New America Foundation, 2010) (http://health.newamerica.net/blogmain).

66. John Yoo, *The "Individual Mandate" an Intrusion on Civil Society* (Washington: AEI, 2010) (www.aei.org/publication/the-individual-mandate-an-intrusion-on-civil-society/).

67. John E. Calfee, *Pricing Out Private Insurance* (Washington: AEI, 2010) (www.aei.org/publication/pricing-out-private-insurance/).

68. Charles R. Kesler, *From the Archives: Kesler on Repealing Obamacare* (Upland, Calif.: Claremont Institute, 2010).

69. Kathryn Nix, "Side Effects: Medical Devices Tax Will Cost Jobs," *Daily Signal*, March 30 2010 (http://dailysignal.com//2010/03/30/side-effects-medical-devices-tax-will-costs-jobs).

70. Herbert I. London, *Healthcare Sends America down the Path of Tyranny* (Washington: Hudson Institute, 2010) (www.hudson.org/index.cfm?fuseaction=publication_details&id=6865).

71. Irwin Stelzer, *United States Is Looking More and More European* (Washington: Hudson Institute, 2010) (www.hudson.org/index.cfm?fuseaction=publication_details&id=6864&pubType=Health).

72. Catherine Holahan, *Health Care Reform: Who Wins and Who Loses* (Dallas: National Center for Policy Analysis, 2010) (www.ncpa.org/sub/dpd/index.php?Article_ID=19134).

73. Kate Pickert, "Understanding the Health-Care Debate: Your Indispensable Guide," *Time*, August 17, 2009 (www.time.com/time/healthcaredebate).

74. Carmen Cox, "White House Pushes Back against McKinsey Healthcare Report," *ABC News Radio*, June 8, 2011 (http://abcnewsradioonline.com/business-news/white-house-pushes-back-against-mckinsey-healthcare-report.html).

75. Nancy-Ann DeParle, "Getting Insurance at Work," *White House Blog*, June 8, 2011 (www.whitehouse.gov/blog/2011/06/08/getting-insurance-work).

76. Democratic National Committee, "Next to You: Someone You Know Has Been Helped by Health Reform," video (http://origin.healthcare.democrats.org/video/?source=DHL); Democratic Party, "We Stand for Health Care" (www.democrats.org/issues/health_care).

77. Jennifer Haberkorn, "In RNC Speech, Mitt Romney Gives Passing Mentions to Health Care, Medicare," *Politico*, August 30, 2012 (www.politico.com/news/stories/0812/80509.html).

78. John Presta, "Bill Clinton Debunks the Mitt Romney and Paul Ryan Arguments against Obamacare," *Examiner*, September 6, 2012 (www.examiner.com/article/bill-clinton-debunks-the-mitt-romney-and-paul-ryan-arguments-against-obamacare).

79. Bowen Garret and Matthew Buettgens, "Employer-Sponsored Insurance under Health Reform: Reports of Its Demise Are Premature," *Timely Analysis of Immediate*

Health Policy Issues (Urban Institute, January 2011) (www.urban.org/uploaded pdf/412295-Employer-Sponsored-Insurance.pdf).

80. John Holahan and Bowen Garret, "How Will the Affordable Care Act Affect Jobs?," *Timely Analysis of Immediate Health Policy Issues* (Urban Institute, March 2011) (www.urban.org/UploadedPDF/412319-Affordable-Care-Act-Affect-Jobs.pdf).

81. Health Policy Center, "Health Care Reform" (www.urban.org/health_policy /health_care_reform/).

82. January Angeles, *Hatch-Upton Report on Costs to States of Expanding Medicaid Relies on Seriously Flawed Estimates* (Washington: CBPP, 2011) (www.cbpp.org/files/3 -16-11health.pdf).

83. Rory Thompson and Matt Broaddus, *Employer-Based Health Coverage Declined Sharply over Past Decade* (Washington: CBPP, 2010) (www.cbpp.org/cms/index.cfm ?fa=view&id=3335).

84. Henry J. Aaron, *Multiple Fictions Drive Opposition to Health Law* (Brookings, 2011) (www.brookings.edu/opinions/2011/0119_health_opposition_aaron.aspx).

85. Corinne Rieder, and others, *Achieving Better Chronic Care at Lower Costs Across the Health Care Continuum for Older Americans* (Brookings, Engelberg Center for Health Care Reform, 2010) (www.brookings.edu/~/media/research/files/papers/2010 /10/28-long-term-care/final-ltc-paper-102810.pdf).

86. Alice M. Rivlin, *Health Reform: Last Call for Competitive Markets?* (Brookings, 2010) (www.brookings.edu/blogs/up-front/posts/2010/09/07-health-reform -markets-rivlin).

87. "Health" (www.epi.org/issues/category/health_care/).

88. *Health Reform Works: A Presentation on Why We Need Health Care Reform* (Washington: CAP, 2010) (www.americanprogress.org/issues/healthcare/news/2010 /06/10/7993/health-reform-works/).

89. Isabel Perera and Lesley Russell, *Better Health Means Better Business: How Minority-Owned Small Businesses Benefit from Health Care Reform* (Washington: CAP, 2011) (www.americanprogress.org/issues/healthcare/report/2011/06/08/9770 /better-health-means-better-business/).

90. Tony Carrk, *The Anniversary of the Affordable Care Act: A Year Later, the False Attacks Continue* (Washington: CAP, 2011) (www.americanprogress.org/issues/health care/report/2011/03/21/9279/the-anniversary-of-the-affordable-care-act/).

91. David A. Hyman and William M. Sage, *Do Health Reform and Malpractice Reform Fit Together?* (Washington: AEI, 2011) (http://webcache.googleusercon tent.com/search?q=cache:BMyGGMJcv4oJ:https://www.aei.org/publication/do -health-reform-and-malpractice-reform-fit-together/+&cd=1&hl=en&ct=clnk&gl =us).

92. R. Glenn Hubbard, John F. Cogan, and Daniel Kessler, *ObamaCare and the Truth about "Cost Shifting"* (Washington: AEI, 2011) (www.aei.org/publication/obama care-and-the-truth-about-cost-shifting/).

93. Anthony Lo Sasso and others, "The Secondary Spending Effects of More Primary Health Care," video (AEI, February 17, 2011) (www.aei.org/event/100371).

94. Diana Furchtgott-Roth, *Tackling the Runaway Medicare Train* (Washington: Hudson Institute, 2011) (www.realclearmarkets.com/articles/2011/04/14/tackling _the_runaway_medicare_train_98965.html).

95. Hanns Kuttner, *Politicizing Health Insurance* (Washington: Hudson Institute, 2010) (www.hudson.org/index.cfm?fuseaction=publication_details&id=6973); Critical Condition, *National Review*, April 30, 2010 (www.nationalreview.com/critical -condition/47291/politicizing-health-insurance-hanns-kuttner).

96. Richard Epstein, "Obamacare's Next Constitutional Challenge," *Backgrounder no. 2554, Hoover Daily Report*, June 7, 2011 (www.hoover.org/research/obamacares -next-constitutional-challenge).

97. Paul Winfree, *Obamacare Tax Subsidies: Bigger Deficit, Fewer Taxpayers, Damaged Economy* (Washington: Heritage Foundation, 2011) (www.heritage.org/Research /Reports/2011/05/ObamaCare-Tax-Subsidies-Bigger-Deficit-Fewer-Taxpayers-Damaged -Economy).

98. Rita E. Numerof, "Why Accountable Care Organizations Won't Deliver Better Health Care—and Market Innovation Will," *Backgrounder no. 2546*, April 18, 2011 (www.heritage.org/Research/Reports/2011/04/Why-Accountable-Care-Organiza tions-Wont-Deliver-Better-Health-Care-and-Market-Innovation-Will).

99. Robert A. Levy, *The Case against President Obama's Health Care Reform: A Primer for Nonlawyers* (Washington: Cato Institute, 2011) (www.cato.org/publications /white-paper/case-against-president-obamas-health-care-reform-primer-nonlawyers).

100. Michael D. Tanner, *Bad Medicine: A Guide to the Real Costs and Consequences of the New Health Care Law* (Washington: Cato Institute, 2011) (www.cato.org/publica tions/white-paper/bad-medicine-guide-real-costs-consequences-new-health-care-law).

101. Michael D. Tanner and Justin Owen, *Costs of Health Care Reform Becoming More Apparent* (Washington: Cato Institute, 2011) (www.cato.org/publications/com mentary/costs-health-care-reform-becoming-more-apparent).

102. "Analysis of Individual Mandate," Technical Report TR-562/1 (Santa Monica, Calif.: RAND Corporation) (www.rand.org/pubs/technical_reports/TR562z1/analy sis-of-individual-mandate.html).

103. "Few Health Reform Options Would Have Covered More People at Lower Cost than New Law," News Release, June 8, 2010 (www.rand.org/news/press/2010/06/08. html).

104. Christine Eibner and others, "Employer Self-Insurance Decisions and the Implications of the Patient Protection and Affordable Care Act as Modified by the Health Care and Education Reconciliation Act of 2010 (ACA)," Technical Report TR-971 (Santa Monica, Calif.: RAND Health, 2011) (www.rand.org/content/dam/rand/pubs /technical_reports/2011/RAND_TR971.pdf).

105. "How Will Health Care Reform Affect Costs and Coverage," Research Brief 9589 (Santa Monica, Calif.: RAND Health, 2011) (www.rand.org/content/dam /rand/pubs/research_briefs/2011/RAND_RB9589.pdf).

106. See "It's Official: U.S. Is in a Recession," *MSNBC Online*, December 1, 2008 (www.nbcnews.com/id/27999557/#.VdQGfs7vgxU); Frank Newport, "Most Americans

Say U.S. Is Now in Economic Recession," Gallup, March 19, 2008 (www.gallup.com /poll/105109/Most-Americans-Say-U.S.-Now-Economic-Recession.aspx); and *What's Driving the High Price of Oil?* (Washington: Hoover Institution, 2007) (www.hoover .org/research/focusonissues/focus/11841471.html). Also *The World Factbook: United States* (Washington: Central Intelligence Agency) (www.cia.gov/library/publications /the-world-factbook/geos/us.html).

107. Michelle Bussenius, *America's Tax Burden* (Washington: Hoover Institution, 2008) (www.hoover.org/research/focusonissues/focus/17442454.html).

108. Federal Open Market Committee, "Press Release," Board of Governors of the Federal Reserve System, December 16, 2008 (www.federalreserve.gov/newsevents /press/monetary/20081216b.htm).

109. Michelle Bussenius, *Recession and the U.S. Economy* (Washington: Hoover Institution, 2008) (www.hoover.org/research/focusonissues/focus/14776626.html); Federal Open Market Committee, "Press Release"; Heather Stewart, "U.S. Federal Reserve Keeps Interest Rates at Near-Zero Level," *Guardian*, January 28, 2009 (www .guardian.co.uk/business/2009/jan/28/federal-reserve-interest-rates-low-levels).

110. Stewart, "U.S. Federal Reserve Keeps Interest Rates at Near-Zero Level."

111. Ibid.

112. John H. Makin, *The Fed's Dilemma* (Washington: AEI, 2008) (www.aei.org /publication/the-feds-dilemma/).

113. *Determination of the December 2007 Peak in Economic Activity* (Cambridge, Mass.: Business Cycle Dating Committee, NBER (www.nber.org/cycles/dec2008 .html).

114. Bussenius, *Recession and the U.S. Economy.*

115. Martin Neil Baily, Douglas W. Elmendorf, and Robert E. Litan, *The Great Credit Squeeze: How It Happened, How to Prevent Another* (Brookings, 2008) (www .brookings.edu/research/papers/2008/05/16-credit-squeeze).

116. Ibid.

117. Ibid.

118. Scott Lilly, *Pumping Life Back into the U.S. Economy: Why a Stimulus Package Must Be Big and Targeted* (Washington: CAP, 2009) (www.americanprogress.org /wp-content/uploads/issues/2009/01/pdf/lilly_stimulus.pdf).

119. Will Straw and Michael Ettlinger, *How to Spend $350 Billion in a First Year of Economic Stimulus and Recovery* (Washington: CAP, 2008) (www.american progress.org/issues/economy/report/2008/12/05/5307/how-to-spend-350 -billion-in-a-first-year-of-stimulus-and-recovery/).

120. Baily, Elmendorf, and Litan, *The Great Credit Squeeze.*

121. Martin Neil Baily, *Don't Blame the War for the Economy* (Brookings, 2008) (www.brookings.edu/opinions/2008/04/20_war_economy_baily).

122. Bussenius, *America's Tax Burden.*

123. Ibid.

124. Isabel V. Sawhill, *Candidate Issue Index: Fiscal Responsibility* (Brookings, 2008) (www.brookings.edu/research/papers/2008/07/02-fiscal-responsibility-sawhill-opp08).

125. Jeffrey Miron, "Path to Recovery," *Harvard International Review* 4, no. 30 (Winter 2009) (http://hir.harvard.edu/archives/1847).

Chapter Four

1. CNN, "Timeline: N. Korea Nuclear Dispute," *CNN.com*, February 13, 2007 (http://www.cnn.com/2005/WORLD/asiapcf/02/10/nkorea.timeline/index.html); Fred Kaplan, "Rolling Blunder," *Washington Monthly*, May 2004 (www.washington monthly.com/features/2004/0405.kaplan.html).

2. CNN, "Timeline: North Korea's Nuclear Weapons Development," *CNN.com*, August 20, 2003 (http://www.cnn.com/2003/WORLD/asiapcf/east/08/20/nkorea .timeline.nuclear/).

3. BBC, "Timeline: North Korean Nuclear Stand-Off," *BBC News*, December 6, 2007 (http://news.bbc.co.uk/2/hi/asia-pacific/2604437.stm).

4. CNN, "Timeline: North Korea's Nuclear Weapons Development."

5. Associated Press, "Timeline: North Korea's Nuclear Development," *New York Times*, October 9, 2006 (www.nytimes.com/2006/10/09/world/asia/10chronocnd.html? _r=1&scp=1&sq=north%20korea%20timeline&st=cse).

6. CNN, "Timeline: North Korea's Nuclear Weapons Development."

7. Ibid.

8. CNN, "Timeline: North Korean Nuclear Stand-Off" (www.cnn.com/2013/10 /29/world/asia/north-korea-nuclear-timeline—fast-facts/index.html).

9. Ibid.

10. Ibid.; also Jayshree Bajoria, *Obama's North Korea Dilemma* (Washington: Council on Foreign Relations, 2008) (www.cfr.org/publication/18056/obamas_ north_korea_dilemma.html?breadcrumb=%2Fregion%2F478%2Fnortheast _asia).

11. CNN, "Timeline: North Korean Nuclear Stand-Off."

12. David Brunner and Sean Maguire, "North Korea Finalizing Launch Preparations: Officials," *Yahoo! News*, April 3, 2009 (http://news.yahoo.com/s/nm/20090403 /ts_nm/us_korea_north).

13. Choe Sang-Hun and David Sanger, "North Koreans Launch Rocket over the Pacific," *New York Times*, April 5, 2009 (www.nytimes.com/2009/04/05/world/asia /05korea.html?ref=asia).

14. Neil McFarquhar, "U.N. Council May Rebuke North Korea," *New York Times*, April 11, 2009 (www.nytimes.com/2009/04/12/world/asia/12nations.html?scp=3&sq =north%20korea&st=cse).

15. Elise Labott, "U.S. Issues Warning to North Korea for Expelling Inspectors," *CNN.com*, April 16, 2009 (www.cnn.com/2009/WORLD/asiapcf/04/16/nkorea .nuclear.inspectors.out/index.html?iref=newssearch).

16. BBC, "Timeline: North Korea," *BBC News*, September 29, 2011 (http://news .bbc.co.uk/2/hi/asia-pacific/1132268.stm).

17. "Conflict on the Korean Peninsula: Ignore Us at Your Peril," *The Economist*, November 25, 2010 (www.economist.com/node/17582000).

18. BBC. "Timeline: North Korea"; Choe Sang-Hun and Rick Gladstone, "North Korean Rocket Fails Moments after Liftoff," *New York Times*, April 12, 2012 (www .nytimes.com/2012/04/13/world/asia/north-korea-launches-rocket-defying-world -warnings.html?pagewanted=all).

19. Richard D. Fisher, *Fixing Jimmy Carter's Mistakes: Regaining the Initiative against North Korea* (Washington: Heritage Foundation, 8 July 1994) (www.heritage .org/Research/AsiaandthePacific/asb131.cfm).

20. Baker Spring and James H. Anderson, *Making the Case for Missile Defense* (Washington: Heritage Foundation, 1998) (www.heritage.org/Research/MissileDefense /BG1225.cfm).

21. CNN, "Timeline: North Korea's Nuclear Weapons Development."

22. William J. Taylor, *North Korea: Avoid another Crossroads* (Berkeley, Calif.: Nautilus Institute, 13 March 2001) (www.nautilus.org/fora/security/0102F_Taylor .html).

23. People for the American Way, "Right Wing Affiliations of Bush Officials" (www .pfaw.org/pfaw/general/default.aspx?oid=6250).

24. CNN, "Timeline: North Korea's Nuclear Weapons Development."

25. BBC, "Timeline: North Korea"; Balbina Y. Hwang, *Giving In to Nuclear Black-mail* (Washington: Heritage Foundation, 2004) (www.heritage.org/Press/Commentary /ed100304c.cfm).

26. Fisher, *Fixing Jimmy Carter's Mistakes.*

27. Balbina Y. Hwang, Larry M. Wortzel, and Baker Spring, *North Korea and the End of the Agreed Framework* (Washington: Heritage Foundation, 2002) (www .heritage.org/Research/AsiaandthePacific/bg1605.cfm); Balbina Y. Hwang, *Overcoming the Stalemate on the Korean Peninsula* (Washington: Heritage Foundation, 2002) (www.heritage.org/Research/AsiaandthePacific/HL750.cfm).

28. George Shultz, "George Shultz Describes Concept of Peace-Seeking Eagle in Talk at MIT," lecture at Massachusetts Institute of Technology, Boston, April 11, 2003. (http://web.mit.edu/newsoffice/2003/shultz.html).

29. "A Conversation with George Shultz," *Atlantic Monthly*, April 18, 2007 (www .theatlantic.com/doc/200704u/schultz-interview). Shultz and Rice studied at Stanford at the same time and therefore have a shared academic past.

30. CNN, "Timeline: North Korea's Nuclear Weapons Development"; Andy McCarthy, "The North Korea Deal Stinks," *National Review Online, the Corner*, February 13, 2007 (http://corner.nationalreview.com/post/?q=YmJkNDdkYTJjNjBmZ DdlOWZjNWQ4ZDFiODFmMDg2NDQ=).

31. AEI, "Biography: John R. Bolton" (www.aei.org/scholars/filter.all,scholarID.121 /scholar2.asp); Edward Cody, "Tentative Nuclear Deal Struck with North Korea," *Washington Post*, February 13, 2007 (www.washingtonpost.com/wp-dyn/content/article /2007/02/12/AR2007021200086_pf.html).

32. Bruce Klingner, *Conservative Landslide Marks New Era in South Korea* (Washington: Heritage Foundation, 2007) (www.heritage.org/Research/AsiaandthePacific /wm1758.cfm).

33. Bruce Klingner, *North Korea Nuclear Verification: Has the U.S. Blinked?* (Washington: Heritage Foundation, 2008) (www.heritage.org/Research/AsiaandthePacific /wm2120.cfm).

34. See www.heritage.org/Research/AsiaandthePacific/sr0037.cfm.

35. Council on Foreign Relations, *Preparing for Sudden Change in North Korea* (Washington: Council on Foreign Relations, 2009) (www.cfr.org/content/publications /attachments/North_Korea_CSR42.pdf), pp. 33–35.

36. Bruce Klingner, *North Korea Leadership Instability: Power Struggle in Pyongyang* (Washington: Heritage Foundation, 2012) (www.heritage.org/research/reports /2012/07/power-struggle-in-pyongyang).

37. Dan Blumenthal, "Coming to Asia's Defense," *Wall Street Journal*, April 16, 2009 (http://online.wsj.com/article/SB123982618778522187.html).

38. Ibid.

39. Dan Blumenthal and Leslie Forgach, *Testing a Missile and an Alliance* (Washington: AEI, 2009) (www.aei.org/publications/filter.all,pubID.29662/pub_detail.asp).

40. Sun-Won Park, *North Korea's Third Attempt to Launch a Long-Range Missile and the Last Opportunity to Prevent It* (Brookings, 2009) (www.brookings.edu/papers/2009/~ /media/Files/rc/papers/2009/0323_north_korea_park/03_north_korea_park.pdf).

41. Richard Bush, *The Mind of Kim Jong Il* (Brookings, 2009) (www.brookings.edu/ opinions/2009/0401_north_korea_bush.aspx).

42. Sun-Won Park, *Pyongyang Fails Again: North Korea's Third Missile Launch and Kim Jong Il's Miscalculation* (Brookings, 2009) (www.brookings.edu/search.aspx?doQuery =1&sort=date:D:S:d1&q=North+Korea&start=0&num=10).

43. Tianjian Shi and Meredith Wen, *Avoiding Mutual Misunderstanding: Sino-U.S. Relations and the New Administration* (Washington: Carnegie Endowment for International Peace, 2009) (www.carnegieendowment.org/files/china_us_relations.pdf).

44. Ibid.

45. "Clinton Backs Six-Party Talks for Ending North Korean Nuclear Program," *Voice of America*, January 14, 2009 (www.voanews.com/english/2009-01-14-voa2.cfm).

46. Susan E. Rice, *We Need to Talk to North Korea* (Brookings, 2005) (www .brookings.edu/opinions/2005/0603northkorea_rice.aspx).

47. "North Korea Space 'Launch' Fails," *BBC News*, April 5, 2009 (http://news.bbc .co.uk/2/hi/asia-pacific/7984254.stm).

48. Douglas H. Paal, *North Korea: Land of Lousy Options, Again* (Washington: Carnegie Endowment Publications, 2012) (www.carnegieendowment.org/sada/2008 /08/12/interview-with-ali-al-rashed-kuwaiti-national-assembly-member-and-candi date/a7dud).

49. Ted Barrett, "Congress Forms Panel to Study Iraq War: Panel to Recommend Iraq Policy to Congress, White House," *CNN.com*, March 15, 2006 (www.cnn.com /2006/POLITICS/03/15/iraq.study/); James A. Baker Institute for Public Policy, "James A. Baker" (http://bakerinstitute.org/Per_Honorary_Chair.cfm); Woodrow Wilson International Center for Scholars, "Lee H. Hamilton" (www.wilsoncenter.org /index.cfm?fuseaction=director.about).

50. Barrett, "Congress Forms Panel to Study Iraq War."

51. See www.usip.org/isg/fact_sheet.html.

52. Ibid.

53. James A. Baker III, Lee H. Hamilton, and others, *The Iraq Study Group Report* (Washington: USIP, 2006) (http://media.usip.org/reports/iraq_study_group_report .pdf).

54. Paul Reynolds, "Iraq Report Sets Stage for Changes," *BBC News*, December 6, 2006 (http://news.bbc.co.uk/2/hi/americas/6209802.stm).

55. Fredrick W. Kagan and Jack Keane, *The Right Type of "Surge": Any Troop Increase Must Be Large and Lasting* (Washington: AEI, 2006) (http://aei.org/publications /pubID.25356,filter.all/pub_detail.asp).

56. Frederick W. Kagan, *Choosing Victory: A Plan for Success in Iraq* (Washington: AEI, 2006) (www.realclearpolitics.com/RCP_PDF/ChoosingVictory.pdf).

57. "Fact Sheet: The New Way Forward in Iraq," White House: Office of the Press Secretary, January 10, 2007 (http://georgewbush-whitehouse.archives.gov/news/releases /2007/01/20070110-3.html).

58. "President's Address to the Nation: 10 January 2007," White House (www .whitehouse.gov/news/releases/2007/01/20070110-7.html).

59. Johns Hopkins University, "General Jack Keane" (www.jhuapl.edu/POW/bios /keane.htm); AEI, "Frederick W. Kagan" (www.aei.org/scholars/filter.all,scholarID.99 /scholar.asp).

60. Peter Baker and Jon Cohen, "Americans Say U.S. Is Losing War; Public, Politicians Split on Iraq Panel's Ideas," *Washington Post*, December 13, 2006 (www.proquest .com.ps2.villanova.edu).

61. Rupert Cornwell, "Cracks Appear between Bush and Blair over Talks," *Belfast Telegraph*, December 8, 2006 (www.belfasttelegraph.co.uk/news/world-news/article 2056247.ece).

62. Ibid.

63. James Jay Carafano and James Philips, *Iraq: Pause in Troop Drawdown Makes Sense* (Heritage Foundation, 2008) (www.heritage.org/Research/Iraq/wm1871.cfm).

64. Jason Campbell, Michael O'Hanlon, and Amy Unikewicz, "The State of Iraq: An Update," *New York Times*, December 28, 2008 (www.nytimes.com/2008/12/29 /opinion/29ohanlon.html).

65. Peter Baker, "With Pledges to Troops and Iraqis, Obama Details Pullout," *New York Times*, February 27, 2009 (www.nytimes.com/2009/02/28/washington/28troops .html).

66. National Commission on Terrorist Attacks upon the United States, "Frequently Asked Questions" (http://govinfo.library.unt.edu/911/about/faq.htm).

67. Ibid., "Thomas H. Kean" (http://govinfo.library.unt.edu/911/about/bio_kean .htm).

68. Ibid., "Lee H. Hamilton" (http://govinfo.library.unt.edu/911/about/bio_hamilton .htm); Barrett, "Congress Forms Panel to Study Iraq War."

69. National Commission on Terrorist Attacks upon the United States, "Richard Ben-Veniste" (http://govinfo.library.unt.edu/911/about/bio_ben-veniste.htm).

70. Mike Allen, "Bush Picks a Replacement for Harriet Meirs," *Time*, January 8, 2007 (www.time.com/time/nation/article/0,8599,1575066,00.html); National Commission on Terrorist Attacks upon the United States, "Fred Fielding" (http://govinfo.library.unt.edu/911/about/bio_fielding.htm).

71. National Commission on Terrorist Attacks upon the United States, "Jamie Gorelick" (http://govinfo.library.unt.edu/911/about/bio_gorelick.htm).

72. Ibid., "Slade Gorton" (http://govinfo.library.unt.edu/911/about/bio_gorton.htm).

73. Ibid., "Bob Kerrey" (http://govinfo.library.unt.edu/911/about/bio_kerrey.htm).

74. Ibid., "John Lehman" (http://govinfo.library.unt.edu/911/about/bio_lehman.htm); Foreign Policy Research Institute, "Board of Directors" (www.fpri.org/about/people/board.html).

75. National Commission on Terrorist Attacks upon the United States, "Timothy Roemer"; Embassy of the United States—New Delhi (http://newdelhi.usembassy.gov/ambroemertjbio.html); Biographical Directory of the U.S. Congress, "Roemer, Timothy John" (http://bioguide.congress.gov/scripts/biodisplay.pl?index=R000385).

76. National Commission on Terrorist Attacks upon the United States, "James R. Thompson" (http://govinfo.library.unt.edu/911/about/bio_thompson.htm).

77. Ibid., "Main Page" (http://911commission.gov); National Commission on Terrorist Attacks upon the United States, *The 9/11 Commission Report* (http://govinfo.library.unt.edu/911/report/911Report.pdf).

78. Mike Allen and Dan Eggen, "Bush May Move Soon on 9/11 Report: President Close to Announcing Plans for Revamping Intelligence System," *Washington Post*, July 29, 2004 (www.proquest.com.ps2.villanova.edu).

79. Scot J. Paltrow and Greg Hitt, "Final 9/11 Report Urges Changes and Avoids Blame," *Wall Street Journal*, July 23, 2004 (www.proquest.com.ps2.villanova.edu).

80. Peter Grier and Faye Bowers, "Failure of 'Imagination' Led to 9/11: The 9/11 Final Report Assigns Little Blame, But Cites Many Errors, and Lays Out Bipartisan Steps to Avert Future Terror Acts," *Christian Science Monitor*, July 23, 2004 (www.proquest.com.ps2.villanova.edu).

81. Frank James, "Parties Eager to Act on 9/11 Panel's Ideas; GOP Switches to Accelerated Speed," *Chicago Tribune*, July 30, 2004 (www.proquest.com.ps2.villanova.edu).

82. Nick Anderson, "Congress Passes Bill to Create Commission on Terrorist Attacks; President's Signature Is Expected; the Panel, Called for by Victims' Families, Will Report on Failures Leading to 9/11," *Los Angeles Times*, November 16, 2002 (www.proquest.com.ps2.villanova.edu).

83. Mike Allen and Dan Eggen, "Bush May Move Soon on 9/11 Report; President Close to Announcing Plans for Revamping Intelligence System," *Washington Post*, July 29, 2004 (www.proquest.com.ps2.villanova.edu).

84. "Fact Sheet: Progress on the 9/11 Commission Recommendations," White House, December 5, 2005 (www.whitehouse.gov/news/releases/2005/12/20051205-5.html).

85. Save Darfur, "The Genocide in Darfur—Briefing Paper" (Washington, June 2008) (www.savedarfur.org/pages/background).

86. Stephanie Hanson, *Negotiating Peace in Darfur* (Washington: Council on Foreign Relations, 2007) (www.cfr.org/publication/13171/negotiating_peace_in_darfur.html).

87. Maggie Farley, "U.N. Puts Darfur Death Toll at 300,000," *Los Angeles Times,* April 23, 2008 (http://articles.latimes.com/2008/apr/23/world/fg-darfur23); "Quick Guide: Darfur," *BBC News,* September 6, 2006 (http://news.bbc.co.uk/2/hi/africa /5316306.stm).

88. Hudson Institute, "Michael Horowitz" (www.hudson.org/learn/index.cfm?fuse action=staff_bio&eid=HoroMich).

89. Allen D. Hertzke, "The Shame of Darfur," *First Things,* October 2005 (www .firstthings.com/article.php3?id_article=239).

90. Ibid.

91. Christopher Preble, *A Regional Solution for Darfur* (Washington: Cato Institute, 2004) (www.cato.org/pub_display.php?pub_id=2744).

92. James Phillips, *Pressure Sudan to Halt Oppression in Darfur* (Washington: Heritage Foundation, 2004) (www.heritage.org/Research/Africa/em943.cfm).

93. Center for American Progress, "Enough! The Project to End Genocide and Crimes against Humanity" (www.enoughproject.org/).

94. John Prendergast, John Norris, and Jerry Fowler, *President Obama's Immediate Sudan Challenge—Letter* (Washington: Enough Project, Center for American Progress, 2011) (www.enoughproject.org/publications/president-obama-immediate-sudan -challenge).

95. In an interview in Nashville in July 2007, President Bush admitted that his decision to not send troops into Darfur was made "in consultation with allies as well as members of Congress and activists"; Peter Baker, "Bush Says He Considered Action in Darfur," *Washington Post,* July 20, 2007 (www.washingtonpost.com/wp-dyn/content /article/2007/07/19/AR2007071902294.html).

96. See senate.gov/~foreign/testimony/2007/RiceTestimony070411.

97. "Biden Calls for Military Force in Darfur," *MSNBC.com,* April 11, 2007 (www .msnbc.msn.com/id/18059937/).

98. See www.cfr.org/publication/16359/presidential_candidates_statement_on _darfur.html?breadcrumb=%2Fregion%2F197%2Fsudan.

99. Ray Walser, *Courting Khartoum: The Obama Administration's Sudan Policy, No. 2660* (Washington: Heritage Foundation, 2009) (www.heritage.org/Research/Africa /wm2660.cfm).

100. Roberta Cohen, "Darfur Debated," *Forced Migration Review* 29 (December 2007), pp. 55–57 (www.fmreview.org/FMRpdfs/FMR29/55-57.pdf).

101. Rachel Zoll, "Evangelicals Lobby Bush on Sudan Crisis," *Washington Post,* October 18, 2006 (www.washingtonpost.com/wp-dyn/content/article/2006/10/18/AR 2006101801236.html).

102. *CNN.com,* April 26, 2006 (http://articles.cnn.com/2006-04-27/politics/darfur .clooney_1_sudan-s-darfur-clooney-syriana?_s=PM:POLITICS).

103. Jim Puzzanghera, "Clooney Puts Star Power to Work; The Actor Helps Draw Attention to Bipartisan Congressional Efforts on Sudan's Genocide Crisis," *Los Angeles Times,* April 28, 2006 (www.proquest.com.ps2.villanova.edu).

104. Tina Daunt, "The World: Clooney Leads Darfur Mission," *Los Angeles Times*, December 12, 2006 (www.proquest.com.ps2.villanova.edu).

105. Sudarsan Raghavan, "Crisis in Darfur Is Expected to Draw Thousands to Mall; Rallies Promoting End to Genocide Planned for 17 Other Cities," *Washington Post*, April 30, 2006 (www.proquest.com.ps2.villanova.edu).

106. "President Meets with Darfur Advocates," White House, April 28, 2006 (www.whitehouse.gov/news/releases/2006/04/20060428-5.html).

107. Michelle Vu, "Evangelicals Carry Darfur Torch," *Christian Post*, December 11, 2007 (www.christianpost.com/article/20071211/30433_Evangelicals_Carry_Darfur -Olympic_Torch.htm).

108. Mia Farrow, "China Can Do More on Darfur," *Wall Street Journal*, October 5, 2007 (www.proquest.com.ps2.villanova.edu); Mia Farrow, "A Critical Moment for Darfur," *Wall Street Journal*, December 11, 2007 (www.proquest.com.ps2.villa nova.edu).

109. "'Buy U.S.' Threat to U.K. Defence Jobs," *BBC News*, June 17, 2003 (http:// news.bbc.co.uk/2/hi/business/2997960.stm).

110. "Steely Biden Tells Critics: Buy into 'Buy American,'" *New York Post*, January 30, 2009 (www.nypost.com/seven/01302009/news/politics/steely_biden_tells_critics __buy_into_buy_152732.htm).

111. David Sanger, "Senate Agrees to Dilute 'Buy America' Provisions," *New York Times*, February 4, 2009 (www.nytimes.com/2009/02/05/us/politics/05trade.html? _r=1&scp=1&sq=%22buy%20america%22%20provision&st=cse).

112. Louis Uchitelle, "'Buy America in Stimulus (but Good Luck with That)," *New York Times*, February 20, 2009 (www.nytimes.com/2009/02/21/business/21buy.html ?scp=3&sq=%22buy%20america%22%20provision&st=cse).

113. Alane Kochems, *"Buy America" Provisions Don't Help Homeland Security or National Defense* (Washington: Heritage Foundation, 2005) (www.heritage.org/Research /HomelandSecurity/wm769.cfm).

114. Christopher S. Robinson, *Beyond the "Buy America" Debate: Sustaining America's Industrial and Technological Edge amid the Challenges of Globalization* (Brookings, 2007) (www.brookings.edu/~/media/Files/rc/papers/2007/07defense_robinson /robinson20070731.pdf).

115. Personal communication from Dr. C. Fred Bergsten, senior fellow and director emeritus, Peterson Institute for International Economics, Washington, D.C., February 11, 2009. See the policy brief he refers to at www.petersoninstitute.org/publications /pb/pb09-2.pdf.

116. Ibid.

117. "That 'Buy America' Provision," *New York Times*, February 11, 2009 (http:// roomfordebate.blogs.nytimes.com/2009/02/11/that-buy-american-provision/?scp=2 &sq=%22buy%20america%22%20provision&st=cse#sherrod).

118. Gary Clyde Hufbauer and Jeffrey J. Schott, *Buy American: Bad for Jobs, Worse for Reputation* (Washington: Peterson Institute for International Economics, 2009), p. 5 (www.petersoninstitute.org/publications/pb/pb09-2.pdf).

119. Ibid.

120. Ibid.

121. Ibid., p. 4.

122. Michael Crowley, *Barack in Iraq—Can He Really End the War?* (Washington: Center for a New American Security, 2008) (www.cnas.org/node/429).

123. James Phillips, "President Obama Takes the Middle Road on Iraq Troop Drawdown," *The Foundry: Conservative Policy News Blog*, February 27, 2009 (http://blog.heritage.org/2009/02/27/president-obama-takes-the-middle-road-on-iraq-troop-drawdown/).

124. Jesse Lee, "President Obama's Address on the End of the Combat Mission in Iraq," White House, August 31, 2010 (www.whitehouse.gov/blog/2010/08/31/president-obamas-address-end-combat-mission-iraq).

125. Phillips, "President Obama Takes the Middle Road on Iraq Troop Drawdown."

126. Lawrence J. Korb, *Impressions from Iraq: Part One* (Washington: CAP, 2009) (www.americanprogress.org/issues/2009/10/korb_iraq_one.html).

127. Lawrence J. Korb, *Obama and the United States: One Year after the Elections* (Washington: CAP, 2009) (www.americanprogress.rg/issues/2009/12/korb_italy_speech.html).

128. Brian Katulis, *Attacks Highlight Uneven Progress in Iraq* (Washington: CAP, 2009) (www.americanprogress.org/issues/2009/12/uneven_progress/html).

129. Ibid.

130. Crowley, *Barack in Iraq*.

131. Anthony Cordesman, *Observations from a Visit to Iraq, Memorandum for the Record* (Washington: Center for Strategic and International Studies, 2009) (http://csis.org/files/publication/090612_iraqitripmemo.pdf).

132. Anthony Cordesman, *Iraq: A Time to Stay? Memorandum for the Record* (Washington: Center for Strategic and International Studies, 2009).

133. Crowley, *Barack in Iraq*.

134. For more information concerning Obama-era Iraq diplomacy, see ibid.; Michael Crowley, *New CNAS Report Assesses Obama's Engagement Strategy* (Washington: Center for a New American Security, 2010) (www.cnas.org/node/4486); Korb, *Impressions from Iraq: Part One*; Katulis, *Attacks Highlight Uneven Progress in Iraq*; Brian Katulis, Marc Lynch, and Peter Juul, *Iraq's Political Transition after the Surge* (Washington: Center for American Progress, 2008) (www.americanprogress.org/issues/2008/09/iraq_transition.html); Lawrence Korb, *Impressions from Iraq: Part Two* (Washington: Center for American Progress, 2009) (www.americanprogress.org/issues/2009/10/korb_iraq_three.html); Korb, *Obama and the United States*.

Chapter Five

1. Buyant E. Khaltarkhuu and Federico Escaler, "The Fast Changing World of Information and Communications Technology," *World Bank Data Blog*, June 27, 2013 (http://blogs.worldbank.org/opendata/fast-changing-world-information-and-communications-technology).

2. Luke Martell, "The Third Wave in Globalization Theory," *International Studies Review* 9, no. 2 (2007), pp. 173–96.

3. Diane Stone, *Globalisation and the Transnationalisation of Think Tanks* (Washington: Asian Development Bank Institute, 2005) (www.adbi.org/discussion-paper/2005/09/09/1356.think.tanks/globalisation.and.the.transnationalisation.of.think.tanks/).

4. Ibid.

5. Stella Ladi, *Globalisation, Policy Transfer, and Policy Research Institutes* (Cheltenham, U.K.: Edward Elgar Publishing, 2005).

6. Union of International Organizations, "The Yearbook of International Organizations" (www.uia.org/yearbook).

7. Meirav Mishali-Ram, "Powerful Actors Make a Difference: Theorizing Power Attributes of Nonstate Actors," *International Journal of Peace Studies* 14 (2009) (www.gmu.edu/programs/icar/ijps/vol14_2/MMRAM%2014n2%20IJPS.pdf).

8. Freedom House, "Freedom in the World—Electoral Democracies," *Freedom in the World 2013* (Washington: Freedom House, n.d.) (https://freedomhouse.org/sites/default/files/Electoral%20Democracy%20Numbers,%20FIW%201989-2013_0.pdf).

9. Thomas L. Friedman, "Globalization, Alive and Well," *New York Times*, September 22, 2002 (www.nytimes.com/2002/09/22/opinion/globalization-alive-and-well.html).

10. Richard Rose, "How People View Democracy: A Diverging Europe," *Journal of Democracy* 12 (2001), p. 105.

11. Grant Cameron, "What Would a Global Partnership for a Data Revolution Look Like?," *World Bank Data Blog*, October 8, 2013 (http://blogs.worldbank.org/opendata/what-would-global-partnership-data-revolution-look).

12. Charles Chase, "Using Big Data to Enhance Demand-Driven Forecasting and Planning," *Journal of Business Forecasting* 32, no. 2 (2013).

13. James Maniyka and others, *Big Data: The Next Frontier for Innovation, Competition, and Productivity* (San Francisco, Calif.: McKinsey & Company, 2011).

14. Claire Provost, "Poorer Countries Need Privacy Laws as They Adopt New Technologies," *Guardian*, December 4, 2013 (www.theguardian.com/global-development/2013/dec/04/poorer-countries-privacy-laws-new-technology).

15. Manuel Castells, *Rise of the Network Society* (West Sussex, U.K.: Wiley Blackwell Publishing, 2009), p. 1969.

16. Jessica E. Vascellaro, "Twitter Trips on Its Rapid Growth," *Wall Street Journal*, May 26, 2009.

17. Richard Holt, "Twitter in Numbers," *Telegraph*, March 21, 2013 (www.telegraph.co.uk/technology/twitter/9945505/Twitter-in-numbers.html).

18. Thomas Carothers, "The End of the Transition Paradigm," *Journal of Democracy* 13, no. 1 (2002). "Third wave democracy" refers to the third major surge of democracy in history. Huntington discusses the idea fully in *The Third Wave: Democratization in the Late Twentieth Century* (University of Oklahoma Press, 1991).

19. "Eroding Trust in Government: Confidence Crumbles," *The Economist*, November 16, 2013 (www.economist.com/news/international/21589902-confidence-crumbles).

20. "Internet Protests: The Digital Demo," *The Economist*, June 29, 2013.

21. Rick Dakin, "Coalfire's Top Five Information Security and Compliance Predictions for 2014," *Business Wire*, December 18, 2013 (www.businesswire.com/news /home/20131218005276/en/Coalfire's-Top-Information-Security-Compliance-Pre dictions-2014).

22. Peter W. Singer, *Cybersecurity Threats and Basic Cyber Hygiene* (Brookings, 2014) (www.brookings.edu/research/interviews/2014/01/03-cybersecurity-threats-basic -cyber-hygiene-solutions-singer).

23. World Bank, "WB Urges Developing Countries to Safeguard Economic Growth, as Road Ahead Remains Bumpy" (www.worldbank.org/en/news/press-release /2013/01/15/wb-urges-developing-countries-safeguard-economic-growth-road-ahead -remains-bumpy).

24. "When Giants Slow Down," *The Economist*, July 27, 2013.

25. A. T. Kearney, "Economic Shift from Global North to South" (www.atkearney .com/gbpc/global-business-drivers/economic-shift-from-global-north-to-south).

26. Ibid.

27. Jean-Pierre Lehmann, "Bridging the 21st Century's North-South Divide," *Globalist Perspective*, March 12, 2012.

28. Nancy Birdsall, Christian Meyer, and Alexis Sowa, "Global Markets, Global Citizens, and Global Governance in the 21st Century," CGD Working Paper 329 (Washington: Center for Global Development, September 2013) (www.cgdev.org/publication /global-markets-global-citizens-and-global-governance-21st-century-working-paper -329-0).

29. John Bolton, "Edward Snowden's Leaks Are a Grave Threat to U.S. National Security," *Guardian*, June 18, 2013 (www.theguardian.com/commentisfree/2013/jun /18/edward-snowden-leaks-grave-threat).

30. Victor Anderson, "Addressing Short-Termism in Government and Politics," *Guardian*, March 2, 2011 (www.theguardian.com/sustainable-business/government -politics-short-termism-unsustainability).

31. George Papandreou, "Rediscover the Lost Art of Democracy," *CNN.com*, October 20, 2013 (www.cnn.com/2013/10/20/opinion/papandreou-ted-democracy/).

32. Alejandro Chafuen, "Think Tanks for Freedom: A Snapshot of the U.S. Market," *Forbes*, February 2, 2013 (www.forbes.com/sites/alejandrochafuen/2013/02/13 /think-tanks-for-freedom-a-snapshot-of-the-u-s-market/).

33. European Think Tank Summit Think Tanks in a Time of Crisis and Paralysis: On the Sidelines or Catalysts for Ideas and Action?, Euro Think Tank Summit Report, November 20, 2012 (http://repository.upenn.edu/cgi/viewcontent.cgi?article=1009 &context=ttcsp_summitreports).

34. Elizabeth Lopatto, "American Nobel Winners Say Research Threatened by Cuts," *Bloomberg.com*, October 8, 2013 (www.bloomberg.com/news/2013-10-08/ameri can-nobel-winners-fear-for-research-as-funding-cut.html).

35. Munyaradzi Makoni, "African Think Tanks Feel Funding Pinch," *Research Limited*, January 28, 2013 (www.researchresearch.com/index.php?option=com_news &template=rr_2col&view=article&articleId=1287105).

36. James McGann, "Think Tanks: Catalyst for Ideas and Action," *Diplomatic Courier Magazine* 5, no. 4 (Fall 2011), p. 68.

37. Ken Silverstein, "The Secret Donors behind the Center for American Progress and Other Think Tanks," *Nation* (www.thenation.com/article/174437/secret-donors -behind-center-american-progress-and-other-think-tanks-updated-524).

38. Troy, "Devaluing the Think Tank."

39. Enrique Mendizabal, "Supporting Think Tanks Series: From Core and Institutional Support to Organizational Development Grants," *OnThinkTanks.org*, June 3, 2013 (http://onthinktanks.org/2013/06/03/supporting-think-tanks-series-from-core -and-institutional-support-to-organizational-development-grants/).

40. Ibid.

41. Edward Lopez, "Ranking Think Tanks: The Challenge of Specialization," *Political Entrepreneurs*, March 19, 2013 (http://politicalentrepreneurs.com/ranking-think -tanks-the-challenge-of-specialization/).

42. James McGann, "Think Tank Challenge: Surviving the Competition," *Asia Pathways* (Washington: ADBI, 2013) (www.asiapathways-adbi.org/2013/08/think -tank-challenge-surviving-the-competition/).

43. Tavis D. Jules and Michelle Morais De Sá E Silva, "How Different Disciplines Have Approached South-South Cooperation and Transfer," *Society for International Education Journal* 5, no. 1 (2008), p. 45 (www.tc.columbia.edu/sie/journal/Volume_5 /jules.pdf).

44. Jeremy D. Taylor, "The Dilemma of Specialization vs. Diversification," *Western Independent Bankers* 67 (January 2013) (www.wib.org/publications__resources/directors _resources/directors_digest/jan13/taylor.html).

45. James McGann, *Q&A with Dr. McGann on the 2012 Go-To Report and Chinese Think Tanks* (Philadelphia: Think Tanks and Civil Societies Program, 2013) (http:// gotothinktank.com/a-qa-with-dr-mcgann-on-the-2012-go-to-report-and-chinese -think-tanks/).

46. Alejandro Chafuen, "Think Tanks in America: Occupying a Unique Space," *Forbes*, April 10, 2013 (www.forbes.com/sites/alejandrochafuen/2013/04/10/think -tanks-in-america-occupying-a-unique-space/#4ae05fb2b113AU).

47. Ibid.

48. Andrew Selee, "Can Think Tanks Influence Public Opinion and Improve Policy?," *World Financial Review*, July 13, 2013 (www.worldfinancialreview.com/?p=696).

49. Alejandro Chafuen, "15 Ways of Measuring Think Tank Policy Outcomes," *Forbes*, April 24, 2013 (www.forbes.com/sites/alejandrochafuen/2013/04/24/15-ways -of-measuring-think-tank-policy-outcomes/#687168e57555).

50. Selee, "Can Think Tanks Influence Public Opinion and Improve Policy?"

51. "Helping Think Tanks Measure Impact," *Redstone Strategy Group*, September 15, 2013 (www.redstonestrategy.com/wp-content/uploads/2013/09/2013-09-30 -IDRC-Helping-think-tanks-measure-impact.pdf).

52. George Monbiot, "Who's Paying?" (http://bit.ly/LcQnKC) (www.monbiot.com /2006/09/26/whos-paying/).

53. Bruce Bartlett, "The Alarming Corruption of the Think Tanks," *Fiscal Times*, December 14, 2012 (www.thefiscaltimes.com/Columns/2012/12/14/The-Alarming -Corruption-of-the-Think-Tanks).

54. Jennifer Rubin, "Jim DeMint's Destruction of the Heritage Foundation," *Washington Post*, October 21, 2013 (www.washingtonpost.com/blogs/right-turn/wp/2013 /10/21/jim-demints-destruction-of-the-heritage-foundation/).

55. Ibid.

56. Paul Krugman, "Think Tank Transparency," *New York Times* (http://nyti.ms /1eKJIAw).

57. Holly Yeager, "Center for American Progress Releases Donor List," *Washington Post* (http://wapo.st/1dnECHU); HI, "Reply to our Critics" (http://bit.ly/1lBSbdF).

58. Gerry Hassan, "The Limits of the 'Think Tank' Revolution" (www.opendemoc racy.net/article/yes/the-limits-of-the-think-tank-revolution).

59. Tom Medvetz, "Think Tanks as an Emergent Field" (www.ssrc.org/publications /view/a2a2ba10-b135-de11-afac-001cc477ec70/).

60. James McGann, Keynote Address, "Shanghai and Beijing, China, August 2013," Global Trends and Transitions in Think Tanks and Policy Advice, Think Tanks & Civil Societies Program; James G. McGann, *Think Tanks and Policy Advice in the United States: Academic, Advisors and Advocates* (London: Routledge, 2007).

61. Donald E. Abelson and Christine M. Carberry, "Following Suit or Falling Behind? A Comparative Analysis of Think Tanks in Canada and the United States," *Canadian Journal of Political Science* 31, no. 3 (1998), pp. 525–55.

62. "Digital Strategy and Tools for Think Tanks," *OnThinkTanks.org*, March 27, 2012 (http://onthinktanks.org/2012/03/27/digital-disruption-the-internet-is-changing -how-we-search-for-information/).

63. Pew Research Center, "Do You Ever Get News Online or Not?," August 8, 2013 (www.pewresearch.org/topics/news-sources/2013/).

64. Enrique Mendizabal, "Digital Think Tanks," *OnThinkTanks.org*, June 14, 2012 (http://onthinktanks.org/2012/06/14/digital-think-tanks/).

65. Ibid.

66. Nick Scott, "Digital Strategy Can Support Communications in Think Tanks. But Can It Also Improve Their Research and Management Too?," *OnThinkTanks.org*, June 15, 2012 (https://onthinktanks.org/articles/digital-strategy-can-support-communi cations-in-think-tanks-but-can-it-also-improve-their-research-and-management-too/).

67. Kathleen McNutt and Gregory Marchildon, "Think Tanks and the Measuring Visibility and Influence," *Canadian Public Policy* 35, no. 2 (2009), pp. 219–36.

68. Sami Atallah and Orazio Bellettini Cedeño, "Democracy Think Tanks in Action: Translating Research into Policy in Young and Emerging Democracies," *Network of Democracy Research Institutes* (Washington: National Endowment for Democracy, 2013) (www.ned.org/events/democracy-think-tanks-in-action-translating-research-into -policy-in-young-and-emerging-democr).

69. Subrat Das, "Balancing Research and Advocacy: Subrat Das," *OnThinkTanks .org*, October 3, 2013 (http://onthinktanks.org/?s=advocacy).

70. Natasha Singer, "You've Won a Badge (and Now We Know All about You)," *New York Times*, February 4, 2012 (www.nytimes.com/2012/02/05/business/employers -and-brands-use-gaming-to-gauge-engagement.html?_r=0).

71. Jeff Knezovich and Melissa Julian, "Taking Think Tank Communications to the Next Level: Determining What Goes Where," *OnThinkTanks.org*, October 8, 2013 (https://onthinktanks.org/articles/taking-think-tank-communications-to-the-next -level-determining-what-goes-where-part-2/).

72. Andrew Rich, *Think Tanks, Public Policy, and the Politics of Expertise* (Cambridge University Press, 2004); Hartwig Pautz, "Think Tanks in Scotland," paper presented at the Fifty-Fifth Political Studies Association Annual Conference. Leeds, U.K., April 4–7, 2005.

73. James Allen Smith, *The Idea Brokers: Think Tanks and the Rise of the New Policy Elite* (New York: Free Press, 1993).

74. Joseph Stiglitz, "Scan Globally, Reinvent Locally: Knowledge Infrastructure and the Localization of Knowledge," in *Banking on Knowledge: The Genesis of the Global Development Network*, edited by Diane Stone (London: Routledge, 2000), pp. 24–43.

75. "Emerging Markets: The Rise of Emerging-Market Think-tanks," *The Economist*, January 26, 2011 (www.economist.com/blogs/schumpeter/2011/01/rise_emerging -market_think_tanks).

76. Hussein Elkamel, "A Presentation on November 8–9, 2010," Africa Think Tank Regional Meeting, Egyptian Cabinet Information and Decision Support Center (IDSC), Cairo (www.thinktanking.idsc.gov.eg/InternatioanlConf/Openning%20Ses sion/Session%201/Elkamel/Information%20Report_Ambassador%20Elkamel%20 final.pdf).

77. Enrique Mendizabal, "How a Digital Strategy Can Enhance Think Tank Management, Research and Communication," *OnThinkTanks.org*, June 21, 2012 (http:// onthinktanks.org/2012/06/21/how-a-digital-strategy-can-enhance-think-tank-manage ment-research-and-communication/).

78. Diane Stone, Andrew Denham, and Mark Garnett, eds., *Think Tanks across Nations: A Comparative Approach* (Manchester University Press, 1998).

79. Andrea Moncada, "New Blood Means New Challenges for U.S. Think Tanks," *OnThinkTanks.org*, June 12, 2012 (http://onthinktanks.org/2012/06/12/new-blood -means-new-challenges-for-u-s-think-tanks/).

80. "The Good Think-Tank Guide," *The Economist*, December 21, 1991–January 3, 1992, p. 49.

81. McGann, *Think Tanks and Policy Advice in the United States*.

Index

Aaron, Henry J., 101

AARP (American Association of Retired Persons), 12

Abelson, Donald: on categorization of think tanks, 6–8; on Franklin Institute, 23; on hybrid think tanks, 167; on influence of think tanks, 54; on presidential campaigns influenced by think tanks, 70–71; on revolving door effect, 77; on think tank proliferation after World War II, 27

Academic think tanks, 14, 16

Advisory Council on Social Security (1994–96), 80

Advocacy think tanks, 8, 16

AEI. *See* American Enterprise Institute

Affordable Care Act. *See* Patient Protection and Affordable Care Act of 2010

Africa, think tanks in, 33, 39, 161, 171

African National Congress (South Africa), 17

African Union Mission in Sudan, 136

Aid to Families with Dependent Children (AFDC), 85, 86

Albania, think tanks in, 37

Albright, Madeleine, 76, 140

Aldy, Joe, 113

Alexander, Gerard, 74

Al Jazeera, 157

Allen, Richard V., 28

American Association of Retired Persons (AARP), 12

American Clean Energy and Security Act of 2009, 113

American Enterprise Institute (AEI): and Affordable Care Act, 95, 97, 102; categorization of, 14; and Clinton health care reform, 90, 91, 94; and economic stimulus package (2008), 107; funding for, 20, 21; influence of, 45; and North Korea nuclear weapons, 119, 120, 121; profile, 179; and revolving door effect, 67; and Social Security reform, 81, 84; and "surge" strategy in Iraq, 123–25

American Political Science Association, 23

American Security Project, 162

American the Vulnerable: Our Military Problems and How to Fix Them (FPRI), 133

Amnesty International, 176

Anarchist movements, 157–58

Anderson, James, 118

Anderson, Martin, 28

Antholis, William, 67

Arab Awakening movement, 157, 159

Armitage, Richard, 72